# Detailing for Landscape Architects

# Detailing for Landscape Architects

## Aesthetics • Function • Constructibility

**Tom Ryan, Edward Allen, and Patrick Rand**

Drawings by
Edward Allen, Joseph Iano,
Patrick Rand, and Tom Ryan

WILEY

John Wiley & Sons, Inc.

*Library of Congress Cataloging-in-Publication Data*

Ryan, Thomas, 1952-
  Landscape architectural detailing : constructibility, aesthetics, and sustainability / Thomas Ryan, Edward Allen, and Patrick Rand.
      p. cm.
  Includes index.
  ISBN 978-0-470-54878-3 (pbk.); 978-0-470-90274-5 (ebk); 978-0-470-90276-9 (ebk); 978-0-470-90460-2 (ebk); 978-0-470-90461-9 (ebk); 978-0-470-90462-6 (ebk)
  1. Landscape architecture.   2. Architecture–Details.   I. Allen, Edward, 1938-   II. Rand, Patrick, 1950-   III. Title.
  SB472.R93 2011
  712´.3–dc22
                                                                                2010019501

Printed in the United States of America

10  9  8  7  6  5  4  3  2  1

# CONTENTS

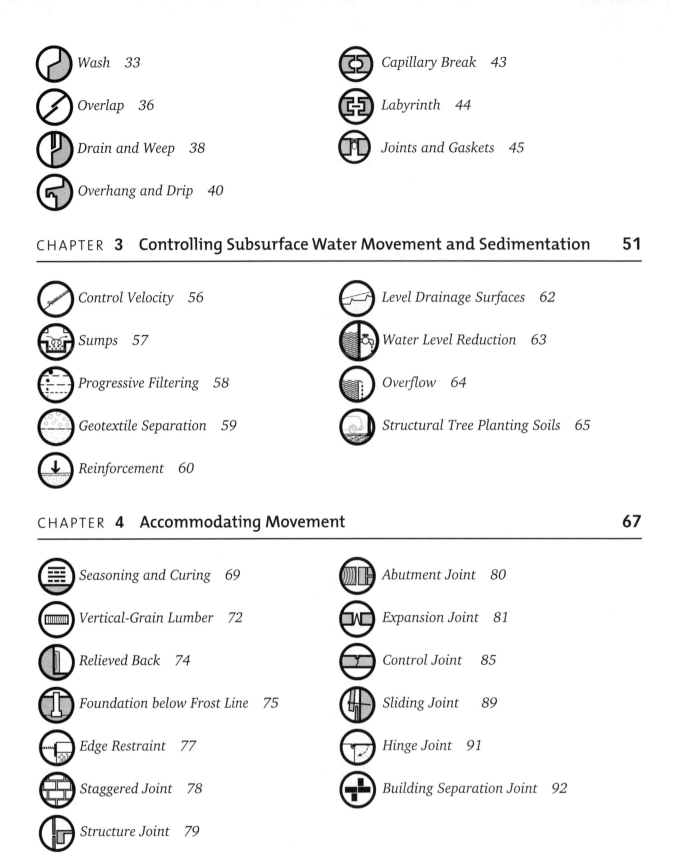

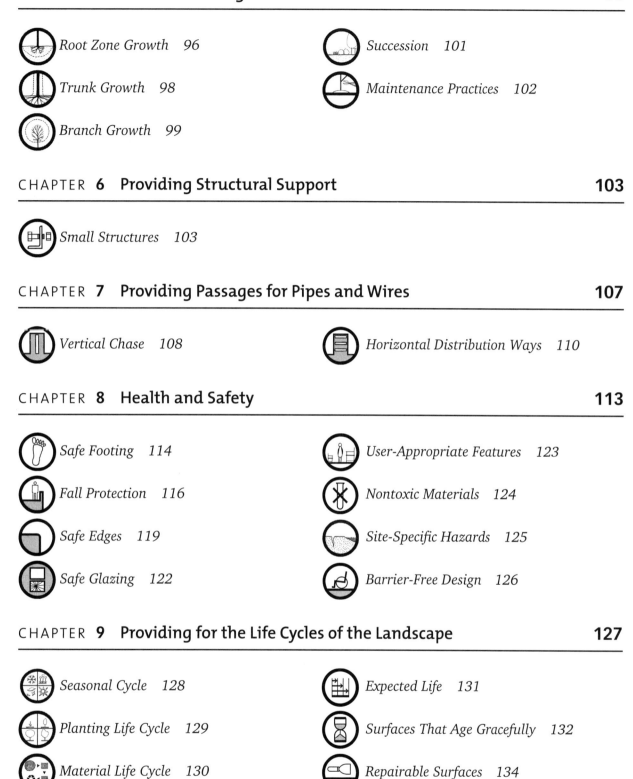

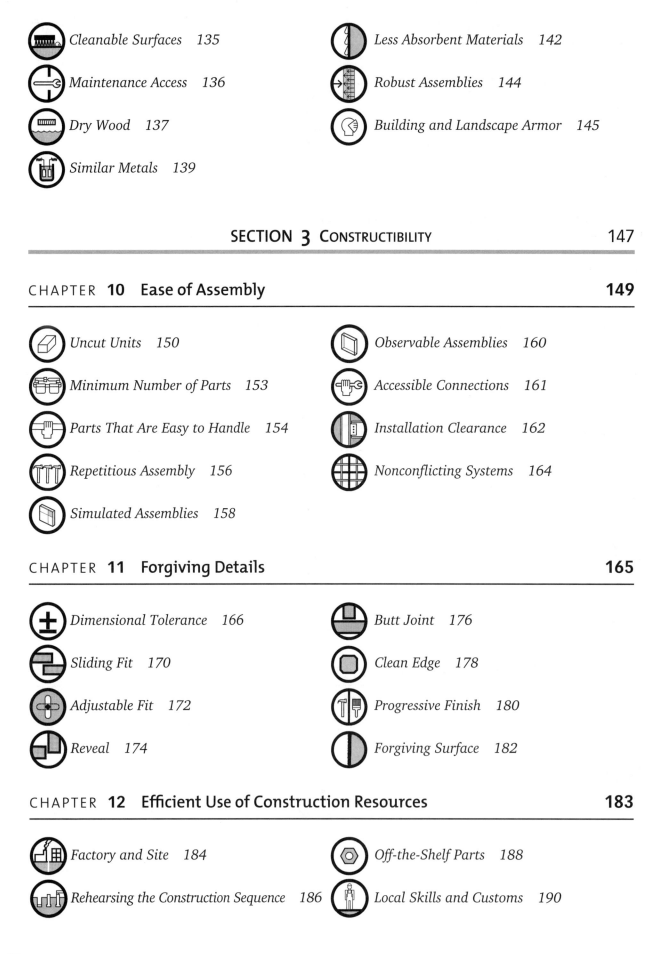

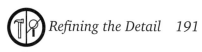 

# ACKNOWLEDGMENTS

This book is based upon the second edition of *Architectural Detailing: Function, Constructibility, Aesthetics* by Edward Allen, Patrick Rand and Joseph Iano published in 2007. Tom Ryan adapted and expanded the material for landscape architects with Ed and Pat's assistance and guidance.

Edward Allen thanks his longtime colleague Joseph Iano, who prepared many of the original versions of the drawings for this book and reviewed the majority of the original manuscript and illustrations. Joe's comments and ideas have strengthened the book in many important ways. Ed is very grateful for the wisdom, experience, and fresh point of view of Patrick Rand, who joined him as coauthor for the second edition of the parent book on architectural detailing. He has long regarded Pat as one of the finest teachers of architectural technology in the world today. Ed's special thanks go to Tom Ryan for a remarkable job of adapting the book to the specialized subject of landscape detailing. Tom's expertise, exceptional drawing skills, and good humor have been exemplary throughout the process of preparing this new book.

At John Wiley & Sons, Inc., Margaret Cummins, senior editor, guided all phases of the preparation and publication of the current edition of this book with wisdom, patience, and good humor; Karin Kincheloe applied her limitless talent and resourcefulness to the design of the original edition. Many thanks to Doug Salvemini who was the production editor for this book. Lu Wendel Lyndon, Maynard Hale Lyndon, and Mary M. Allen were his informal advisors throughout the writing and illustrating of the book. To all these friends and coworkers, he extends sincere thanks. He also expresses his profound gratitude to his many students in detailing classes at the Massachusetts Institute of Technology and Yale University, who helped sharpen the focus of this book.

Patrick Rand thanks Edward Allen, generous mentor to a generation of architectural educators, for this opportunity to collaborate once again. Ed shows us all how to make the most important aspects of our craft vivid and accessible, empowering countless young designers to make architecture. Pat thanks Tom Ryan for his initiative to undertake this project, and for his vision demonstrating that good design principles are not limited in terms of scale setting or design discipline. Pat is also grateful to his many students, whose ambitious designs and probing questions helped him grow. He also thanks Christine Nalepa for her patience, support, and candid critiques of word and image.

Tom Ryan would like to thank Ed Allen for his generous encouragement and support, Pat Rand for his insight and tenacity, and both of them for the patient collaboration with an inexperienced author and part-time educator. Additional thanks are also due to Alan Aukeman, Lauren Bubela, Elliot Ryan, and Heather Thompson-Ryan for assistance and support with the writing and illustrating of this book. Tom would also like to thank Chuck Harris and Jim Corner for support in believing in his teaching ability and supporting him in developing the ideas in this book through classes at Penn and Harvard. He would also like to thank his past employers, partners, employees, co-workers, and students who have challenged his thinking and helped form the opinions buried in many of these patterns.

Much of the text and a number of the drawings in this book are based on text and illustrations in Allen and Rand's *Architectural Detailing: Function, Constructability, Aestetics,* 2nd ed. (2007). They have been adapted for this volume with the permission of the publisher, John Wiley & Sons, Inc.

E. ALLEN
*South Natick, MA*

P. RAND
*Raleigh, NC*

T. RYAN
*Lexington, MA*

# INTRODUCTION

As a way of guiding the transition from landscape architectural idea to built reality, a landscape architect designs and draws for each project a set of details that show how it will be put together.

How does the landscape architect know if these details will achieve the desired result? Will the project that they represent go together easily and economically? Will it drain? Will plant material thrive? Will the details look good with one another and with the overall form and space of the project? Will the details grow old gracefully, and will it last for the requisite period of time? There are many more questions of similar importance.

The experienced landscape architect does not leave the answers to chance. Each detail, no matter how special or unprecedented, is designed in conformance with universal, timeless patterns that, given competent execution on the construction site, virtually guarantee satisfactory performance. These *detail patterns* are the subject of this book.

Detail patterns are elemental fragments that are present in all successful details. They represent an accumulation of centuries of wisdom about what works in site construction and what does not. Many of the patterns are firmly grounded in scientific theory. Others are based just as solidly on common sense and the realities of human performance. The experienced landscape architect employs all these patterns automatically, as if by instinct, when designing details. The patterns provide a framework and a vocabulary to the concepts that underlie "good detailing."

Good detailing is an opportunity to advance the concepts, symbols, and aesthetic themes of the basic design. The detail patterns can be used to edit the schematic design, celebrating its strengths and eliminating features that are not contributing to the central ideas. The patterns clarify the issues relevant to a particular detail but avoid stating what the solution should be. They are meant to provoke the designer to discover many possible solutions, and to provide a clear process through which each can be assessed.

Details are rarely designed from scratch, a pure response to a situation, as if it never existed before. More often, we build upon precedents. The landscape architect uses the detail patterns as a reliable means of analyzing and understanding existing details. They are helpful in reviewing one's own work, in checking the work of other detailers in the office, in judging the quality of manufactured building components, and in diagnosing problems in existing landscapes. The absence of attention to a particular detail pattern, or the presence of a feature that contradicts a pattern, usually indicates a problem or a potential problem that should be corrected.

The detail patterns are straightforward and easy to learn. There are fewer than a hundred of them. Each is irreducibly simple. The first section of this book introduces each of the patterns in turn, explains it, and illustrates several instances of its use. Each pattern is given a simple descriptive name and a graphical icon to assist in its memorization.

The patterns are arranged in three main groups: Aesthetics, Function, and Constructibility, corresponding to the three major concerns of the detailer. Under each of these groupings, the patterns are further categorized by similarity of intent. The first category of patterns under Function, for example, is Controlling Water Movement, comprising eleven detail patterns that offer a complete strategy for accomplishing this important task.

The second portion of the book demonstrates the use of the detail patterns during the process of designing the details of three different landscapes: a plaza, a rooftop, and a residence.

The book closes with an annotated listing of publications recommended for the detailer's own reference shelf and a list of websites of particular interest. Exercises for self-study or classroom use are also provided.

The many sketches and drawings are intended to be illustrative of the elements and natural phenomena being addressed. They are not working drawings. Some information has been intentionally deleted or added to make the drawings effective instructional tools. For instance, anchors securing a masonry veneer to the backup are drawn in these sections, whereas they might only be identified in specifications or only in a large-scale detail in a set of working drawings produced in an office.

It is assumed that the reader has a general background in the materials and methods of site construction and is familiar with the conventions of landscape architectural drawing.

# PART
# I

# DETAIL
# PATTERNS

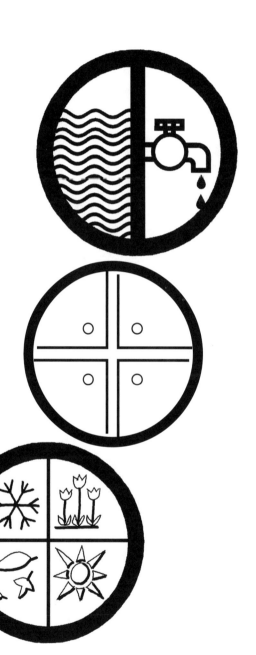

# SECTION
# 1
# AESTHETICS

A landscape should please the eye. Its details play a large role in this important function. Every truly great landscape has great details: details that contribute to the aesthetic themes of the site, that complement one another, and that create beauty out of the ordinary materials and necessities of construction. A landscape with a splendid thematic idea can fail as landscape architecture if it has poor details: details that are badly matched to its primary aesthetic, that do not relate strongly to one another, or that fail to lift their materials above the ordinary.

The detail patterns that relate to aesthetics are few in number, but each is powerful, far-reaching, and requires greater effort and insight to implement than any of the patterns relating to function and constructibility. The foremost aesthetic requirement for detailing is that all of the details of a landscape should contribute to its formal and spatial theme. Aesthetics drive what one should detail as well as how that detail will be developed. That development is based in ideas. Without strong and clear design ideas, the detailer's work is much more difficult. There is little basis for deciding how to configure a detail. Should the space feel enclosed, or expansive? What elements are the most important and which ones are subordinate? Should the joints between materials accentuate their differences or downplay them? Aesthetic features of individual details should be as appealing in future years as when they were built. These requirements are developed in the following detail patterns:

*Contributive Details (p. 5)*
*Timeless Features (p. 7)*

Details may be elaborated to feature certain inherent characteristics, or they may be decorative for purely visual effect:

*Hierarchy of Refinement (p. 8)*
*Intensification and Ornamentation (p. 10)*
*Active Details and Recessive Details (p. 12)*
*Continuous and Discontinuous Details (p. 14)*

Lastly, details may be developed whose role is solely to unify and give order to the visual composition of landscape elements that otherwise might seem disjointed or unrelated. This role is introduced in the following patterns:

*Formal Transitions (p. 15)*
*Composing the Detail (p. 17)*

These eight patterns serve to focus the detailer's attention on some important aesthetic issues that arise in detailing. They constitute a small part of a much larger field of study, visual composition that will amply repay as much time as the detailer can devote to its study.

The body of built landscape from antiquity to the present provides evidence of the importance of the link between art and craft. Classical Greeks originated the notion of *techne*, derived from the Greek verb *tikto*, meaning to produce. This term means the simultaneous existence of both art and craft, deliberately avoiding distinction between the two.

Landscape architectural details can convey to the observer in literal terms the facts about the form and how it is made. They can also reveal what is latent within the form—features so subtle that they are not consciously noticed by the casual observer. In these patterns, the term "aesthetics" will be used to describe features that recognize the inextricable link between art and craft, between the ideal and the circumstantial, between the concept and its tangible embodiment. In landscape architectural detailing, ideas must be made real.

The detailer is challenged to find solutions that solve the specific technical requirements of a given detail, while also showing affinity with the landscape's central aesthetic themes. Some details may seem to have no solutions, others may have many. The best solutions are functional, convey meaning, and reward the senses.

Although the emphasis in this section is on the visual qualities of a landscape and its details, the detailer should always look for opportunities to delight the other human senses. Tactile qualities of materials are important: the feel of decomposed granite underfoot; the shiny precision of a stainless steel and glass railing; deep, luxurious cushions on a bench; or the rough texture of a split stone wall. Auditory qualities are also vital: Should a particular space seem hushed and quiet? Should it be vast and echoey? Should one's footsteps resound throughout a space, or would it be more appropriate for one to tread softly, as if floating noiselessly? Would it enhance the users experience if one heard the sounds of splashing water, of birdsongs, of wind in trees, or of children chattering, in lieu of traffic noise? And consider the opportunities for olfactory delight in a landscape: the fragrance of thyme underfoot, the perfume of flowers, the freshness of mown grass, the moist breezes off a pond. Once again, the designers of the greatest landscapes have considered these possibilities and have often used them to their advantage.

CHAPTER **1** Aesthetics

![column icon] *Contributive Details*

All of the details of a landscape should contribute to its formal and spatial theme. They support and embellish the main design ideas in a landscape.

**1.** Many details are associated with a style. The style may be the incidental byproduct of practical actions, as might be found in good vernacular design, or the intentional expression of a particular body of work such as the California Modernists of the 1950s and 1960s. The flowing concrete patios and walls, redwood decks and fences all contributed to the "look" of the modern gardens of that time. They were a departure from the symmetry and ornament of the Beaux Arts that preceded it, and the detailing complimented the new aesthetic. Styles in landscape architecture are not always as well defined as in architecture, but the aesthetic sensibilities of a time are reflected in landscape architecture as well as the other arts.

**2.** In similar fashion we can analyze the details associated with any landscape architectural style: Baroque landscapes, which used highly finished materials with ornate profiles that were unified in balanced symmetrical compositions directly contrasted with Contemporary design, where elements may instead juxtapose machined and unprocessed materials in asymmetrical unresolved compositions with overlapping forms.

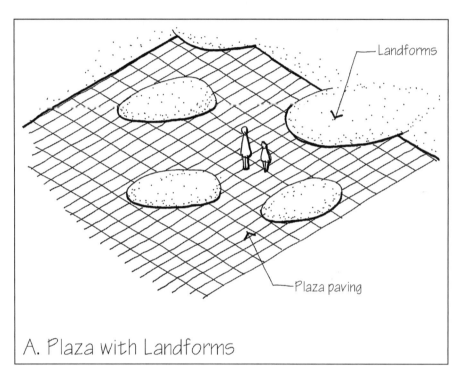

A. Plaza with Landforms

Landforms

Plaza paving

**3.** Every designer of landscapes works in his or her own manner or style. It may not have a name, but it has a consistent personality, sensibility, or a guiding ethic. This personality or ethic stems from an approach to space, form, light, color, and to details. The style of the details must be integral with the style of the landscape. As a designer's manner evolves and changes with each project, so must the details. The details must contribute their proportional share to the character and content of the landscape. For some landscape architects, a particular material or detail is the seed from which the landscape's design grows. Even if not the source of the central design concept, details are the voice of the concept, the means through which the concept is expressed. They are evident in the earliest conceptual drawings and must be developed as the design evolves. ▷

**4.** A landscape's details should be all of a family. It will not do to copy one detail from one source, another detail from another, and patch together a set of details that function well but bear no visible resemblance to one another. The designer should develop a matched set of the most important details as an ongoing part of the overall design process. This set of key details should then serve to guide the preparation of every other visible detail in the project. Details may become related by sharing a common compositional approach, which may be evident in their proportions, materiality, alignment, and orientation.

**5.** Dissimilar elements and architectural palettes can also be joined. Special attention must be given to their technical and compositional compatibility. One paving pattern may spill out over another. The details of the edges are the key to expressing either a low-key harmonious transition or to accentuate the tension and drama of the contrast between two different patterns and forms. Landforms marching across a plaza should have an edge detail that makes it clear that the landforms are dominant and overlapping the plaza below as opposed to rising up from below (see A and B). ■

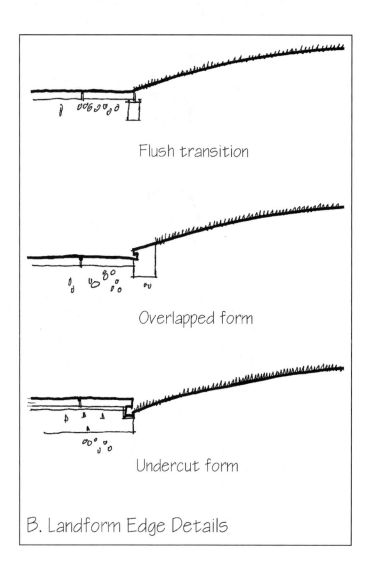

Flush transition

Overlapped form

Undercut form

B. Landform Edge Details

Details embody all that we know from the past, they respond to the certainty of the present, and they will serve an unknown future. They should be designed with this broad time frame in mind, not focused too narrowly on the present.

**1.** Nothing grows wearisome faster than a trendy detail or material treatment. The longer the life expectancy of the project, the more timeless its materials and details should be. It is usually inappropriate to detail a park or institutional landscape which will have a long life in the public realm, in the fleeting fashion of the day. However, it may be appropriate to do so in a hotel or retail project that will be continually renovated to stay new, or for an individual's garden where the aesthetic expression is personal and specific to the changing preferences of the owner. Well-designed details, made using durable materials and installed using appropriate workmanship, have a timeless quality.

**2.** Timeless details are more likely to be understood and appreciated by people in the future, much as good literature or music is appreciated by successive generations in a culture. A landscape with well-proportioned forms and spaces, a logical plan, and meaningful and well-made details will live a long time, almost certainly longer than the initial program. Owners in the future will become the landscape's stewards, maintaining it, introducing new elements with care, and being respectful of its basic ordering principles. Such landscapes should not be made with features that become aesthetically obsolete in a short period of time.

**3.** To be timeless, a detail does not need to have been done previously, or selected from a catalog of stock solutions. Innovation remains essential. New details and materials will always be part of a landscape architect's work. New details should be based on sound compositional principles, contribute to the overall themes of the design, have a grasp of the relevant physical phenomena, and should not waste human or material resources. If this is done, the details will likely achieve this timeless quality.

**4.** The means of production and "best practices" *du jour* often become a date stamp on the project. As industry introduces new materials and processes, or as new methods of construction are introduced at the construction site, eager designers explore their technical and aesthetic possibilities. Each designer nudges the envelope of authentic insights regarding the new material or process. Initial uses of new materials and tools are often ersatz imitations of their predecessors. Insight follows imitation: plastic was first used to imitate ivory products, such as billiard balls and piano keys; only later were the unique possibilities (and limitations) of plastics discovered. As light sources have become smaller and more energy-efficient, the design of light fixtures has expanded the range of lighting options tremendously. Detailers should actively participate in the exploration of new materials and construction processes, striving to distinguish between formal possibilities that are timeless and those that are merely today's fashion. ■

When designing a project, landscape architects usually establish a hierarchy of importance for spaces and elements, reflecting the importance of each part of the landscape in relation to the other parts. The level of refinement of details within the project should be consistent with this hierarchy.

**1.** Important spaces are often finished and detailed more lavishly or specially than other spaces of lesser stature. The front entrance of an office building is more extensively detailed than the loading dock. Plazas and squares are more refined than the pathways leading to them.

**2.** Details that will be viewed at close range are generally more refined than those that will be seen from far away and may also be designed for tactile olfactory qualities. The details of pedestrian ways are inherently more intricate than of vehicular ways, acknowledging differences in distance and speed of the viewer.

**3.** In elements with layered forms of construction, the visible outer surfaces are typically detailed with much more refinement than those that are concealed within the assembly, where only

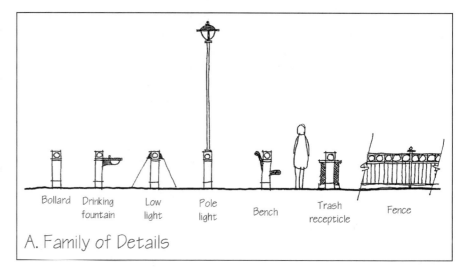

A. Family of Details

Bollard  Drinking fountain  Low light  Pole light  Bench  Trash recepticle  Fence

technical issues are relevant. A concrete block backer wall that supports a veneer of brick or stucco need not be aesthetically pleasing because it will be concealed by a visible outer finish. See *progressive finish,* p. 180.

**4.** No detail should fail to meet its functional obligations and all details must be constructible, but the degree of refinement may vary in order to enhance the detail's symbolic or experiential content. Some details are to be celebrated in the landscape, while others are quietly competent, func-

tional but simple. Resources that are conserved in making the routine details are then available for the special ones. Pathways paved with asphalt and edged with simple concrete curbs can subsidize an intersection with stone pavement and decorative curbing.

**5.** Differences between details should be thought of as variations on a basic theme. This will make all the details part of a family, and will make it easier for the observer to detect the intended relationship between them (see A).

**6.** At one time, refined building materials were wrought from raw materials; stone details were carved from rough blocks; a squared wood column was laboriously shaped from a log with an adze and plane from a log. High refinement was the mark of a skilled craftsperson, bestowing honor and respect to the artifact. With injection-molded plastics, aluminum extrusions, and computer-controlled laser cutters, we can now produce precise, refined pieces with unprecedented ease. We may ask: How much precision and refinement is enough? If every surface and detail is equally refined, none is more important than another. Meaning is diminished when there is no differentiation of refinement. Architectural philosopher John Ruskin advocated in his *Stones of Venice,* first published in 1851–53: "There should be no refinement of execution where there is no thought, for that is slave's work, unredeemed. Rather choose rough work to smooth work so only the practical purpose be answered, and never imagine

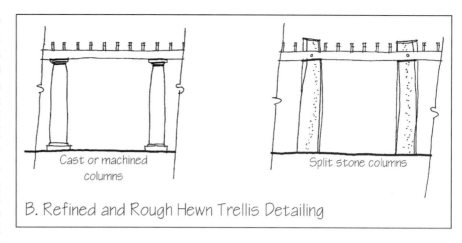

Cast or machined columns

Split stone columns

B. Refined and Rough Hewn Trellis Detailing

there is reason to be proud of anything that may be accomplished by patience and sandpaper." Our attraction to precision, crisp details, and smooth surfaces may be a vestige of the pre-industrial and predigital ages, when the means of production made such refinements rare and expensive. Many times it is the rough and un-machined elements that are now expensive and rare. A site element can be detailed utilizing machined or rough hewn material such as the trellis above. The effect of the material choice is integral to the design. The detailer should continue to reserve the most special, custom-made details for the most important elements in the landscape, and make other details in a manner consistent in quality and cost with their level of importance (see B). ■

Details can be embellished to add to the visual richness of a landscape.

**1.** Since the beginning of civilization, makers of things have evidenced love of their work by adding nonfunctional elements to their forms. Weavers have added textures, colors, and patterns. Tile makers have added brightly decorated glazes. Carpenters have chamfered and carved their work. Shinglers have added scallops and sawtooth patterns. Masons have laid delightful patterns of headers, soldiers, rowlocks, and corbels in their walls. The results of these efforts are often very beautiful, sometimes because they bring out inherent beauties of material and craft, and sometimes because they are simply beautiful in the abstract.

**2.** If we examine an ancient decorated Greek vase, we find two sets of patterns painted on it. One set is made up of circumferential stripes and bands that were created by holding a paintbrush against the clay vase as it spun on the potter's wheel. These stripes generally

Unadorned form    Intensification with striping    Ornamentation

A. Analysis of a Greek Vase

were applied at locations that were significant in relationship to the curvature of the vase—a change in the radius or direction of curvature. This practice might be termed intensification, because it is purposefully related to the process of making the vase and to its form, and thus it intensifies the vase's aesthetic. The bands and stripes express the pragmatic and formal qualities of the vase. The

other set of patterns consists of scenes of animals, warriors, athletes, gods, and goddesses—whatever suited the mood or mission of the potter. These bear little or no relationship to the manufacture or form of the vase, and might be termed ornamentation. Both intensification and ornamentation contribute to the beauty of the vase, but they sprang from different inspirations (see A).

**3.** Intensification and ornamentation have their places also in the work of the building trades. The carpenter's chamfers reduce the likelihood of splinters along the edges of a post or beam, so they have a function to perform. However, they also bring the long, straight edges more prominently to our view, and their beveled facets add sculptural interest to the timbers. A chamfer could not continue into a joint between members without creating unsightly gaps, so carpenters developed stylish ways of terminating chamfers short of the end of the member, in devices such as sinuous lamb's tongues or various angular notches. In the joints themselves, most of the artistry of the carpenter was necessarily concealed in mortises, tenons, and laps, but pleasing patterns could be created of exposed pegs and brackets. All this might be considered intensification, because it sprang from necessity but went beyond it to create a delight that enhances our understanding of the making of the building. If the carpenter went on to carve scenes or mottoes on the sides of the beams, this was ornamentation, because as attractive and contributive to the overall aesthetic of the structure as it might be, it was not directly related to necessity (see B).

**4.** The detailer should look first to intensification as a way of enhancing the aesthetic impact of details. The sources of inspiration are many: the need to put control joints into a concrete slab or stucco wall surface; the need to use form ties and rustication strips to create satisfactory surfaces of architectural concrete; the need to add brackets and bolts to connect members of steel or timber; the need to contain modular pavers; the need to install a lintel to support masonry over an opening in a garden wall; or the need to cover the gaps between fence boards to control

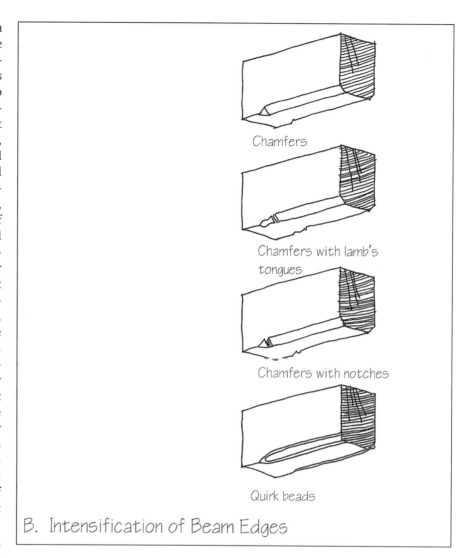

Chamfers

Chamfers with lamb's tongues

Chamfers with notches

Quirk beads

B. Intensification of Beam Edges

sound and sight. Each of these is an opportunity to intensify the form of a portion of the project by such strategies as adding lines or moldings to junctions between planes, creating rhythms and patterns of fasteners or seams, exaggerating sizes or numbers of things such as bolts or brackets, or adding contrasting colors. Each such effort is a celebration of the necessary, a virtuoso cadenza, a sharing of the joy of assembling a landscape with the viewer, who was not involved in its construction.

**5.** Ornamentation can be equally as effective as intensification, but it requires more dexterity and judgment, because it does not arise from a specific, tangible feature of the project but is derived from some other source or is created from scratch. Often intensification alone is sufficient to carry the landscape into the realm of the special, and applied ornament can look superficial, even awkward or tasteless if it is badly done or is at odds with the intrinsic features of the composition. ■

Details can actively contribute visually to the overall form or geometry of the design, visually asserting its presence against the surrounding field, or it can recess and blend quietly into its surroundings.

**1.** A simple paver edge detail can be either active or recessive. A recessive detail may include a plastic edge restraint that contains the pavers below grade and allows the pavers to abut the surrounding landscape directly. A complementary paving pattern could be a simple field unadorned with headers (see A).

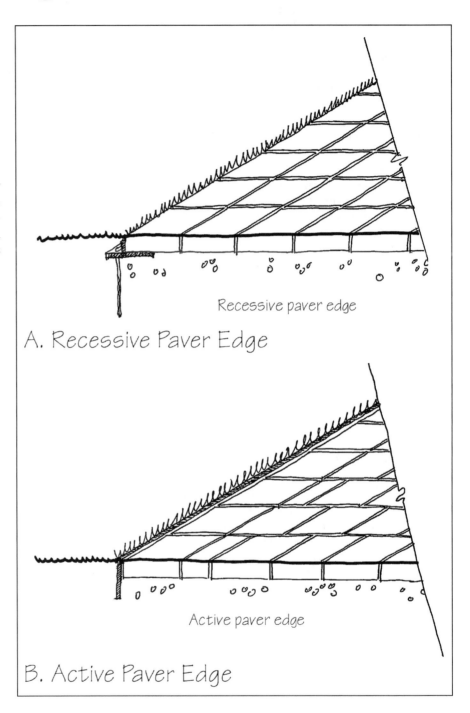

Recessive paver edge

A. Recessive Paver Edge

Active paver edge

B. Active Paver Edge

An active detail containing the same elements might also include a plastic or steel edge, but one that expresses itself at the surface (see B). A very active edge may extend above the face of the pavers to allow the paver surface to be slightly depressed below the edge of the surrounding landscape (see C). The paver surface could be further intensified with a header at the edge ornamented with an inscription or be enhanced by an additional decorative layer of stone or other contracting material.

**2.** The detailer weighs many factors when deciding whether a particular feature should be active or recessive. A largely transparent deck railing overlooking a spectacular view should include visually simple details that recede and don't compete with the view. On the other hand, guardrails and edges of steps and walls should be appropriately detailed in a very active manor to accentuate the differences between these elements and their surroundings and make them more visible. In these locations, the functional need for safety is more important than aesthetic concerns. ∎

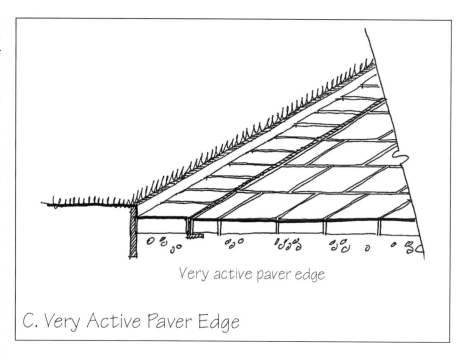

Very active paver edge

C. Very Active Paver Edge

Element profiles or patterns can be repeated in a family of details. The continuity or discontinuity of this repetition can be used to reinforce design ideas.

**1.** A stone bollard can be mimicked in a paving pattern, in a wall insert, and in bench supports all following an overriding pattern and/or module in the design. As the pattern of stone elements overlays the landscape, they can morph into bollards, benches, light posts, and so forth with all these elements sharing details that are applied continuously over the site (see A).

**2.** An element can also be detailed to accentuate its differences with its surrounding. Discontinuous details introduce contrast to the landscape, accentuating its difference. When the prevailing pattern of the landscape is not followed, it draws attention to the uniqueness or importance of the discontinuous element (see B). ■

A. Continuous Details

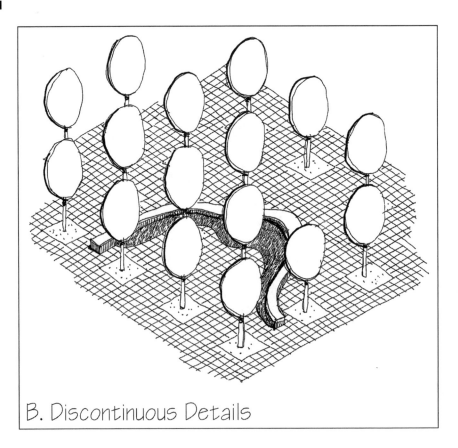

B. Discontinuous Details

Details can help to unify the visual composition of landscape elements that might otherwise seem disjointed or unrelated.

**1.** The masses and forms of a well-designed element generally merge pleasingly and require no further attention from the detailer, but occasionally a detail can help to correct the appearance of an awkward junction. A circular plaza at the junction of three paths may be weak as a diagram. Minor changes in the paving and edge detailing can celebrate the forms and focus attention on the shape of the plaza, establishing the prominence of the hierarchy of spaces at the site (see A).

**2.** An unarticulated transition from a stucco wall to a precast cap appears indecisive. The addition of recessed panels with a decorative border and the overhanging of the cap with a base trim below and at the base of the wall, breaks down the mass of the wall into component parts covered with a unifying top and base (see B).  ▷

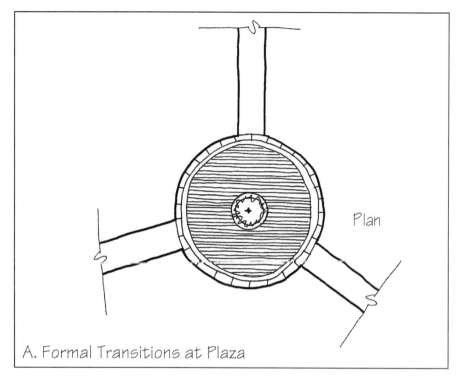

Plan

A. Formal Transitions at Plaza

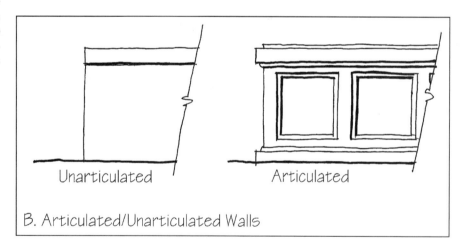

Unarticulated    Articulated

B. Articulated/Unarticulated Walls

**3.** In wood construction, a square cut rafter that simply extends beyond a supporting beam looks visually weak. A contouring of the rafter end can be a much stronger transition to the leading edge of a trellis overhang. Similarly, the connection of a column to beam can also appear weak and abrupt. The introduction of a capital can visually strengthen the transition (see C).

**4.** There are many details that benefit from a graceful termination of a form: a finial on a newel post, a volute at the termination of a cheekwall, a pier at the end of a wall. In none of these examples is it visually satisfactory merely to chop off the member that is being terminated (see D). ■

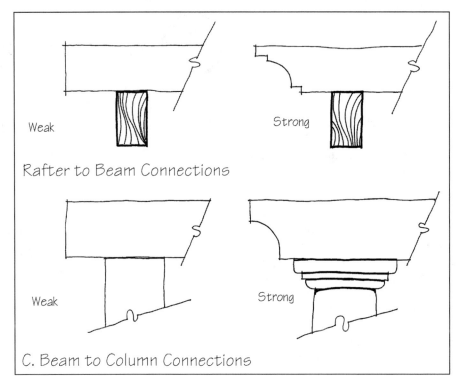

Rafter to Beam Connections

C. Beam to Column Connections

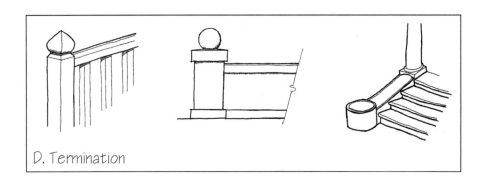

D. Termination

Aesthetic goals are often catalysts for exploration of a detail's technical possibilities. The detailer fuses aesthetic composition and technical exploration to find the best solution.

**1.** In the best landscapes, the details go beyond the technical realm to convey important compositional qualities and meaning. A well-composed detail can capture the essence of the design in a vivid way and can explain the relationships between the elements it joins. The brick paving that is scribed to meet the irregular face of an existing rock outcrop tells us that the outcrop is the dominant element, anchoring the composition. The detail demonstrates the basic design concept.

**2.** Detailers must resolve countless compositional questions such as whether an expressed joint is desired. In a low Cor Ten steel retaining wall, the steel panels can be fit into an expressed frame that is partially hidden, or supported with the most minimally visible frame. What the detail looks like and how the detail is made are inseparable aspects (see A).
▷

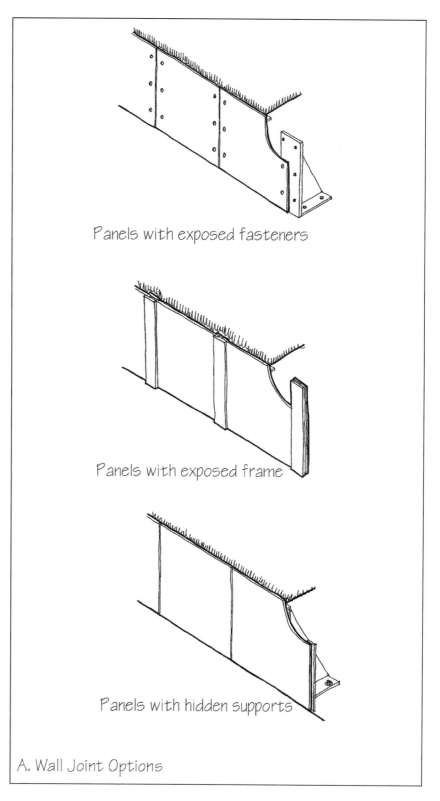

Panels with exposed fasteners

Panels with exposed frame

Panels with hidden supports

A. Wall Joint Options

**3.** Many landscapes have one little feature that people can fall in love with. The potency of the detail as a memorable element of the landscape is sometimes underestimated. Details that are seen up close or touched have the greatest potential to positively influence the observer. Whimsical inserts of castings or tile into paving or walls can personalize a space, making a connection between the designer and the users, inserting a little humor onto the landscape.

**4.** Details must be visualized in three dimensions. It is wise to develop details in three-dimensional sketches or models to visualize completely their forms and implications. Three-dimensional development also helps to explore how each detail turns the corner or intersects another element (see B).  ■

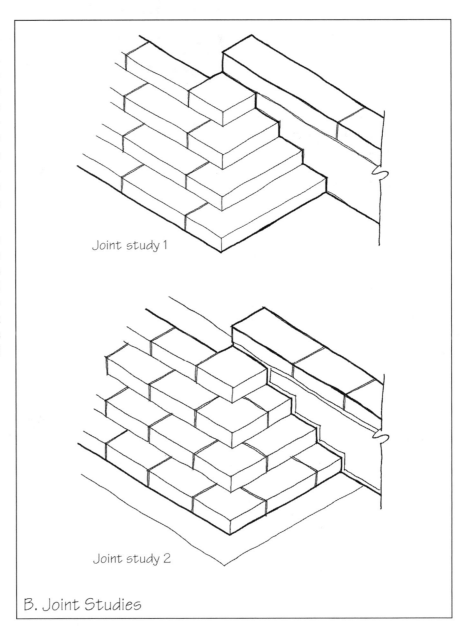

Joint study 1

Joint study 2

B. Joint Studies

# SECTION

## 2

# FUNCTION

For a landscape to function well, its details must function well. When designing details for a landscape, there are countless choices to make and no prescribed path toward the best solution. This portion of the book guides the detailer along this path by describing factors that affect the functional performance of details.

In landscape architecture, function certainly includes the technical performance of the details that contribute to making a site safe and secure for its users. But function also includes features that affect the qualities of the forms, surfaces, and spaces that compose the landscape. A space that is fully handicapped accessible and infiltrates all of the rain water that falls upon it but cannot withstand hard use and is expensive to maintain does not function as well as it could.

The detailer is challenged to address the functional needs of the site when it is new but also long into the future and sometimes beyond the lifetime of those who designed or constructed it. The detailer must remember that landscapes constantly change in response to natural forces, such as the daily cycles of temperature and light, as well as in response to seasonal changes. A basic grasp of physics and of biological and chemical processes are part of the detailing process, so too is knowledge of the functions which concern the users who engage with the site every day, altering it through countless actions.

The detail patterns that relate to function address the breadth of these topics. They are organized into thematic groups to focus the detailer's attention on each topic individually. Each pattern builds awareness of the issue and includes directions toward possible solutions. The patterns describe the natural processes involved, as well as the codes, standards, and conventional practices that are relevant to discovering appropriate detailing solutions.

CHAPTER **2** # Controlling Water Movement

## INTRODUCTION

When detailing elements in the landscape, some general principles should be kept in mind.

- All landscape elements are directly exposed to water.
- Water moves through a landscape driven by gravity, wind, and the pressure exerted by moving water.
- Water moves across the surface of non-porous materials and both across and through porous ones.
- Water is needed for plant growth, but can be detrimental to root growth if too much water displaces the air in the voids between soil particles. Excessive moisture can also foster decay in some organic materials that are in contact with the soil.
- Too much or too little water can weaken the bearing capacity of soil and can cause it to contract or expand.
- In cold climates, the presence of water in materials subject to freezing can cause movement and cracking.

In landscape architectural detailing, the detailer should be able to trace the path of water through the detail, repelling it in some areas and allowing it to penetrate in others. The patterns described in this chapter are grouped into two categories. One group describes patterns that repel water and keep it from penetrating vulnerable elements and assemblies. The other group describes patterns that allow for movement of water through details.

This group of details is also integrally connected to grading. All exterior surfaces must slope to accommodate drainage. Those slopes are the fundamental basis of detailing to accommodate the movement of water. Sectional drawings that indicate a level surface must be sloped in another axis. Landscape architectural details are fundamentally different than architectural details in this regard. In landscape architectural detailing, all horizontal surfaces are sloped and subject to the extremes of precipitation, where many architectural details deal with level surfaces sheltered from moisture and large temperature fluctuations.

## WATER PENETRATION

For water to penetrate through an assembly (building, pavement, and the like) three conditions must all occur at the same time:

1. There must be an opening through the assembly.
2. There must be water present at the opening.
3. There must be a force to move the water through the opening.

If any one of these three conditions is not met, water will not penetrate the assembly. In designing any exterior detail, therefore, we can pursue one or more of three strategies:

1. We can try to eliminate openings in the assemblies.
2. We can try to keep water away from openings in assemblies.
3. We can try to neutralize forces that move water through openings in the assemblies.

Complete success in any one of these three strategies will result in the complete elimination of water leakage. But sometimes in detailing we pursue two of these strategies, or even all three of them at the same time, because this gives added security in case one of them fails due to poor workmanship or material deterioration. Let us consider each of these strategies briefly and list the detail patterns that relate to each.

## 1. ELIMINATING OPENINGS IN ASSEMBLIES

Every assembly is full of openings. A shingled fence has an opening under each shingle. A concrete slab has a potential opening at every crack or joint. A brick and stone wall has cracks around joints between the units of material from which the wall is made. Additional cracks and holes may form as the elements age and deteriorate. We can attempt to eliminate all these openings by using preformed gaskets and sealants. As a sole strategy this is unreliable. Gaskets may not seal securely if they are the wrong size or resiliency, or if the surfaces they touch are rough or unclean. Sealants may fail to adhere properly if the materials to which they are applied are not scrupulously clean and properly primed or if the installer does not compress the sealant fully into the joint. Both sealants and gaskets can deteriorate from weathering and from the flexing and stretching they may undergo as the building ages. A surface that relies on sealants and gaskets alone for watertightness will leak sooner or later. Furthermore, even a small defect in a sealant or gasket that is exposed to the weather can leak very large amounts of water, just as a small hole in a hose can create a very large puddle and the defect will tend to grow.

Sealants and preformed gaskets are extremely useful, however, as components of an overall strategy for making a surface watertight. Therefore, it is important to know how to detail sealant joints and gasket joints correctly and how to incorporate them into more complex schemes for controlling water penetration. The detail pattern that relates to eliminating openings in assemblies is discussed in the following section:

*Joints and Gaskets* (p. 45)

## 2. KEEPING WATER AWAY FROM OPENINGS IN ASSEMBLIES

There are a number of effective ways to keep water away from openings. Often it is useful to keep most water away from an opening simply by reducing the volume of water that must be dealt with at the opening itself.

The detail patterns that relate to keeping water away from openings in assemblies are:

*Drainage Diversions* ( p. 23)
*Redundant Drainage Systems* (p. 27)
*Foundation Drainage* (p. 29)
*Roof Drainage* (p. 31)
*Wash* (p. 33)
*Overlap* (p. 36)
*Drain and Weep* (p. 38)
*Overhang and Drip* (p. 40)

## 3. NEUTRALIZING FORCES THAT CAN MOVE WATER THROUGH OPENINGS IN ASSEMBLIES

There are four forces that can move water through an opening in an assembly or surface: (1) gravity, (2) surface tension, (3) capillary action, and (4) momentum. In most cases, it is surprisingly easy to detail an assembly so that all four of these forces are neutralized, and the most secure strategies for keeping water out of an assembly are based on this approach.

We have already encountered some of the detail patterns for neutralizing gravity and surface tension, because these same patterns are useful in keeping water away from openings in assemblies. The force of gravity is neutralized by the following patterns that keep water out of assemblies.

*Wash* (p. 33)
*Overlap* (p. 36)

The force of gravity is neutralized by this pattern to expel water from the assembly.

*Drain and Weep* (p. 38)

Surface tension, a force that causes water to cling to the underside of a surface where it can run into an opening, is neutralized by

*Overhang and Drip* (p. 40)

The pattern for neutralizing capillary action is:

*Capillary Break* (p. 43)

The pattern for neutralizing momentum is:

*Labyrinth* (p. 44)

By combining these patterns we can make an assembly entirely waterproof.

Surface water is diverted from travel ways, buildings, and other structures by grading the ground surrounding them to areas that are not susceptible to water damage or don't pose a safety hazard when flooded. Drainage can be dispersed and taken away in a sheet flow or concentrated and removed via a drainage system. Drainage systems are either open (swaled) or closed (piped). In general, the steeper the gradient, the faster the water will flow and the higher the rate of flow can be accommodated for a given cross sectional area (steeper slope = smaller pipe or swale for a given flow rate). On the other hand, the steeper the gradient, the less exfiltration occurs and the drainage system downstream must be sized to take greater flow and volume than one with a shallower gradient. In addition, steeper gradients mean higher runoff velocities and more potential for erosion and scour.

**TABLE 2-1**

| Gradients | Small (flat slope) | Large (steep slope) |
|---|---|---|
| Flow Capacity | Low | High |
| Infiltration | High | Low |
| Erosion Potential | Low | High |

The site grading must strike a balance between the desired slope and its implications on water flow, concentration and dispersal. The detailer should

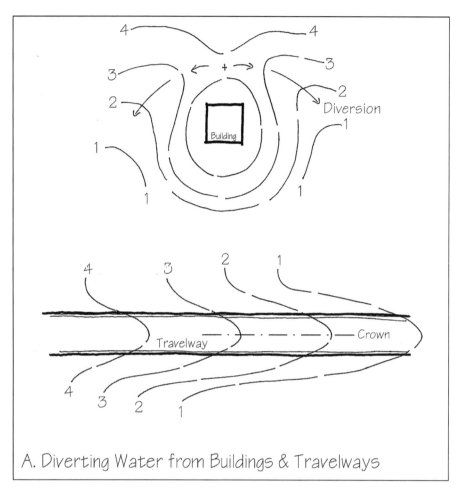

A. Diverting Water from Buildings & Travelways

always be aware of the path water will take through the landscape and through each detail, including its relative volume and velocity.

**1.** The site grading should introduce relative high points or ridges within the landscape to divert water from buildings. The relative high points create diversions or alternate routes for water to flow away from buildings and the crown (ridgeline in the center of the road) of travel ways (see A).  ▷

**2.** The detailer should be familiar with basic drainage configurations. A simple enclosed space such as a flat rooftop with a parapet, courtyard, plaza, and the like can be drained in four basic configurations.

The **first** configuration is a drain in the space's interior with all sides sloping to the drain. This allows all edges to be level and at the same elevation. This configuration concentrates water away from the edges which may be susceptible to water damage from puddling at the drain, but could interfere with travel ways through the space (see B1).

The **second** configuration slopes the entire space to one edge. This configuration can create a uniformly sloping plane without folds and may be aesthetically desirable, but requires a continuous drain (trench or slot drain) along one edge. The low edge and the high edge can be level, but the sides are sloping. This configuration disperses and sheds water from the space, but the edge concentration can jeopardize adjacent structures. Also a trench drain is usally much more expensive than individual inlets (see B2).

The **third** configuration introduces a fold or swale into the space to collect the water and convey it to a single point at the edge. This configuration allows for three level sides and one side sloping to the drain. This configuration is similar to the second, but can be accommodated with a single, usually less-expensive drain (see B3).

The **fourth** configuration introduces a fold and continuous drain at the interior of the space. This configuration has the inherent cost premium of the B1 configuration but without the clean lines of a single plane (see B4).

These four configurations are rarely used individually, but are usually used in combinations or arrays to drain spaces with multiple watersheds.

**3.** There are four basic configurations that relate to drainage of travel ways. These four configurations are distinguished by their cross sections.

The **first** configuration has a level cross section through the pavement and all drainage is carried longitudinally along the travel way. This configuration

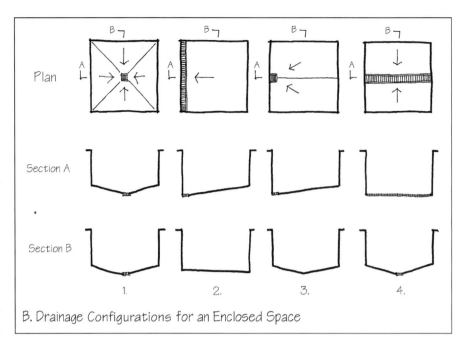

B. Drainage Configurations for an Enclosed Space

provides a consistent sheet flow down the way (see C1).

The **second** configuration introduces a ridge or crown into the center of the travel way and concentrates the water flow at the edge of the pavement. That edge often is defined by a curb or similar hard edge to resist erosion by the concentrated flow. The crown keeps the center of the way dry and free of ice while concentrating the flow at the edges where it can be intercepted by drains (see C2).

The **third** configuration also has a ridge or crown but allows the water to flow off the pavement into an adjacent swale. This configuration concentrates the runoff away from the paved way in an open drainage system, but requires much more width than the previous pattern (see C3).

The **fourth** configuration uses a cross pitch to collect drainage on one side of the pavement. The drainage can be collected at the pavement surface, similar to the second configuration, or run into an open system, similar to the third. This configuration is also used in curving roads, sloping the pavement to

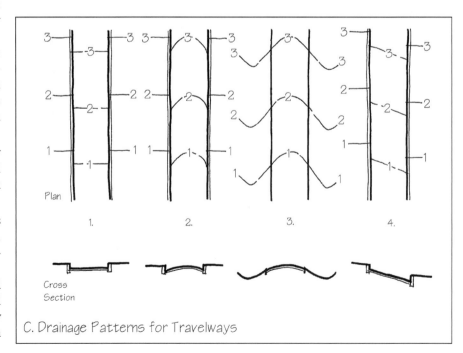

C. Drainage Patterns for Travelways

the inside of the curve to use gravity to counteract a car's centrifugal force, thus keeping them on the road. The cross pitch is called superelevation (see C4).

**4.** Every site drainage system is designed to accommodate a certain design storm intensity. Design storm intensities are usually described as 1, 2, 5, 10, 50, or 100-year storms (or the rate of rainfall that could be reasonably expect, in a peak event that would occur in a 1, 2, 5, 10, 50, or 100-year period). Drainage systems that are designed for a 1-year storm have smaller drains, with smaller pipes and swales than a 100-year storm and would be expected to be overwhelmed much more often than a 100-year storm design, but will be much less expensive. Drains also require some ponding over their tops to operate at peak efficiency. This ponding, or free-board, over the drain must be worked into the detailing of parapets, curbs, walls, ramps, and so forth to allow for a certain amount of water to puddle over drains without backing up and jeopardizing buildings or travel ways. Waterproofing is extended well above drains in roof conditions; drains are kept below the tops of retaining walls; and handicapped ramps are located away from drainage structures to allow for this ponding (see D).

**5.** Sheet flow in sufficient volume and velocity can cause erosion on a slope that is not sufficiently armored (see *Building and Landscape Armor,* p. 145) to resist the erosive forces. As an alternate to armoring the slopes, water can be intercepted and conveyed away to one or more catch swales or interceptor swales. If these are used, armor may be advisable on the surface that blunts the water flow (to the right of the center-line in Drawing E), but not be needed on the other surfaces. (see E). ▷

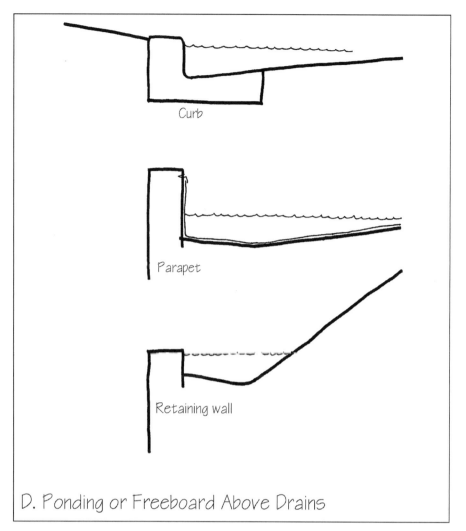

Curb

Parapet

Retaining wall

D. Ponding or Freeboard Above Drains

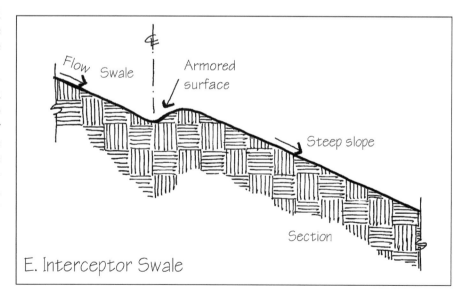

Flow  Swale    Armored surface    Steep slope    Section

E. Interceptor Swale

**6.** In areas where snow is expected, drainage patterns must be designed to function with snow accumulations. Drain inlets are often located in areas where snow removal above the drain is easy (see F). ■

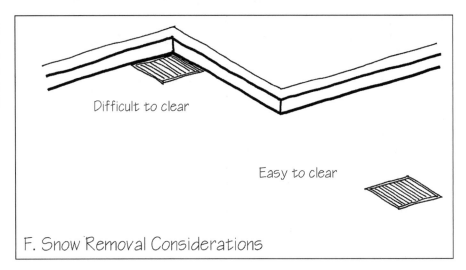

Difficult to clear

Easy to clear

F. Snow Removal Considerations

# Redundant Drainage Systems

Drainage systems sometimes fail. Drainage structures can be clogged with debris, pipes can be crushed or chocked with sediment, and outfalls can be confined with grading or debris. The detailer should be aware of potential failures and include in the design redundant systems to protect buildings and key travel ways from flooding.

**1.** Redundant drains are sometimes required on roof structures. A secondary or overflow drain is located above the primary drain to provide a backup to the primary drain. The secondary drainage system should be visible so as to alert owners to the need to clean or repair the primary system when water flows through the secondary system (see A).

**2.** If the failure of a closed drainage system could flood the building, so it is often backed up with an open swale emergency overflow that will divert water away from the building if the primary drain fails (see B).

**3.** Multiple redundant drains are used to back up one another with the drainage divide between drain watersheds being set below the elevation of any potential flood damage elevation. If one drain fails, water will flow to adjacent drains before it jeopardizes a building (see C).  ▷

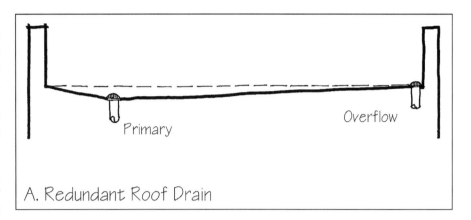

A. Redundant Roof Drain

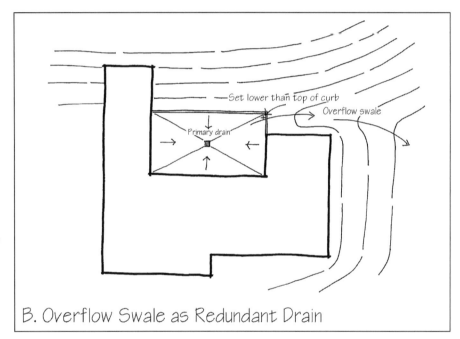

B. Overflow Swale as Redundant Drain

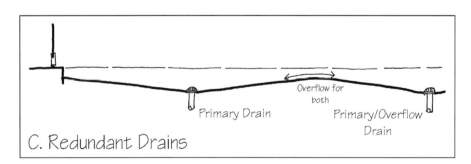

C. Redundant Drains

**4.** In a fountain, standpipes can be used to remove excess stormwater that falls in the pool as well as overflow of displaced water when someone or something enters into the water. The same standpipe can double as a drain inlet when the pipe is removed and the fountain is drained and inactive (see D).

**5.** Dome-shaped roof or planter drains have a "built-in" redundancy when compared with a flat drain. A flat drain is easily clogged with debris, but in a domed drain, if the lower parts of the drain are clogged, the higher portions remain free to function. There are also combined drains that have two inlets in a single structure. This type of drain adds further redundancy when the overflow drain is connected to a separate drain line (see E). ■

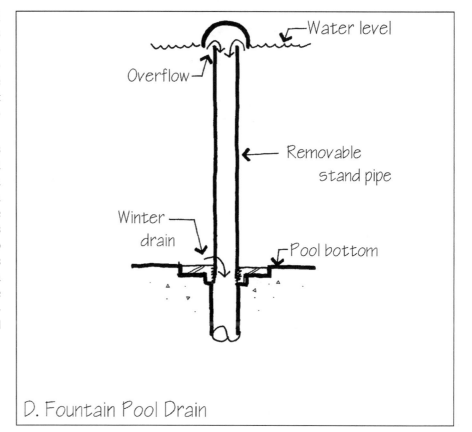

D. Fountain Pool Drain

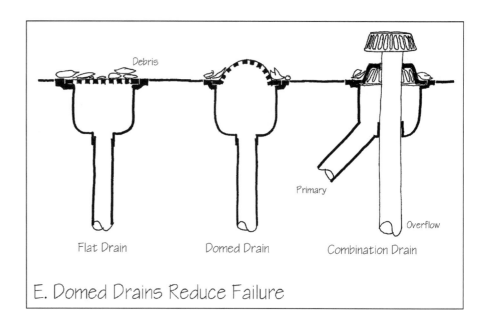

E. Domed Drains Reduce Failure

Basements tend to leak. Water is almost always present in the surrounding soil. There are always openings in basement walls: Concrete and masonry foundation walls are full of cracks, pores, and utility line penetrations, and the joint between a basement floor slab and a foundation wall is difficult to make waterproof. Also present are strong forces to move any water through the openings, especially hydrostatic pressure. Removing water from the soil around a basement by means of foundation drainage is the surest way to keep the basement from leaking. Foundation drainage has the added benefit of reducing or eliminating the water pressure that tends to collapse the basement walls. These principles also apply to buildings without basements because groundwater can also harm slabs on grade and crawl space foundation systems.

**1.** Surface drainage is a first line of defense against water around a basement forcing surface water to drain away from the basement rather than toward it. Gradients of 2 to 10 percent are recommended for a distance of at least 6 ft (1.83 m) from a building. Also part of the first line of defense are roof drainage systems (either perimeter gutters or internal roof drains), which keep roof water away from the foundation and basement by collecting it and diverting it (see A).  ▷

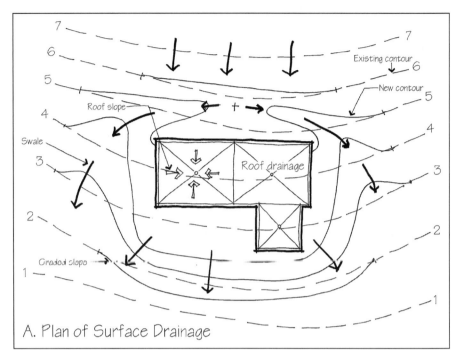

A. Plan of Surface Drainage

**2.** The second line of defense against water around a basement consists of open drainage pipes that are laid in porous material at the base of the basement wall. Sometimes on very wet sites drainage pipes are laid under the floor slab as well. The porous material against the wall may be either a gap graded crushed stone (a mix of stone sizes that has a gap in one or more size, allowing water to move through that gap) and/or a thick panel or mat of synthetic material that contains large internal voids for the passage of water. When water moves through the ground toward the basement wall, it first reaches the porous layer, where gravity pulls it rapidly downward. As the water accumulates at the base of the wall it enters the open drainage pipe and flows by gravity either to an outlet down slope from the building or to a sump in the basement floor from which it is ejected by an automatic pump (see B).

The drainage pipe has a line of holes or slots in it to allow water to enter. The function of the pipe is to provide an unobstructed lateral passage for water through the crushed stone. Pro-

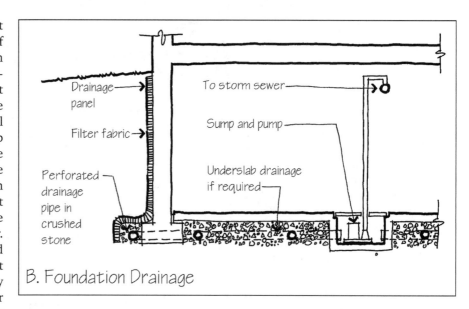

B. Foundation Drainage

vided the pipe is placed lower than the slab of the basement it is protecting, it makes no difference whether the holes face up, down, or sideways, except that downward-facing holes allow water to enter the pipe at a lower elevation than the other orientations.

Fine soil particles can be carried into the drainage layer by water percolating through the soil. Eventually, these particles may clog the pores of the drainage material. To prevent this, it is good practice to provide a synthetic filter fabric compatible with the soil texture between the drainage material and the soil. The fabric allows water to pass freely while straining out the fine soil particles. For further discussion, see Chapter 3, *Controlling Subsurface Water Movement and Sedimentation*. ■

Water sometimes leaks into a structure because of an inadequate or poorly maintained drainage mechanism. Designers should trace the path of water from where it first contacts the structure to its point of discharge to be sure that the path will be effective. The best drainage systems in these instances remove the water swiftly and directly. Special attention is called for when the drainage lines are concealed inside of walls or under slabs, because they are difficult to detect and expensive to repair.

**1.** Once water is collected in a drainage mechanism, keep it moving smoothly to the discharge point by avoiding flat slopes or circuitous paths. Even short distances where water is stationary can allow waterborne sediment to collect, slowing the flow of water. Anticipate where an obstruction may occur and include features that minimize its threat. Use rainfall intensity data for the building location to calculate the volume of water to be carried by the drainage system; include a safety factor in case unusual weather, ice damming, or poor maintenance occurs. The safety factor should double if multiple adverse factors are expected. Scale gutters, leaders, scuppers, and drains generously and avoid extreme reductions in the size of the channel that carries the water. Provide accessible cleanouts at the locations where obstruction is most likely. Where possible, include details that separate waterborne debris from the moving water. Filters or strainers at the point where water enters a roof drain, gutter, leader rain barrel, or drain are a common solution but require periodic maintenance to remove debris (see A).

**2.** At the point where the downspouts meet the ground, the rainwater must be dispersed and directed away from the foundation with a splashblock or other armored surface, collected in a drainage system, or harvested in a cistern. After

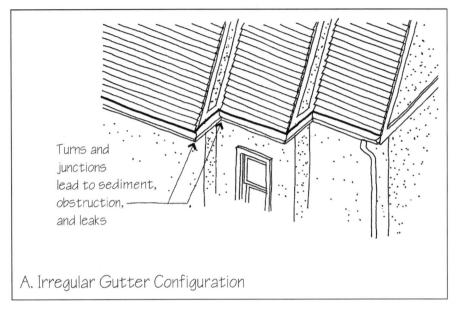

A. Irregular Gutter Configuration

Turns and junctions lead to sediment, obstruction, and leaks

the initial flush washes away airborne dirt, rainwater is a very desirable source of water for reuse (see B).

**3.** The joints in water drainage systems for precipitation, snowmelt, and condensation typically are not sealed as tightly as plumbing pipes that contain water under pressure. When drainage channels are obstructed, water may collect to sufficient depth to cause these joints to leak. Drainage lines concealed within a wall cavity or under a pavement should be watertight to avoid leaks that are difficult to find and correct. ▷

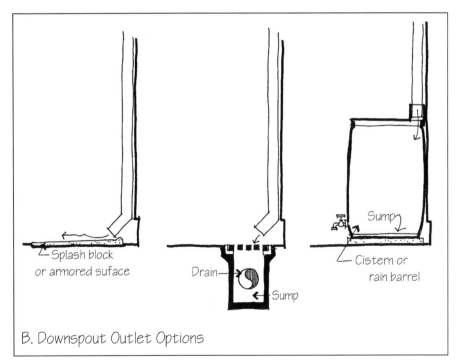

B. Downspout Outlet Options

Splash block or armored suface

Drain—

Sump

Sump

Cistern or rain barrel

**4.** Capillary action can be used to transfer water from a roof to a drain or swale on the ground by means of a chain or series of connected funnels. Often chosen for their aesthetic qualities, these systems are not as effective at conveying water to the ground as a downspout. There can be substantial overflow and splash from the chains or funnels, particularly in high-volume or high-wind storms. The basins or inlets that receive the water should be sized accordingly (see C). ■

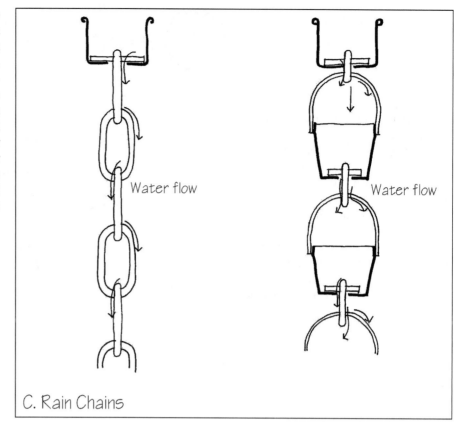

C. Rain Chains

# Wash

A wash is a slope given to a horizontal surface to drain water away from vulnerable areas of an assembly.

**1.** The coping on a retaining wall parapet has a wash to keep standing water away from the seams and cracks in the parapet. Usually the wash drains away from the exposed face, to minimize water staining (see A).

**2.** Another special case of the wash is indicated on architectural drawings by the note "pitch to drain." The rain gutter at the eave of a roof is usually pitched (sloped) to drain water toward the nearest downspout. Common slopes used for gutters are ⅛ in. or ¼ in. per foot (1:100, 1%, or 1:50, 2%). A steeper slope gives a greater capacity to handle water in a heavy rainstorm. Care should be taken to detail the end of the downspouts, tying them into subsurface systems or providing a splashblock to armor the soft surface of the ground against erosion (see B). ▷

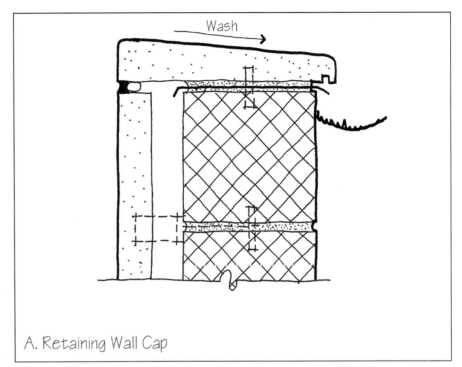

A. Retaining Wall Cap

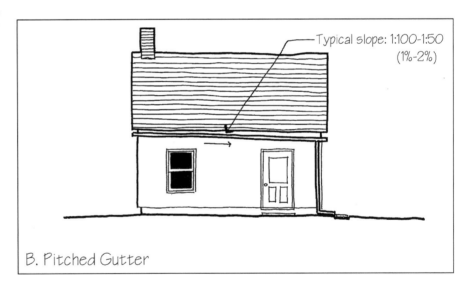

Typical slope: 1:100-1:50 (1%-2%)

B. Pitched Gutter

**3.** If there is no interior floor drain, a residential concrete garage floor is usually pitched so water dripping off a car will run under the garage door and out. Minimum pitch recommendations are ¼ in. per foot (1:50, 2%) (see C).

**4.** Minimum pitches on exterior surfaces are determined by the porosity, and/or roughness of the material as well as the precision in which it can be constructed. Porous materials can be laid almost flat, with water infiltrating through the surface to the soil below. In non-porous surfaces, water will flow with a very shallow pitch when the force of gravity is greater than the surface tension between the water and the pavement. Changes in surface gradients inherent in any rough material must be overcome with steeper pitches. In very shallow pitches, where the surface is not extremely smooth, water will form puddles. Puddling can be caused by rough materials (split stone), by installation (asphalt), and by design (pattern of joints).

Rough stone that has fabrication tolerances of up to 1/8″ should be laid with a minimum slope of 2% to alleviate puddling in the depressions inherent in the surface of the material. Installation of monolithic surfaces also has an acceptable tolerance in surface flatness that can cause puddles in very shallow slopes. Asphalt paving is typically installed without formboards and the surface is finished with a roller that can further distort the surface, so asphalt tolerances are up to ¼″ per 10' and a recommended minimum slope is

Typical pitch: 1:50 (2%)

Pitch to drain

C. Garage Slab Pitched to Drain

**TABLE 2.2**

| Surface | Minimum Slope | Maximum Slope |
|---|---|---|
| Concrete, textured/exposed aggregate finish | 2% | |
| Concrete, broomed finish | 1.5% | |
| Concrete, troweled finish | 1% | |
| Brick/Stone with flame finish | 1% | |
| Stone with split finish | 2% | |
| Fine crushed aggregate (decomposed granite, limestone screenings etc. without binder) | 1.5% | 3% |
| Asphalt with finish course | 1.5% | |
| Roadway longitudinal slope | 0.5% | 12% |
| Roadway cross slope | 0.5% | 6% |
| Roadway crown | 2% | 3% |
| Parking space cross slope | 0.5% | 5% |
| Concrete gutters | 0.25% | |
| Sidewalk longitudinal slope | 0.5% | 10% * |
| Sidewalk cross slope | 1% | 4% |

* 5% or 8% (with rails) if accessible by the disabled

2%. Concrete paving is usually cast with formboards and finished with more precision than asphalt, so a recommended minimum is 1%. Concrete curbs can be cast with even tighter tolerances due to the narrow width between formboards and the smooth troweled finish common on integral curb and gutter.

Design can also play a role in minimum slopes. A joint pattern with joints running parallel to the slope can be laid in a flatter slope that the same materials with the majority of joints running perpendicular to the slope (see D and E).

**5.** Benches, seatwalls, stadium seats, and other sittable surfaces should have a wash to shed water after a rain. The same is also true of fence posts, caps and top rails, curbs, walls etc. (see F).

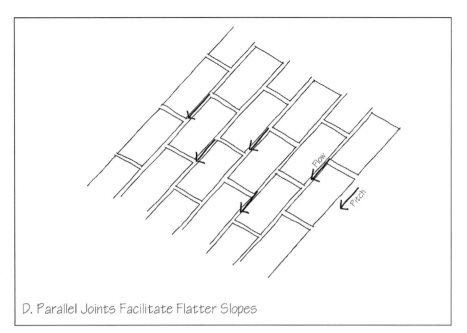

D. Parallel Joints Facilitate Flatter Slopes

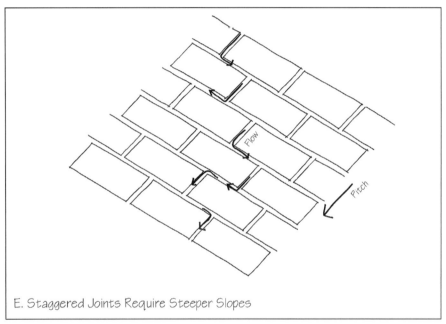

E. Staggered Joints Require Steeper Slopes

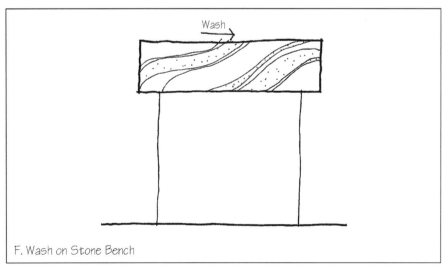

F. Wash on Stone Bench

In an overlap, a higher surface is extended over a lower surface so water moved by the force of gravity cannot run behind or beneath the surface. For an overlap to work, the surfaces must be sloping or nearly vertical. Porous materials need a greater overlap and steeper slope to be effective.

**1.** Roof shingles and tiles keep water out by overlapping in such a way that there is no direct path through or between them. Each unit covers a joint between units in the course below. The overlap only works, however, if the roof surface slopes steeply enough so that water runs off before it can find its way around the backs of the shingles or tiles to the open cracks beneath (see A).

**2.** Wood bevel siding sheds water by overlapping each board over the one below. The weak spots in wood siding are the end joints, which should be caulked and flashed to prevent water penetration (see B).

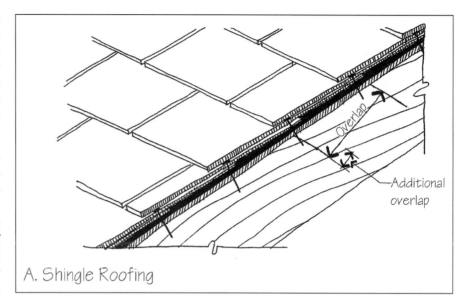

A. Shingle Roofing

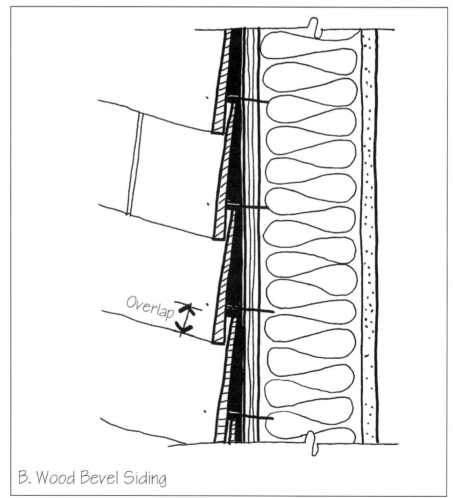

B. Wood Bevel Siding

**3.** A reglet (also called a raggle) is an upward-sloping slot in a vertical surface into which a flashing or the edge of a roof membrane may be inserted. The slope (wash) acts to prevent water from being forced into the vulnerable joint by gravity, and the overlap of the upper lip of the reglet over the flashing keeps water from reaching the joint between the two components. The contemporary type of reglet shown in this drawing is created in a concrete wall or spandrel beam by using a preformed strip of metal or plastic that is nailed lightly to the formwork before the concrete is poured. The opening in the reglet is usually closed temporarily with an adhesive tape or a strip of plastic foam to prevent its being accidentally clogged with concrete. There are many patented profiles for this type of reglet that are intended to interlock securely with a folded edge on the top of the flashing. Diligent inspection is needed just prior to concrete pouring to be sure that the reglet is installed right-side up.

If a reglet is wetted, water may find its way through by capillary action. A continuous bead of sealant between the flashing and the reglet can be helpful in preventing this (see C).

**4.** There are also a number of patented designs of surface-mounted reglets made of plastic or metal. A bead of sealant is intended to keep water from behind the reglet. This is somewhat risky, because the success of the detail is entirely dependent on perfect workmanship in installing the sealant and perfect adhesion of the sealant to the wall.

An overlap is generally very effective in preventing entry of water driven by the force of gravity. If wind is allowed to blow through an overlap, however, it may carry water with it. An overlap is useless against standing water, so it cannot be used on a level surface. When working around the base or on top of buildings, the flashing require-

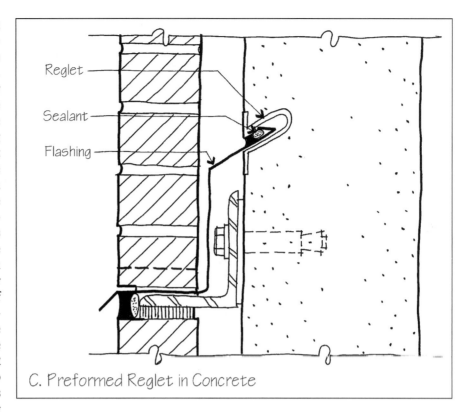

C. Preformed Reglet in Concrete

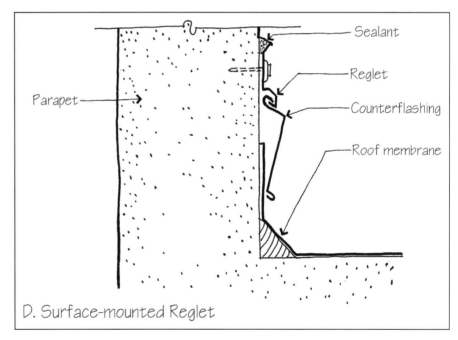

D. Surface-mounted Reglet

ments of the building must be coordinated with the finish grades outside the building and at the building parapets. Flashing in parapets at the edge of veg-

etated roofs on the tops of buildings must also be carefully matched with the elevations of the planting medium (see D). ∎

It is often wise to include provisions for collecting and conducting away any water that may leak through the outer layer of a masonry cavity wall system. This internal drainage system is a frank and useful acknowledgment that things can go wrong in sealants, gaskets, mortar joints, and metal connections, whether caused by faulty materials, inadequate workmanship, movement, or deterioration of materials over time. Such a drainage system also releases any water that condenses inside the assembly or enters it from interior sources. It is inexpensive insurance against the damage that can be caused by uncontrolled leakage and the expense of rebuilding a wall of flawed design. An internal drainage system is comprised of spaces or channels that conduct water by gravity to weep holes or other openings that direct the water back out of the wall.

**1.** The rafter detail of a traditional Redwood-framed greenhouse is extremely simple. The sheets of glass that bear on the rafter are bedded in glazing compound and secured with a strip of Redwood held on with screws. This is not a rain screen detail; any defect in the glazing compound will result in water leakage between the glass and the rafter. Because of surface tension, water that has leaked through will cling to the rafter and run down its sides. This detail furnishes a small drainage gutter milled into the rafter on either side to catch this water and conduct it to the bottom of the rafter, where it is wept to the outdoors. Contemporary manufactured skylights and greenhouse assemblies have similar integral drainage features (see A).

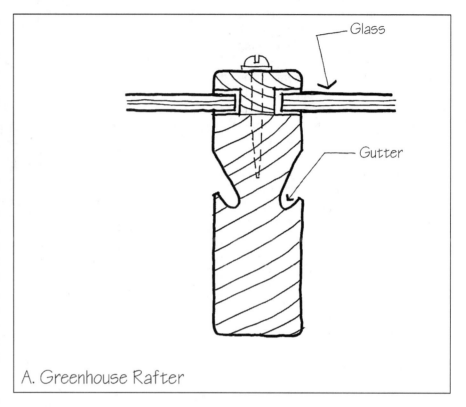

A. Greenhouse Rafter

Glass

Gutter

**2.** The outer wythe of a masonry cavity wall is expected to leak water, especially as the mortar joints age and deteriorate. The leakage drains down the cavity until it encounters an interruption of the cavity such as an opening in the wall, or at the base of the wall. At each of these points, a continuous flashing collects the water and drains it through weep holes that are provided at horizontal intervals of from 2 to 4 ft (0.6 to 1.2 m) (see B). ■

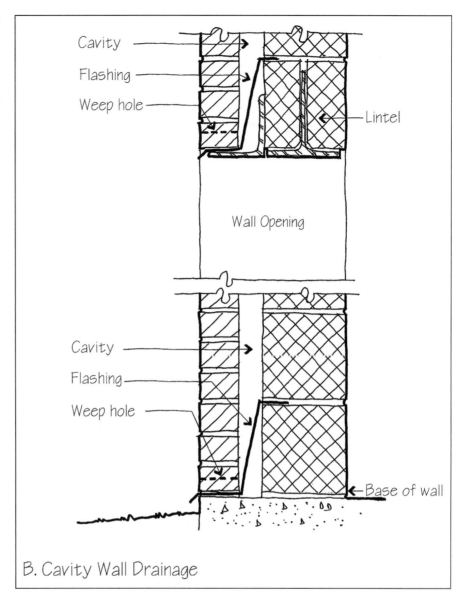

Cavity

Flashing

Weep hole

Lintel

Wall Opening

Cavity

Flashing

Weep hole

Base of wall

B. Cavity Wall Drainage

Adhering drops or streams of water running down a wall can be kept away by a twofold strategy: (1) creating a projecting profile (an overhang) above the opening or at the top of the wall, and (2) creating a continuous groove or ridge in the underside of the projection (a drip) so that gravity will pull the adhering water free of the overhang.

**1.** The size of an overhang is determined by its function. The width of an overhang that protects a seam or joint need not extend far from the face of the surface it is protecting. An overhang that is meant to protect a tall exterior wall must be much wider to be effective. The wider the overhang, the greater the wall area below that will be protected, because wind-driven rain falls at an angle, not straight down. The angle of falling rain during a storm is difficult to predict accurately, but a good rule of thumb is to add 20 to the wind speed [in miles per hour (mph)] at the time of the rain. The sum is the approximate angle from the vertical of the falling rain. Rain falling with a 20 mph (32 kph) wind would fall at an angle of about 40 degrees off of vertical; at 40 mph (64 kph) it would fall at approximately 60 degrees off of vertical. Greater overhang width also moves the splash of the water on the ground below farther from the wall face, decreasing secondary wetting and soiling of the surface (see A and B).

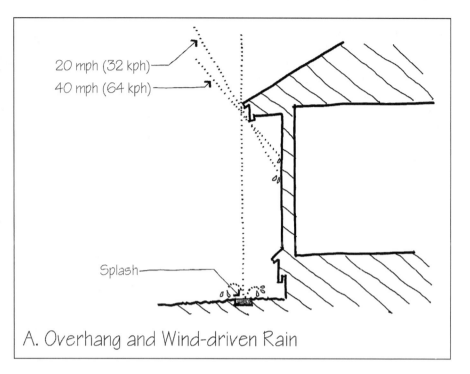

A. Overhang and Wind-driven Rain

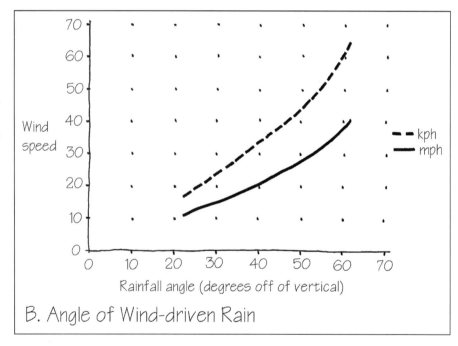

B. Angle of Wind-driven Rain

**2.** Standard exterior details of wood-frame houses contain several examples of the overhang and drip principle. The roof shingles overhang the fascia board and slope upward so that water will drip clear of the joint between the fascia and the shingles. The lower edge of the fascia projects below the horizontal soffit so that water running down the fascia will drip free of the crack between the fascia and the soffit. The whole eave, of course, is a large overhang and drip that keeps water off the vulnerable upper edge of the wall and also gives some protection to window and door openings. At the base of the wall, a traditional water table detail consists of an overhang and drip designed to keep water out of the crack between the wood wall and the foundation. Whether or not a water table is used, the bottom edge of the siding should be spaced away from the foundation wall to create another overhang and drip. Both of these details create a zone of concentrated runoff that can erode a strip along the ground where the dripping water hits the ground. The ground can be armored or the water can be dispersed to alleviate the erosion (see C).

**3.** The stone or concrete coping atop a masonry parapet wall is sloped toward the inside of the building to help prevent staining and leaking of the outer surface of the wall. A generous overhang and drip are provided to keep water out of the mortar joint immediately beneath the coping. Additionally, the metal flashing in this mortar joint projects outward and downward to provide another overhang and drip. A similar detail can be used at the top of a free-standing wall or retaining wall (see D).    ▷

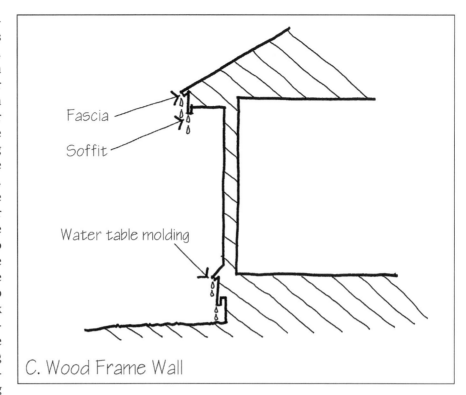

Fascia

Soffit

Water table molding

C. Wood Frame Wall

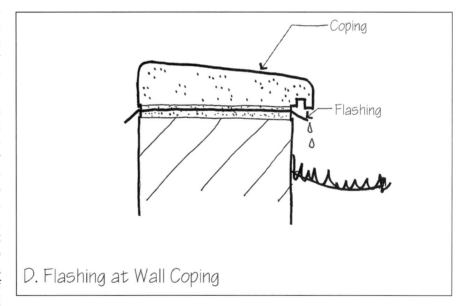

Coping

Flashing

D. Flashing at Wall Coping

**4.** Internal flashings in masonry veneers sometimes catch and divert relatively large volumes of water as the mortar joints in the veneer above age and deteriorate. Each flashing should project completely through the outer face of the masonry by roughly ¾ in. (20 mm) and turn down at 45 degrees to keep the draining water from wetting the mortarless horizontal joint beneath the flashing. The detailer should resist the urge to recess the outer edge of the flashing into the mortar joint. This might look better than a projecting flashing, but it can lead to serious leakage and deterioration problems beneath the flashing (see E). ■

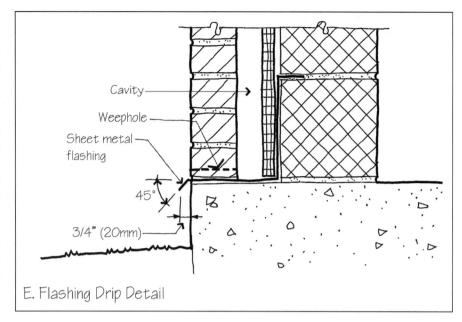

Cavity

Weephole

Sheet metal flashing

45°

3/4" (20mm)

E. Flashing Drip Detail

Water can pull itself by capillary action across and even upward through a narrow crack, but not a wide one. To prevent capillary entry of water, we create a capillary break by enlarging a crack internally to a dimension large enough so that a drop of water cannot bridge across it, at least ¼ in. (6 mm).

**1.** This drawing shows a typical post anchor. The post is fastened ¼ in. above the horizontal surface to prevent water from being pulled into the gap under the post and entering the end grain (see A).

**2.** This beam is resting on a masonry column. The beam is separated from the column surface with a ¼ in. neoprene spacer to prevent moisture from being pulled into the gap below the beam.

A capillary break serves only to neutralize capillary action as a force that can move water through into an assembly. It is a reliable and useful tool for making an assembly watertight, but it is not capable of resisting water penetration caused by gravity, momentum, or wind (see B). ∎

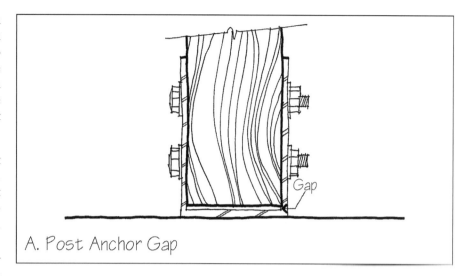

A. Post Anchor Gap

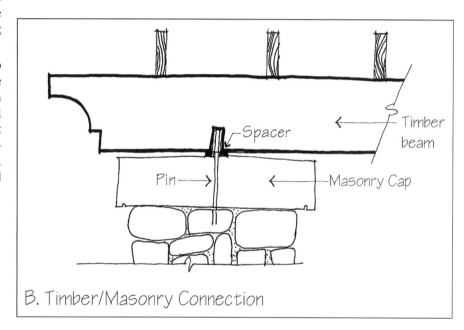

B. Timber/Masonry Connection

 *Labyrinth*

If a joint is designed so that no straight line may be constructed through it without passing through solid material, a raindrop or a snowflake cannot pass through the joint by its own momentum.

**1.** A windblown raindrop or snowflake possesses momentum that can move it through an opening in a fence or free-standing wall. A raindrop striking this open horizontal joint between two stone or precast concrete wall panels, for example, will splatter water through the joint to the back side unless the joint is configured as a simple labyrinth (see A).

**2.** The astragal is a traditional labyrinth design that is used to keep water drops from being blown through the vertical crack between a pair of swinging doors or gates (see B). ■

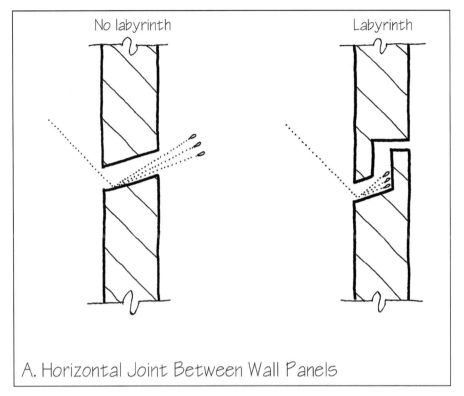

A. Horizontal Joint Between Wall Panels

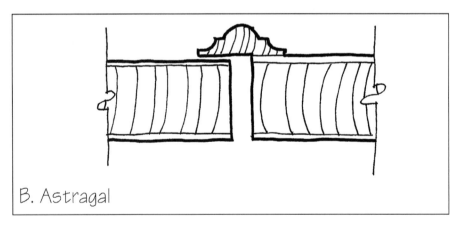

B. Astragal

Sealants and gaskets are elastic materials that can be placed in a joint to block the passage of water and/or air while allowing for relative movement between the two sides of the joint. A gasket is a strip of synthetic rubber that is compressed into the joint. Most sealants are mastic materials that are injected into the joint and then cure to a rubberlike state. A gasket seals against a surface by compressing tightly against it. A sealant seals by adhering tightly to the surface.

**1.** The width and depth of a sealant joint must never be left to chance; they should be determined in accordance with the procedure shown in *Expansion Joint,* (p. 81). The plastic-foam backer rod is a very important part of every sealant joint: It limits the depth of the sealant to the predetermined dimension, provides a firm surface against which to tool the sealant, and imparts to the sealant bead the 1:2 hourglass shape that optimizes the strength and elasticity of the sealant. The backer rod should be at least 20 percent larger than the maximum joint width (see A).

**2.** If the sealant joint is too narrow, normal amounts of movement between the adjoining components can overstretch the sealant and tear it (see B).

**3.** If the sealant bead is too deep, stresses in the bead will be excessive and tearing is likely (see C). ▷

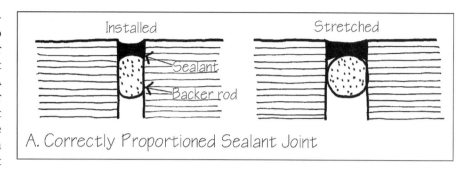

Installed    Stretched

A. Correctly Proportioned Sealant Joint

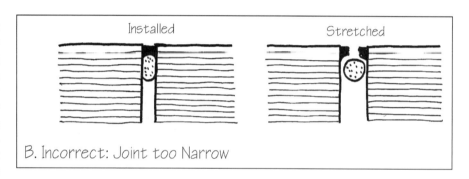

Installed    Stretched

B. Incorrect: Joint too Narrow

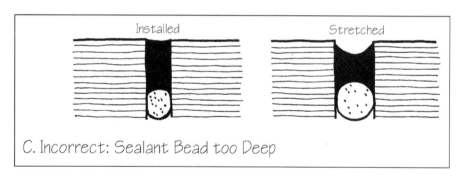

Installed    Stretched

C. Incorrect: Sealant Bead too Deep

**4.** Tooling forces the sealant material to fill the joint, assume the desired profile, and adhere to the adjoining components (see D).

**5.** In a three-sided sealant joint, bond-breaker tape should be applied against the back of the joint to allow for full extension of the sealant bead when the joint opens (see E and F).

**6.** If a sealant joint is too narrow, the sealant may become overcompressed, squeezing it out of the joint and tearing it (see G).

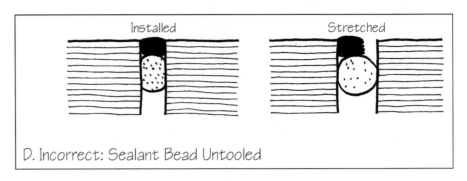

D. Incorrect: Sealant Bead Untooled

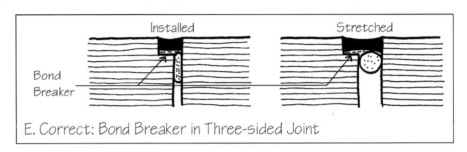

E. Correct: Bond Breaker in Three-sided Joint

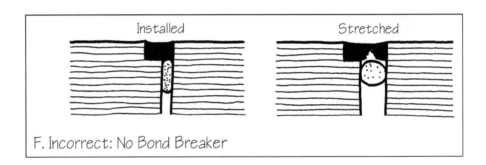

F. Incorrect: No Bond Breaker

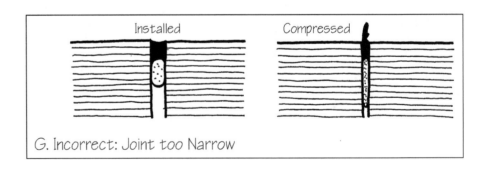

G. Incorrect: Joint too Narrow

**7.** Sealant should be applied at an air temperature that is neither too hot nor too cold. If application at very hot or very cold temperatures is anticipated, the initial joint width should be adjusted to compensate for the seasonal over-stressing that might otherwise occur (see H).

**8.** A sealant lap joint may be dimensioned using the same procedures as for a butt joint (see I).

**9.** This is an example of a preformed synthetic rubber gasket used to close a movement joint in a high-traffic horizontal surface, such as a roadway or a parking garage. The gasket is slightly wider than the joint and must be compressed during installation (see J).  ▷

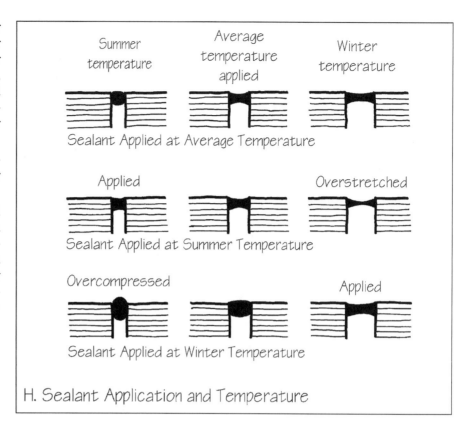

H. Sealant Application and Temperature

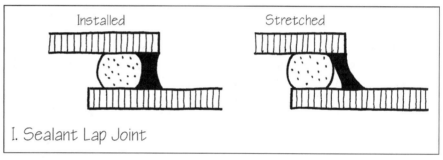

I. Sealant Lap Joint

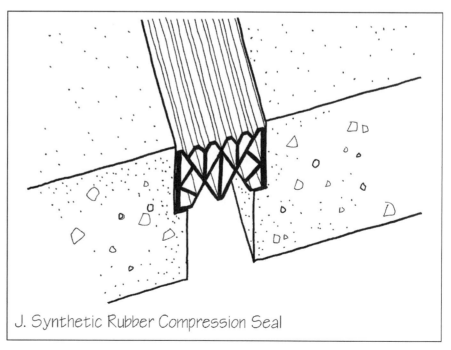

J. Synthetic Rubber Compression Seal

**10.** The waterstop is a preformed synthetic rubber gasket used to seal pour joints and movement joints in concrete foundation walls or pool walls. The example shown here features a center tube that allows the waterstop to stretch or compress considerably in response to movement in the concrete walls. Many other shapes of synthetic rubber waterstops are also manufactured, along with alternative designs made of rigid plastic, metal, mastic, and even bentonite clay, which expands and seals when wetted (see K). ■

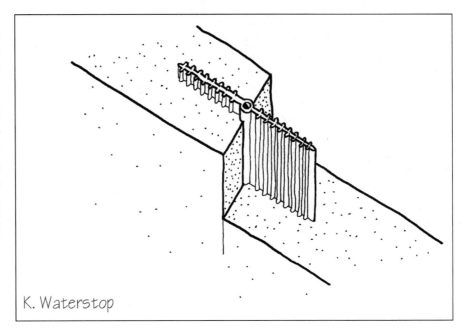

K. Waterstop

## PROPORTIONING SEALANT JOINTS

Sealant joints should be provided at frequent enough intervals in a surface so that the expected overall movement in the surface is divided into an acceptably small amount of movement in each joint. Usually sealant joint spacing is determined by the desired sizes of the panels or sheet materials that make up a wall.

Generally, a sealant joint should not be narrower than ¼ in. (6 mm). A joint narrower than this is difficult to make and has little ability to absorb movement. Joints can be as wide as 1 to 2 in. (25 to 51 mm), depending on the ability of the sealant not to sag out of the joint before it has cured. The depth of sealant in a joint should be equal to half the width of the joint but not less than ¼ in. (6 mm) or more than ½ in. (13 mm). Thus, a ¼ in. wide joint should be ¼ in. deep (6 × 6 mm), a ¾ in. wide joint should be ⅜ in. deep (19 × 9 mm), and a 1-¼ in. wide joint should be ½ in. deep (32 × 13 mm).

To determine the required width for a sealant joint in a particular location in a wall or pavement, many factors must be considered. The spacing between movement joints, the particular materials used, and the climate at the site are some of the factors.

A complete discussion of this topic, including example calculations of sealant joints, follows in Determining Widths of Sealant Joints.

## DETERMINING WIDTHS OF SEALANT JOINTS

Calculations of expansion joint intervals and sealant joint widths are interdependent. The width of a sealant joint should be determined by the designer of the project, the detailer, the specifications writer, the suppliers of the components or materials on either side of the joint, and the structural engineer. These collaborators work together using all available information on temperature extremes at the building site, the time of year when the sealant will be installed, the properties of the materials on either side of the joint, and the properties of the sealant itself. For preliminary purposes, the following equation may be used to determine the width of any sealant joint:

$$W = \frac{100}{X}(\varepsilon L \triangle T + M_0) + t$$

where

$W$ = required width of sealant joint

$X$ = percent plus or minus movement capability of sealant, expressed as a whole number

$\varepsilon$ = coefficient of expansion of wall or pavement material

$L$ = length of wall or pavement between joints

$\triangle T$ = annual range between extreme high and low temperatures. If specific temperature data are lacking, assume that $\triangle T$ is 130°F (54°C)

$M_0$ = anticipated movement due to such nonthermal factors as structural deflections, creep, or moisture expansion and contraction

$t$ = construction tolerance

This formula may be used with either conventional or SI units. Following are three examples of its use.

### TABLE 2-3: Coefficients of Linear Thermal Expansion of Common Building Materials

| | | in./in./°F | mm/mm/°C |
|---|---|---|---|
| **Wood (seasoned)** | | | |
| Douglas fir | parallel to grain | 0.0000021 | 0.0000038 |
| | perpendicular to grain | 0.0000320 | 0.0000580 |
| Pine | parallel to grain | 0.0000030 | 0.0000054 |
| | perpendicular to grain | 0.0000190 | 0.0000340 |
| Oak | parallel to grain | 0.0000027 | 0.0000049 |
| | perpendicular to grain | 0.0000300 | 0.0000540 |
| Maple | parallel to grain | 0.0000036 | 0.0000065 |
| | perpendicular to grain | 0.0000270 | 0.0000486 |
| **Masonry and Concrete** | | | |
| Limestone | | 0.0000044 | 0.0000079 |
| Granite | | 0.0000047 | 0.0000085 |
| Marble | | 0.0000073 | 0.0000131 |
| Brick | | 0.0000036 | 0.0000065 |
| Concrete masonry units, normal aggregate | | 0.0000052 | 0.0000094 |
| Concrete masonry units, lightweight aggregate | | 0.0000043 | 0.0000077 |
| Concrete | | 0.0000055 | 0.0000099 |
| **Metals** | | | |
| Steel | | 0.0000065 | 0.0000117 |
| Stainless steel, 18-8 | | 0.0000099 | 0.0000173 |
| Aluminum | | 0.0000128 | 0.0000231 |
| Copper | | 0.0000093 | 0.0000168 |
| Tin | | 0.0000161 | 0.0000290 |
| Titanium | | 0.0000050 | 0.0000090 |
| Zinc | | 0.0000172 | 0.0000310 |
| **Finish Materials** | | | |
| Glass | | 0.0000050 | 0.0000090 |
| Acrylic glazing sheet | | 0.0000410 | 0.0000742 |
| Polycarbonate glazing sheet | | 0.0000440 | 0.0000796 |
| Polyethylene | | 0.0000850 | 0.0001530 |
| Polyvinyl chloride | | 0.0000400 | 0.0000720 |

*Example 1:* Calculate the required width of a sealant joint between white granite wall panels that are 4 ft, 7 in., or 55 in. (1397 mm), in maximum dimension. The annual range of air temperature is from –10° to 110°F (–23° to 43°C). The wall structure will be of reinforced concrete, and the structural engineer estimates that creep in the frame will eventually reach about 0.03 in. (0.76 mm) per panel, but that structural deflections will be insignificant. The sealant will have a movement capability of ±25 percent. The supplier and installer of the granite panels expect to work to an accuracy of ± ³⁄₁₆ in. (4.76 mm).

From the table above, we find a coefficient of thermal expansion for granite of 0.0000047 in./in./°F (0.0000085 mm/mm/°C). Starting with the given equation:

$$W = \frac{100}{X}(\varepsilon L \triangle T + M_o) + t$$

and substituting,

$$W = \frac{100}{25}[(0.0000047 \text{ in./in./°F})(55 \text{ in.})(120°F) + 0.03 \text{ in.}] + \tfrac{3}{16} \text{ in.}$$

we have W = 0.43 in.; use a ½ in. joint. A depth of ¼ in. is suitable.

Working in SI (metric) units:

$$W = \frac{100}{25}[(0.0000085 \text{ mm/mm/°C})(1397 \text{ mm})(66°C) + 0.76 \text{ mm}] + 4.76 \text{ mm}$$

we have W = 10.93 mm; use an 11 mm joint. A depth of 6 mm is suitable.

**Example 2:** Calculate the required width of a vertical sealant joint in a brick wall with a joint spacing of 21 ft, 4 in., or 256 in. (6.5 m or 6500 mm). The air temperature range is up to 108°F (60°C). The contractor would like to use a sealant that has a movement capability of ±12.5 percent. According to Technical Note No. 18 of the Brick Industry Association, brickwork will expand over time by about 2/100 of 1 percent due to moisture absorption. A construction tolerance of ±¼ in. (6 mm) is expected.

According to the table, the coefficient of thermal expansion of brick masonry is 0.0000036 in./in./°F (0.0000065 mm/mm/°C). Starting with the given equation

$$W = \frac{100}{X}(\varepsilon L \triangle T + M_o) + t$$

and substituting,

$$W = \frac{100}{12.5}[(0.0000036 \text{ in./in./°F})(256 \text{ in.})(108°F) + (0.0002)] + \tfrac{1}{4} \text{ in}$$

We have W = 1.05 in.

Working in SI (metric) units:

$$W = \frac{100}{12.5}[(0.0000065 \text{ mm/mm/°C})(6500 \text{ mm})(60°C) + (0.0002)] + 6 \text{ mm}$$

We have W = 26.28 mm

This is fairly wide, (over 1 in.) which would be very noticeble. If a sealant with a ±25 percent movement capability were used instead, the joint would only need to be just over ½ in. (18 mm) wide, which could be rounded up to 1 in. (25 mm). If a narrower joint is desired, then another sealant with even greater movement capability could be selected or the joints could be spaced closer together.

**Example 3:** Calculate the required width of a horizontal sealant joint in a 5 in. (127 mm) thick concrete slab with a joint spacing of 10 ft, 0 in. or 120 in. (3.5 m or 3048 mm). The air temperature range is up to 108°F (60°C). The contractor would like to use a sealant that has a movement capability of ±25.0 percent. According to the Portland Cement Association's *Concrete Floors on Ground*, by Scott M. Tarr and James A. Farny, typical concrete slabs will contract over time by between 100 and 300 millionths due to shrinkage. A construction tolerance of ± ¼ in. (6 mm) is expected.

According to the table, the coefficient of thermal expansion of concrete is about 0.0000055 in./in./°F (0.0000099 mm/mm/°C). Starting with the given equation:

$$W = \frac{100}{X}(\varepsilon L \triangle T + M_o) + t$$

and substituting,

$$W = \frac{100}{25}[(0.0000055 \text{ in./in./°F})(120 \text{ in.})(108°F) + (120 \text{ in.})(0.000300 \text{ (as worst case)})] + \tfrac{1}{4} \text{ in.}$$

we have W = .54 in.; use a ⅝ in. joint. A depth of ⁵⁄₁₆ in. or ⅜ in. is suitable.

Working in SI (metric) units:

$$W = \frac{100}{25}[(0.0000099 \text{ mm/mm/°C})(3048 \text{ mm})(60°C) + (0.000300 \text{ (as worst case)})] + 6 \text{ mm}$$

we have W=13.24 mm: use a 14 mm. joint. A depth of 7 mm is suitable.

CHAPTER

# 3 Controlling Subsurface Water Movement and Sedimentation

The patterns of this chapter regarding the control of surface water and the movement of sediments depend upon a basic knowledge of subgrade soil and water functions. Following is a brief review of those functions.

Most landscape architectural details are integrally connected to soil and water. Pavements rest upon layers of aggregate and on a compacted subsoil whose strength depend upon an optimum soil moisture; planting details involve layers of soils of different strengths, porosities, and fertilities allowing for the movement of water through the planting soil section; foundations and retaining walls bear upon soil and can be compromised by too much groundwater pressure.

The patterns in this chapter regarding the control of subsurface water movement and sedimentation depend upon a basic knowledge of soils and water movement principles. Following is a brief review of these principles.

## MINERAL COMPONENTS

Natural soils are formed by the weathering of solid rock creating small particles that accumulate over time to create soil. Individual soil structures and many of the physical characteristics of soils are determined by the size of those particles, the distribution of the particle sizes within an individual soil, and the distribution and size of the spaces between those particles (pore

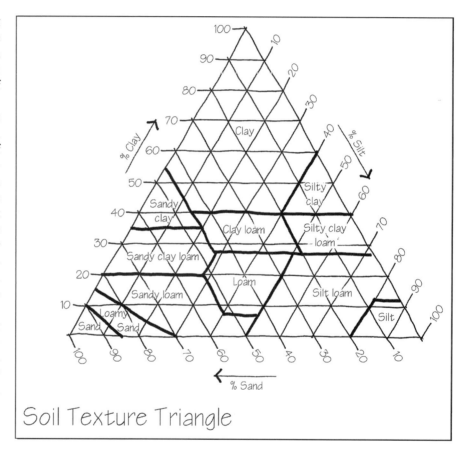

Soil Texture Triangle

space). Soil particles are classified by their size.

Large particles such as sands and gravels tend to behave differently than fines (very fine sand, silt, and clay). Soils made up predominantly of large particles tend to be well draining, have large pore spaces but do not tend to hold nutrients or moisture for plant

growth. Fine soils, on the other hand, can be very poorly draining with small pore sizes but tend to retain both moisture and nutrients. Most soils are made up of a mix of different soil particle sizes and are called loams.

Soil characteristics that are important to detailers include soil-bearing capacity (which varies with soil moisture, see diagram below), soil permeability or infiltration rate, and bulk density. Loam soils that are very wet (mud) or very dry (dust) are usually much less strong than soils of moderate moisture levels. The moisture level in which the soil is strongest is referred to as the optimum moisture content for that soil (see A). As a soil is compacted to increase its density and strength, the pore sizes decrease and permeability decreases. If a soil has a uniform distribution of particle sizes (a uniform or well-graded soil), then the compaction process will cause the fine soil particles to migrate into the voids between the larger particles.

Soils that are missing one or more soil particle sizes (a gap-graded or poorly graded soil) maintain pore space within the soil matrix and resist compaction (see B).

Organic material is valuable as a component of the planting soil but not as a structural soil component. Organic material can hold moisture and nutrients for plant use. It can buffer the pH of the soil allowing more of the nutrients in the soil to be soluble and available for plant use. Organic material breaks down over time and can be absorbed by plants. In some cases, they can exacerbate the effects of the fine soil particles in regards to water movement, degrading a soil's structural capability, but in others, organic material can bind small soil particles together into clumps, improving the overall soil permeability. Microorganisms exist in most natural soils and readily colonize new soils where there is physical space within the soil matrix to accommodate them. In general, beneficial microorganisms that prey on microorganisms that are detrimental to plant growth require large pore sizes. In addition these predator microorganisms, beneficial fungi, and so forth require interconnected areas of large adjacent pore space.

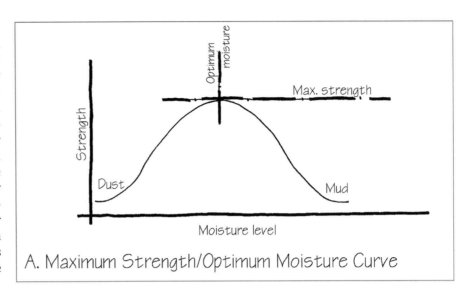

A. Maximum Strength/Optimum Moisture Curve

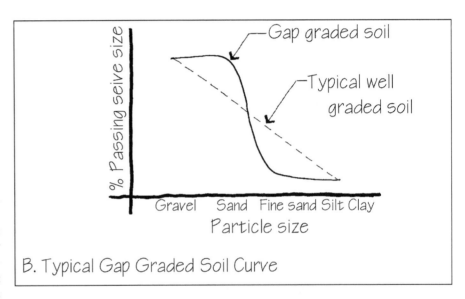

B. Typical Gap Graded Soil Curve

Both water and air within soils are used by plants. Water is incorporated into new cell structures and acts as a medium to convey nutrients to the cells. Air is also necessary in the soil for both plant and microorganism growth. Air is present in the pore structures of soils and is easily pushed aside when new roots grow into them. When the air is displaced with moisture, or in heavily compacted soils, beneficial microorganisms die off and root growth is curtailed.

## SUBSURFACE WATER MOVEMENT

Water is found in all soils and is bound electrically to the surface of all soil particles. The water molecules that tightly surround the soil particles are called hygroscopic water and can only be removed by high heat. Water is only available to plants where there is enough of it to fill all the hygroscopic water needs of the soil and produce a surplus. If this surplus can be moved through the soil via gravity it is not long available to the plants. The water that remains in the soil after it is drained by gravity and is held only by capillary attraction between individual water molecules is called *available water* (see C).

Water enters the soil primarily from above via rain, irrigation, or snow melt. After a rain or irrigation cycle, the entire section of soil achieves *saturation*. Additional water will run off and not soak into the soil (when all the pores are filled with water and displace air within the pores). The water that can be removed from the soil via gravity is called *free water*. Free water is the water that affects a soil's strength and also contributes to optimum moisture levels. As gravity pulls the water downward out of the larger pores, an equilibrium is reached with water remaining in the smaller pores held against the force of gravity by capillary action. This state is called the soil's *field capacity*. Water in the soil is held in place by capillary attraction to the soil particles, but plants are able to overcome this attraction and extract water from the soil. As plants extract the water and air enters the soil and additional water evaporates, the amount of water in the soil decreases. At some point the water volume has decreased enough to leave only water that is tightly bound by electrical attractions to the soil particles; it is no longer available to the plants. This state is called the *wilting point* of the soil.

Plants use the capillary water as a reservoir and a source for dissolved nutrients. They also need a zone of soil that is not saturated to take in oxygen. Beneficial microorganisms also need air to survive and can be replaced by anaerobic bacteria if soils are saturated for long periods of time. Chemical reac-

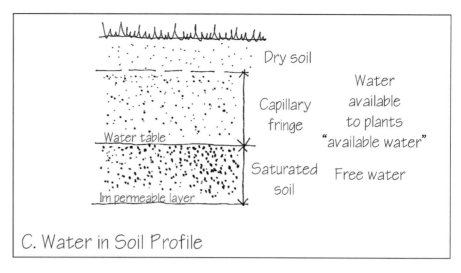

C. Water in Soil Profile

tions occur in overly saturated soils that reduce available nitrogen and increase the formation of harmful gasses such as methane and sulfur dioxide. The chemical reactions that are beneficial to plant growth use both air and water. Plants without enough available water or enough available air often die. Soil drainage problems relating to planting details involve balancing the two for optimum plant growth.

Remediation of drainage problems involves the removal of free water from the soil to maintain soil moisture for optimum strength under pavements and structures or to reduce saturation time in root zones.

In both planting and drainage problems, the capillary forces are the wild card greatly influencing the movement of water horizontally and upwardly. Water moves down through the soil structure by gravitational attraction. If the water encounters a sloping, impervious surface (such as a roof or planter bottom), gravity can move water horizontally only if there is a slope or head (pressure) behind the water. The force moving water horizontally is only a fraction of the gravitational force that moves it downward. Capillary forces, however, can move water slightly hori-

zontally through a soil section but only slightly and very slowly. Capillary forces can also move water up from the water table into the capillary fringe (see D).

Capillary forces can be used to supply available water to plants from below, but also must be overcome to allow water to penetrate filter fabrics or sand drains.

In general, coarse textured soils with larger particle sizes (gravels and coarse sands) have larger pore sizes, greater permeability, and smaller capillary fringe than fine textured soils. Uncompacted soils have more pore space due to a greater number of pores than compacted soils. The rate of movement downward through the soil by gravity is a function of the square of the pore size, so water will move 100 times faster through a coarse sand than through a clay, because the pores in sand are 10 times larger than those of clay and the rate of flow is $10^2$ or 100 times faster.

Water movement depends on the existing moisture content of the soils. Very dry soils will absorb water very quickly, but as the small pores fill with water, the rate will decrease. In soils that have their small pores already filled, the initial rate will be slower.

When two different soil textures are overlaid on one another, the interface between the two soil textures influences the entire section. For example, an underlying compacted clay soil (or construction debris) with low porosity can inhibit drainage of coarser soils above. This can result in an artificial or perched water table extending into the (normally) free-draining upper soil. On the other hand, a heavy clay soil over an open graded gravel may not drain due to a lack of contact points between the many pores in the clay and the very few of the gravel.

## SOIL MOVEMENT

If a force is applied to soil via wind, water, or compaction, individual particles of soil can move. That movement can happen at the surface of the soil resulting in erosion, or it can happen within the soil structure. The deposition of these soil particles is called sedimentation.

### SURFACE EROSION

The distance erosive forces move soil particles is proportional to the mass of the particle. Fine soils will be moved hundreds of times farther than coarser particles that are hundreds of times larger. Clays, silts, and fine sands are much more likely to be moved at the surface of a soil or within a soil. When these fine soils are moved and re-deposited in a layer, this layer of sediment has the characteristic of a much finer soil than a parent material that is a mix of particle sizes. Therefore, eroded sediments tend to cause problems associated with fine textured soils (low porosity, high capillary attraction, and so forth).

### SUBSURFACE SOIL MOVEMENT

Fine soil particles can also move within a soil section. Water can dislodge fine particles (especially in uncompacted soils or soils with poor texture) and move them down through a section

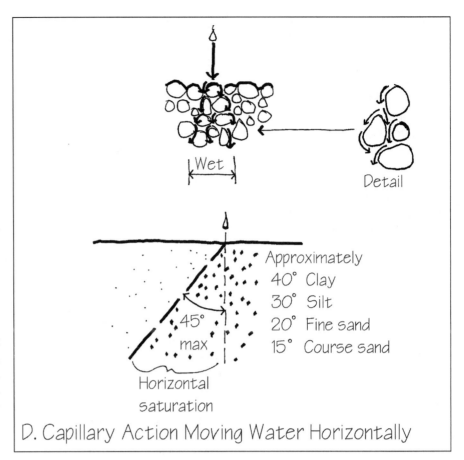

Detail

Approximately
40° Clay
30° Silt
20° Fine sand
15° Course sand

45° max

Horizontal saturation

D. Capillary Action Moving Water Horizontally

into large pores below. This results in a reduction in the size and number of large pores and a change in soil performance at this lower level.

Compaction can also move fine soil particles into large pores. However, compaction can also move soil particles horizontally or laterally and can cause large particles to be pushed into underlying fine-textured soils, thereby reducing the size and number of large pores in the overall soil. Section moisture can accelerate that movement. If gravel or even large stone is placed on wet, fine-textured soil and compacted (e.g. run over by a vehicle) the gravel will be pushed down into the wet fine-textured soil (mud) and take on the structural characteristics of the mud rather than the gravel (see E).

### FILTERS

All soil filters balance two functional criteria. The first is to allow water to freely pass through the filter and the second is to hold back fine soil particles to prevent them from filling the voids in the drainage medium and stopping the movement of water. The first criterion argues for a very porous sand or fabric that will allow a high rate of water transmission. The second criterion argues for a less permeable media that will hold back the small soil particles. Well-functioning filters do both over a long period of time. The way they work is to employ the tendency of soil particles to form small bridges over openings in larger particles below as water washes small particles through the filter. This condition only occurs if the filter holes are relatively close in size to the particles it is filtering. That filter can be in the form of a layer (or progressively coarser layers) of sand or other aggregate, by a filter fabric, or by a combination of fabric and sand filter layer. The filter design must also take into consideration the size of organic material and microorganisms that may also clog the filter.

The patterns that deal with soil particles moving in water across the surface of the land or through a closed drainage system are:

Control Velocity p. 56

Sumps p. 57

The patterns that deal with soil particles moving within the soil matrix are:

Progressive Filtering p. 58

Geotextile Separation p. 59

Reinforcement p. 60

Patterns dealing with water movement through soils are:

Level Drainage Surfaces p. 62

Water Level Reduction p. 63

Overflow p. 64

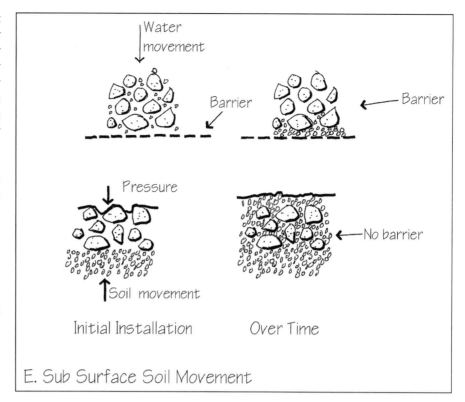

E. Sub Surface Soil Movement

The last pattern of this chapter is an application of the patterns above in a system that supports both tree root growth and pavement support.

Structural Tree Planting Soil p. 65 ■

Sediments are transported in moving water and settle in still water. The detailer can use this phenomenon to design drainage systems that do not clog and erosion control structures that trap sediment onsite. The key to the long-term functionality of these systems is to provide enough slope on the pipes or swales to keep sediment moving through the system and flat slopes in areas that are meant to slow or stop the flow and trap sediment and/or infiltrate water.

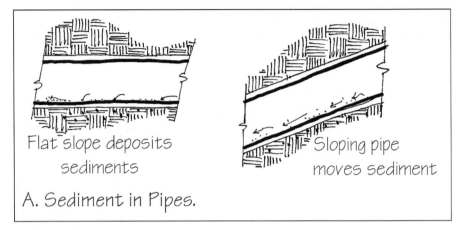

Flat slope deposits sediments

Sloping pipe moves sediment

A. Sediment in Pipes.

Most drainage systems are unpressurized and flow downhill by gravity. The steeper the gradient of the pipe or swale, the faster the velocity of the water. At shallow gradients (low velocities), sediments settle out of suspension and can eventually clog drainage systems. At steep gradients (high velocities), water and soil particles can scour the walls of pipes and erode exposed surfaces. The design of drainage systems needs to balance enough velocity (gradient) against too much. High velocity can also move a higher volume of water than at low velocity, so steeper pipes can move more water than the same size pipe at a shallower slope (see A).

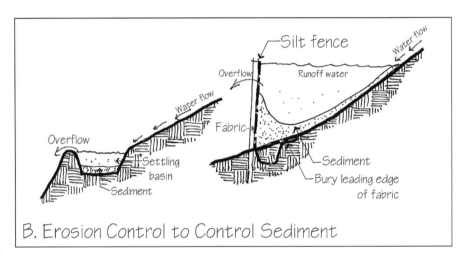

Silt fence

Overflow

Runoff water

Water flow

Water flow

Fabric

Overflow

Settling basin

Sediment

Sediment

Bury leading edge of fabric

B. Erosion Control to Control Sediment

**1.** In closed (subsurface piped) drainage systems, water should maintain a minimum velocity of 2.5 feet (762mm) per second. This translates into a minimum slope of about ½% for small diameter, smooth-surfaced pipes. The minimum slope is flatter for large-diameter pipes. This keeps pipes free of sediment by washing it out through the system. In open (surface) drainage systems using grass-surfaced swales, a minimum slope of 2% should be maintained to facili-

tate flow without sedimentation and ponding. Grass swales are sometimes designed with gradients of 1% to facilitate sedimentation and infiltration as a "bioswale".

**2.** Similarly, roof membranes below green roofs should be sloped a minimum of 1.5 percent to move any sediment that accumulates in the drainage layer to the drains.

**3.** Silt fences at the base of slopes and settling basins at low points in projects should include enough volume to pond sediment-laden water long enough to settle out particles prior to the next storm. Such devices are not permanent solutions. If sediment continues to flow into these basins, they will eventually become filled and need to be cleaned out (see B). ∎

# Sumps

To create a place to intercept sediment and debris in a closed drainage system and prevent sedimentation downstream, a sump is used at the beginning of a drainage system (catch basin) or at locations where the system changes direction—changing horizontal direction or dropping elevation—(manhole). These sumps in the system both protect the downstream system from sedimentation, but also provide excess capacity at vulnerable places in the system (see A). ■

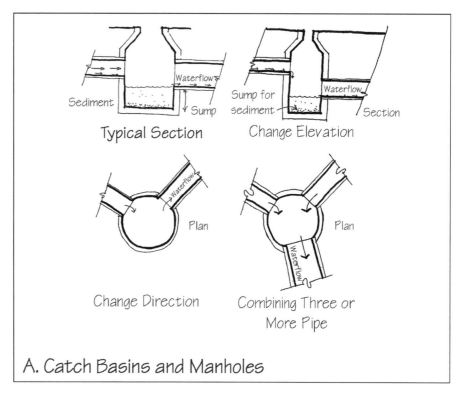

Typical Section

Change Elevation

Change Direction

Combining Three or More Pipe

A. Catch Basins and Manholes

When a soil is overlaid on another soil with different texture, there is the potential for fines to move from one soil into the pores of another. The seam between the soils can inhibit drainage. Water moving from a coarse soil to a fine one will be slowed down as it passes from the more porous soil to the less porous soil. In this case, the water will back up into the coarser soil. When water moves from fine soil to coarse soil, drainage can also be inhibited. Water can be held in a large number of small pores that are not in contact with the larger, less numerous pores of the coarser soil, so they do not have the opportunity to move via capillary action and will stay perched above the coarser soil until it is saturated and the water moves as free water. A progressive filter adds a layer between the coarse and the fine that bridges that gap and allows both to function.

**1.** A layer of sand over a filter fabric can allow the combined drain to filter and drain much finer soils than the fabric or sand alone (see A).

**2.** In many cases, with soils that are less than 50 percent fines (a #200 sieve), a fabric alone can function as the filter between soils. The properties of the fabric must be matched to the individual soil in use on the site. A mockup should be done to test the suitability of the soil and fabric together if there is any question of suitability.

**3.** Filters can fail over time, especially where there is a large predominance of fine particles and when soils do not aggregate into larger peds (clumps of fine soils that behave like large-sized

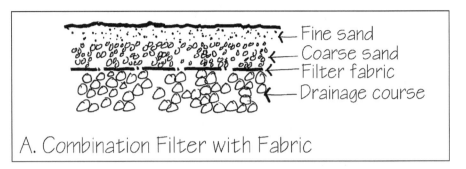

Fine sand
Coarse sand
Filter fabric
Drainage course

A. Combination Filter with Fabric

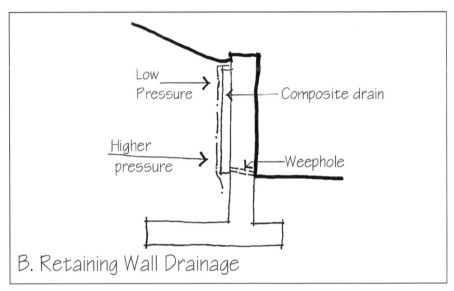

Low Pressure →

Composite drain

Higher pressure →

Weephole

B. Retaining Wall Drainage

particles). Under these conditions, the finer particles can move through the soil and be trapped in the filter. Filters can also be compromised by the presence of high alkaline water, which can lead to a buildup of magnesium, calcium, or sodium; or where there is a high amount of suspended solids or microorganisms on the surface of the filter. Progressive filtering is especially suitable when these conditions exist, because a single filter is likely to be inadequate.

**4.** Filters in all locations can be constructed of either fabric or sand or a combination, but in vertical applications fabrics are usually preferred for two reasons. Fabrics are much easier to install in a vertical position and the added head at the base of the drain, coupled with the tendency of water to move very slowly and not far in the horizontal dimension, add to the safety of the fabric filters (see B). ■

# Geotextile Separation

Fabrics are ideally suited to separating different soil types in a detail.

**1.** When placing a coarse drainage aggregate layer in a porous paving reservoir, a fabric is used to separate the open graded base from a well-graded subsoil. The geotextile separator keeps the fines out of the voids in the base material and allows for water to percolate into the subsoil below (see A).

**2.** In addition, the sides of porous pavement reservoirs are also separated from the surrounding soil via a fabric or impermeable barrier such as a curb or plastic barrier (see B).

**3.** Fabrics are also used to separate free draining materials from sources of sediment. Fabric is almost always an element of an underdrain section included below and on the sides of pipe or wrapped stone drains, but its inclusion on the top of the pipe can inhibit drainage if the material above the drain is incompatible with the drain material (see C).

**4.** Waterproof membranes (not fabrics) can also be used to separate expansive clay soils from sources of excess moisture in areas where the expansion can cause damage such as against a retaining well or building foundation. ■

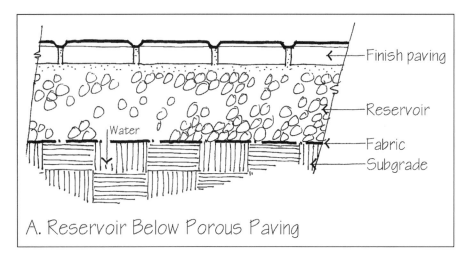

A. Reservoir Below Porous Paving

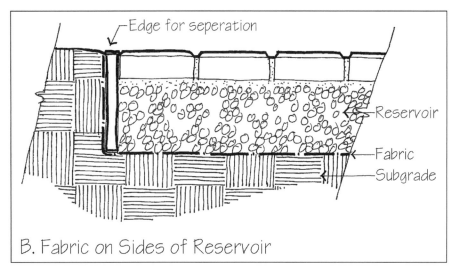

B. Fabric on Sides of Reservoir

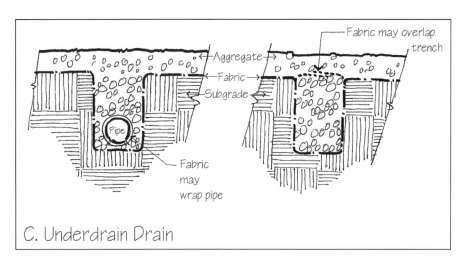

C. Underdrain Drain

Fabrics typically have a high tensile strength while soils (within an optimum moisture range) tend to be very strong in compression, so fabrics are often used to reinforce soils.

**1.** Coarse foundation material for roads or structures can be installed over a layer of fabric and float on soil that would not support the point loads of the larger stone. This is also a technique for constructing foundations on highly organic soils and permafrost (see A).

**2.** Slopes can be reinforced with layers of fabric, or geogrids, to prevent the soil from slumping and sliding (see B).

**3.** Geogrids can also be used as deadmen for retaining walls (see C). In this application, the vertical modules of the masonry or concrete elements used to face the wall corresponds with the grid spacing. To be effective, the back-filled soils must be compacted in place in layers corresponding to the geotextile layers.

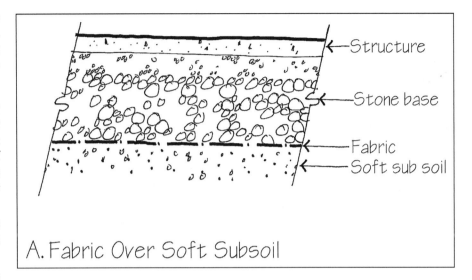

A. Fabric Over Soft Subsoil

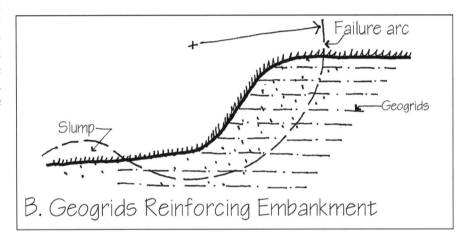

B. Geogrids Reinforcing Embankment

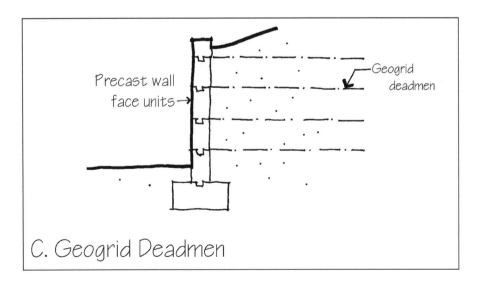

C. Geogrid Deadmen

**4.** Soil-filled fabric tubes interspaced between geogrids can be used to create near vertical embankments. Geogrids are interlayered with soil-filled tubes to anchor them with the weight of the embankment (see D).

**5.** Geotextile and geogrids are often used in erosion control blankets to add strength to the surface of the soil. The fabric or grid is locked into place by the roots of the cover crop and add resistance to scour of the surface by runoff water. These fabrics can be completely biodegradable for temporary reinforcement until the roots of the cover crop can secure the soil. Alternatively, they can be completely nonbiodegradable, or a composite material for longer-term protection. As shown in this example, both types can be combined (see E). ■

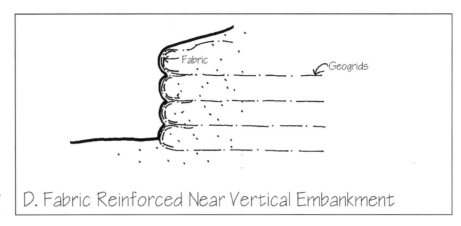

D. Fabric Reinforced Near Vertical Embankment

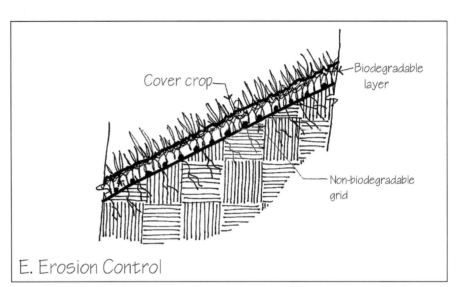

E. Erosion Control

To optimize infiltration from one sub-surface soil layer or reservoir into an underlying soil, the bottom plane of the reservoir should be level. If the bottom slopes, the upper portions will infiltrate much less than the bottom.

**1.** When detailing reservoir areas below sloping surfaces, the bottom surfaces should be a series of cascades separated by level-bottomed cells. The cells contain the water so that it will pass uniformly into the subsoil below. A sloping subgrade would allow subsurface water to flow to a low point before soaking into the subsoil below (see A). ■

A. Reservoirs Below Sloped Pavement

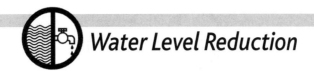

Underdrainage pipe or swales run in parallel lines and can be used to drain free water soil from.

**1.** Agricultural underdrains are usually laid out in a herringbone pattern of sloped, perforated pipes of open ditches. The system lowers the water level to the surface of the drain in the area directly above the drain, but the water table gradually rises as the distance from the drain increases (see A).

**2.** In general, the drains become more efficient with depth, so fewer numbers of deep drains can drain an equivalent area to many shallow drains (see B). ∎

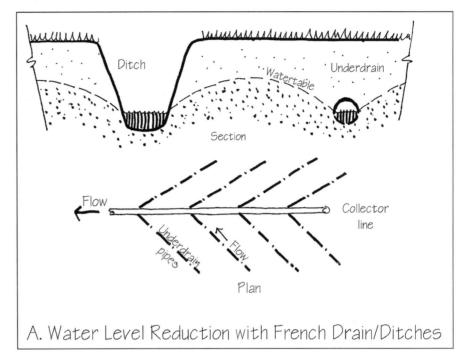

A. Water Level Reduction with French Drain/Ditches

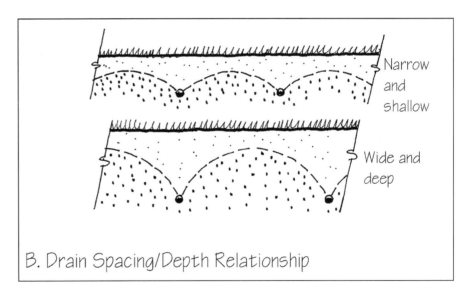

B. Drain Spacing/Depth Relationship

Subgrade reservoirs normally release water into porous soil below, but they should have an overflow to provide a redundant drainage system to prevent failure (see page 27).

**1.** When using aggregate base material to serve as a reservoir for stormwater infiltration, the detailer should provide an overflow to allow the water built up in the reservoir to flow out of the section. The overflow releases excess water before it reaches the finished surface to prevent uplift of the surface and to protect against frost damage (see A).

**2.** When using a drywell for primary drainage, the detailer should provide an overflow to a gravity drain to protect sensitive structures from inundation if the volume of stormwater is more than the soil can infiltrate (see B). ■

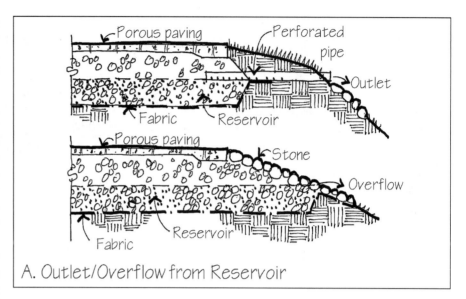

A. Outlet/Overflow from Reservoir

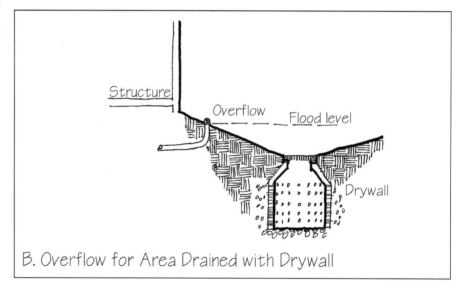

B. Overflow for Area Drained with Drywall

To support paving and allow for a moderated soil environment for root growth, a composite system of open-graded, crushed aggregates, coarse sands, and organic material is used.

**1.** There are many recipes for structural soils that utilize different proportions of soil and stone sizes, organic material, and additives such as super-absorbants. In all of them, the coarse, crushed stone transfers the loads from the finish pavement to the subsoil below while the finer soil partially fills the voids between the stones. These systems allow for the soil to support heavy loads while maintaining a large number of open pores for root growth. The best ones allow for good water infiltration and supplemental moisture holding capacity (see A). ∎

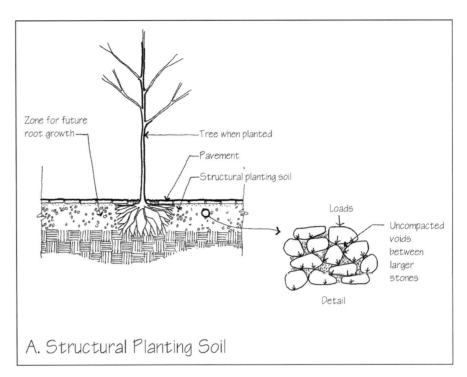

Zone for future root growth

Tree when planted

Pavement

Structural planting soil

Loads

Uncompacted voids between larger stones

Detail

A. Structural Planting Soil

CHAPTER

# 4 Accommodating Movement

A landscape is never at rest. Its movements, though seemingly small, are extremely powerful and can cause irreparable damage unless the elements of the landscape are detailed to accommodate them. There are a number of sources and types of movement that the detailer must keep in mind:

*Temperature movement* is caused by the expansion and contraction of materials with rising and falling temperatures. A material's temperature is chiefly affected by the surrounding air temperature but also is affected by radiant energy, as sunlight strikes a dark surface.

*Moisture movement* occurs in porous materials such as soil, wood, plaster, masonry, and concrete. These materials swell as they absorb moisture from water or humid air and shrink as they dry.

*Phase-change movement* accompanies a change in the physical state of a material. The phase-change movement that is of primary interest to the detailer is the expansion of water as it freezes.

*Chemical-change movement* takes place in certain construction materials as they cure or age. Solvent-release coatings and sealants shrink as they cure. Reinforcing bars that rust expand and can crack the masonry or concrete in which they are embedded.

*Structural deflections* always accompany changes in the loads on landscape elements. Beams, slabs, trusses, and arches sag more as they are loaded more heavily, and sag less as their loads are reduced. Columns become shorter as loads are applied to them. Wind and seismic loads flex and rack free-standing structures, and move those structures laterally by substantial amounts.

*Structural creep* is characteristic of wood and concrete, both of which sag

permanently by a small amount during the first several years after installation and then stabilize.

*Foundation settlement* occurs when the soil beneath a foundation deflects or creeps under loading. All foundations settle; if the settlement is small and is uniform across the entire structure, little movement occurs within the components built on that foundation. If settlement is nonuniform from one wall or column to another, considerable movement must be accommodated.

We can predict, often with impressive accuracy, the magnitude of movement that will occur from many of these sources: Temperature movement can be quantified rather precisely using the expected range of temperature difference and the coefficient of thermal expansion of the material (p. 49). Moisture movement cannot be quantified with such precision, but we can predict it accurately enough to prevent it from causing damage Phase-change and chemical-change movements can be estimated with varying degrees of accuracy. Structural deflections are computed very closely using standard engineering techniques, and structural creep can be quantified to within manageable limits. A geotechnical or foundation engineer can provide enough data regarding expected levels of foundation movement to guide the detailer. During the life of a project, changes in the surrounding soil and water conditions, such as a deep excavation nearby, may call for further analyses.

In detailing a landscape, we concede that most movements are unpreventable and are caused by forces so large that we cannot restrain them. Instead, we provide movement joints between components at such intervals and in

such configurations that the movements can be absorbed without harm in these joints. As designers we must be alert to where movement due to these unpreventable forces is most likely. For instance, thermal movement is likely to be more significant in dark walls or pavements that are exposed to the sun on the south or west elevations (in North America). Moisture movement is likely to be more radical on the base of a free-standing wall, where it is in contact with the ground rather than at its top. Detailing a tall solid fence is different than a short one in terms of anticipated movement, because wind pressure is greater aloft.

If we did not provide movement joints, the forces that cause movement in a wall or pavement would create their own joints by cracking and crushing components until the internal stresses were relieved. At best, the result would be unsightly; at worst, the result would be leaky, unstable, and unsafe.

The detail patterns that relate to accommodating movement in landscapes are associated with several simple strategies. The first of these is to manufacture and configure materials in ways that minimize their tendency to move in undesirable ways. Its associated patterns are:

A second strategy is to separate elements that are likely to move at different rates and in different ways. Its patterns are:

A third strategy is to divide large surfaces that are likely to crack, crush, or buckle into smaller units of such a size that the likelihood of such failures is greatly reduced. This leads to the following patterns:

A fourth and final strategy is used by architects to divide a large building, especially one with a complex geometry, into two or more geometrically simple buildings; each of a size and compactness such that we can reasonably expect it to move as a unit in response to large forces such as foundation settlement and seismic accelerations. Detailing of landscapes that straddle these joints require special care to accommodate the movements required in these joints within the landscapes that are built over them. This leads to the pattern:

Many porous construction materials should be seasoned or cured for a period of time following their manufacture, before they are incorporated into a project. Seasoning or curing allows a material to reach a moisture content equilibrium and to stabilize dimensionally before their movement is restrained by adjoining structural components.

**1.** Wood is the building material that is by far most subject to dimensional change due to changes in moisture content. When live wood is cut, it is fully saturated with water. As it dries, it becomes stronger and stiffer. It also shrinks by very large amounts until it reaches its equilibrium moisture content, at which point it no longer gives off moisture to the air. Wood is seasoned commercially, either by stacking it in loose arrays for a period of many months, to allow it to dry in the air, or by drying it in a kiln over a period of a few days. Kiln drying generally produces a more stable product. Throughout its lifetime, however, a piece of wood seasoned by either method will absorb moisture and expand during humid periods and will give off moisture and shrink during dry periods. Wood shrinkage and expansion in common species of softwoods can be quantified using the Western Wood Products Association's *Dimensional Stability of Western Lumber Products* (see Appendix A, p. 241).

Though made with the same porous materials, engineered wood products, such as glue-laminated beams and parallel strand lumber, tend to undergo much less drying shrinkage or distortion than solid timber. The wood used to make these products is kiln dried before being incorporated into the large wood elements. Distortion is minimized because wood grain direction varies in the members, with no prevailing direction of shrinkage. These products are manufactured and dressed to their final size after drying is complete.

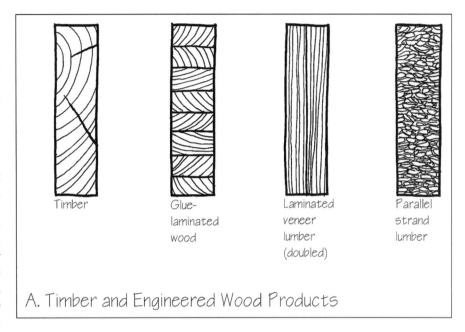

Timber

Glue-laminated wood

Laminated veneer lumber (doubled)

Parallel strand lumber

A. Timber and Engineered Wood Products

Many hardwoods suitable for exterior use are available on the market ranging from tropical hardwoods such as ipe, purpleheart, mahogany and teak to domestic hardwoods such as black locust. These hardwoods tend to have a much lower water content and higher strength, hardness, resistance to rot, and of course cost. These are subject to the same movement issues as softwoods, but to a lesser extent (see A).

**2.** Unseasoned ("green") lumber is sometimes used in construction, especially for rustic railings and fences and other structures. Special care should be taken in detailing the finish components framed with unseasoned lumber, because framing components will shrink by large amounts in the perpendicular-to-grain direction which will apply severe stresses to finish components that are rigidly fixed to the frame. Fasteners such as nails and bolts may loosen as the wood shrinks. Unseasoned lumber is also expected to distort by cupping, warping, and twisting as it dries to its equilibrium moisture content. See *Vertical-Grain Lumber* (p. 72) to see how moisture affects the shape of a piece of wood. Unseasoned lumber should never be used for finish components except in a very rustic style; in fact, finish lumber should be the most carefully seasoned of all, dried to a moisture content that is in equilibrium with the air, usually about 11 percent by weight, but which varies from 4 to 14 percent for different climates and seasons.

**3.** Concrete masonry units are manufactured with moisture content that has been controlled at the plant to reduce drying shrinkage after the units have been laid. Despite this, minor shrinkage is to be expected in concrete masonry units due to drying and carbonation which is an unavoidable result of the curing process. Clay bricks, on the other hand, are devoid of moisture when they come from the kiln and expand very slightly over a period of weeks and months as they absorb small amounts of moisture from the air. It is wise to allow both types of masonry units to season for a time before using them in a wall; this has usually occurred before the units are purchased by the contractor. ▷

**4.** At the time concrete is poured, it contains more water than is needed for curing. This excess water evaporates from the concrete, causing it to shrink slightly. In addition, minor shrinkage is expected in concrete as a natural byproduct of the hydration process. An exception to this is concrete made with an expansive cement that offsets normal initial shrinkage (see B).

In most concrete walls and slabs on grade it is possible to provide control joints to absorb the cracking that will be caused by this shrinkage (see *Control Joint* p. 85). When pouring structural slabs that are very large in area and that cannot have control joints, shrinkage distress can be minimized by pouring in smaller sections, separated by open shrinkage strips. After the sections have cured and dried long enough so that most shrinkage has occurred, the shrinkage strips are poured to complete the slab. Reinforcing bars should be spliced within the shrinkage strips so the separate areas of the slab can move independently while the strips are open. The

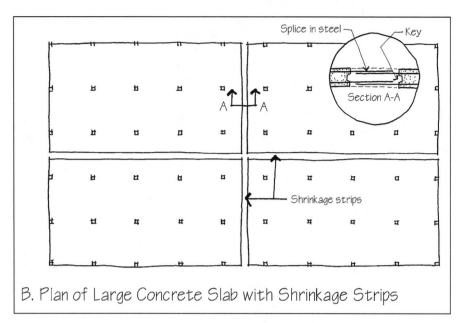

B. Plan of Large Concrete Slab with Shrinkage Strips

concrete in the strips should be keyed mechanically to the slabs on either side. Supporting formwork must be left in place until the concrete in the shrinkage strips has cured. The locations of the shrinkage strips must be determined by the structural engineer.

Shrinkage cracking can also be minimized with the addition of synthetic fibers into the concrete mix. The tiny fibers reinforce the concrete and stop small cracks from growing into big ones.

**5.** Moisture movement of cementitious materials and masonry can be approximated using Table 4-1.

*Example No.1:* About how much will a concrete slab 210 ft (64 m) long shrink during curing and drying?

(210 ft.) (12 in./ft.) = 2,520 in.
(2,520 in.) (0.0005 in./in.) = 1.26 in.

64 m = 64,000 mm
(64,000) (0.0005 mm/mm) = 32 mm

### TABLE 4-1: Moisture Movement of Cementitious Materials and Masonry

| | in./in. (mm/mm) |
|---|---|
| Curing and drying shrinkage of concrete | 0.0005 |
| Curing and drying shrinkage of concrete masonry units | 0.0001– 0.0010 |
| Moisture expansion of brick masonry | 0.0002 |

*Example No. 2:* Approximately how much moisture expansion should be anticipated in a new brick wall 175 ft (53.3 m) long?

(175 ft) (12 in./ft) = 2,100 in.
(2,100 in.) (0.0002 in./in.) = 0.42 in.

53.3 m = 53,300 mm
(53,300) (0.0002 mm/mm) = 10.6 mm

**6.** When combining materials with different movement rates and directions, joints must be detailed to provide needed flexibility. In the example shown above, the wooden rails are attached to a granite post via a steel plate and pin. The plate is attached with screws to the rails and the pin in inserted into holes drilled in the posts. As the rail expands and contracts, the pin can move in and out of the post (see C). In walls containing stone, brick, and concrete masonry, it is important to compare the properties of the particular materials and avoid interspersing materials that will move inconsistently. It is better to insert an entire course of concrete masonry into a brick wall than to insert isolated units at intervals. This simplifies masonry placement and increases the efficiency of the joint. ■

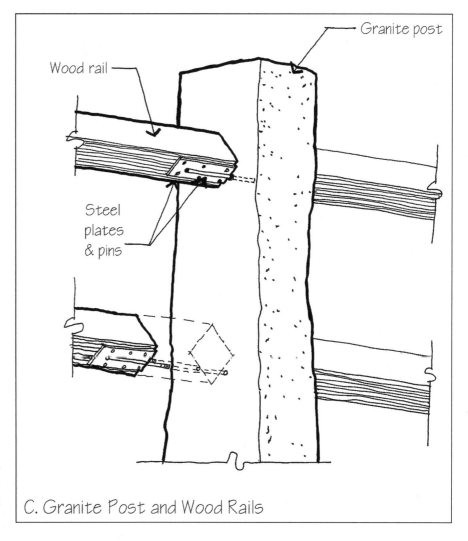

**C. Granite Post and Wood Rails**

Wood rail

Granite post

Steel plates & pins

Lumber used for flat finish components of a deck, fence, trellis, or other structure should be sawn from the log in such a way that the growth rings of the wood run approximately perpendicular to the surface of the board.

**1.** When a log is seasoned, it shrinks very little along its length. It shrinks considerably in its radial direction (perpendicular to the growth rings), and it shrinks most of all in its tangential direction (along the growth rings). The amounts of shrinkage are very large, as the accompanying graph indicates. The amount of shrinkage depends on the difference between the moisture content when milled and when at equilibrium with its place in the structure. Consult references by the American Wood Council and Architectural Woodworking Institute in *The Detailer's Reference Shelf* (p. 241) to find recommendations for a particular location (see A).

**2.** The larger shrinkage in the tangential direction causes a log to check (split along radial lines). It also causes pieces of lumber cut from different parts of the cross section of the log to distort during seasoning in a variety of ways. Checking is more likely if the wood is dried quickly (see B).

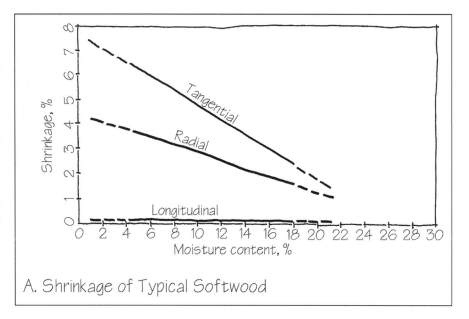

A. Shrinkage of Typical Softwood

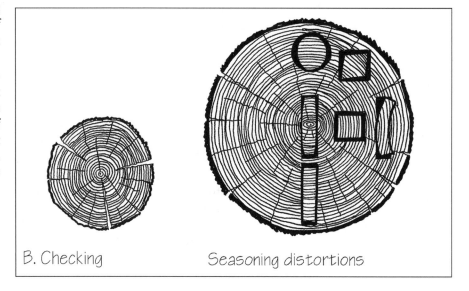

B. Checking          Seasoning distortions

**3.** To avoid seasoning distortions as much as possible, boards and lumber can be cut from the log in such a way that the face of each piece is approximately perpendicular to the annual rings in the wood. This is referred to as rift sawing or quarter-sawing, and lumber cut in this way is often called vertical-grain lumber. Vertical-grain wood is best for finish millwork that must remain flat and straight—fine latticework, for example. Vertical-grain lumber also wears better in site furniture and decking, because the harder summerwood bands occur very close together at the surface of each piece, protecting the soft springwood between from abrasion. Vertical-grain wood takes longer to saw than plain-sawed lumber, however; and it wastes more of the log, so it costs more. For most uses, especially ordinary framing, plain-sawed lumber is a satisfactory and economical choice, despite its tendency to distort. Boards and lumber cut from logs with many knots are more prone to distortion than "clear" pieces that are knot-free and have parallel grain patterns. Small diameter logs are less likely to yield boards or lumber that have all of these desirable features (see C).

**4.** Most outdoor decks are made of plain-sawed decking. If the boards are laid with their bark side up, they will cup in a way that traps water during rainstorms. The proper way to lay decking is bark side down. To predict how a given piece of wood will change, remember that as it dries, the arcing annual rings on the end tend to become straighter (see D). ■

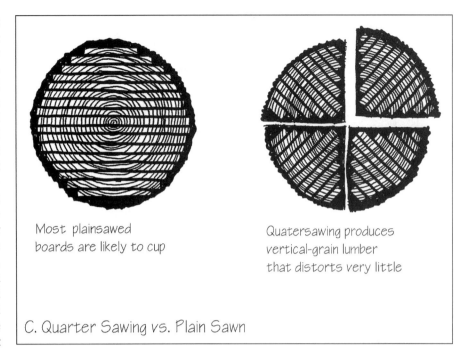

Most plainsawed
boards are likely to cup

Quatersawing produces
vertical-grain lumber
that distorts very little

C. Quarter Sawing vs. Plain Sawn

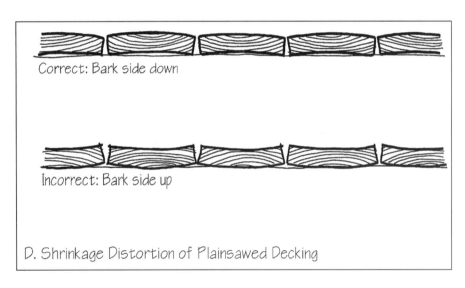

Correct: Bark side down

Incorrect: Bark side up

D. Shrinkage Distortion of Plainsawed Decking

Problems caused by cupping distortions in flat finish pieces of wood can be minimized by using a profile with a relieved back and by back priming each piece for painted or stained finishes.

**1.** Cupping distortion of a wood board is caused by a difference in the amount of shrinkage experienced by the opposite sides of the board. The thinner the board, the less the force that can be exerted on it by this difference in shrinkage. It is common practice to relieve the backs of flat pieces of wood millwork by cutting one or more grooves, thus effectively reducing the thickness of the pieces and diminishing their tendency to cup. If a single, wide groove is cut, it also makes the piece easier to attach to a flat surface, because only the two edges need to touch. In factory-produced millwork the grooves are usually cut by shaping machinery. On the jobsite, it is usually more practical to cut multiple grooves on a portable table saw (see A).

**2.** Back priming, the application of a coat of primer paint to the back side of a board, is also helpful in preventing cupping distortion of flat pieces of wood that will be painted. The effect of back priming is to cause both the front and back surfaces of the board to react to moisture at roughly the same rate. The back priming needs to be done at least a day in advance of installation to give the primer time to dry. It should be noted in the carpentry or millwork section of the specifications and referred to in detail under the painting section. ■

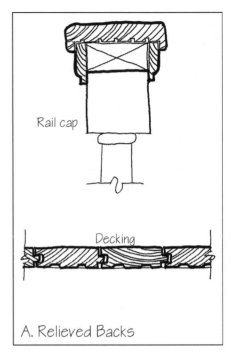

Rail cap

Decking

A. Relieved Backs

# Foundation below Frost Line

One type of movement that we can prevent is frost heaving. It is caused by water freezing in the soil beneath a foundation. Phase-change expansion of the water can cause the soil to expand, lifting the foundation slightly. Larger amounts of lifting can occur due to the growth of long vertical crystals of ice under the foundation under certain temperature and moisture conditions. Similar movement can be caused by excessive moisture in expansive clay soils.

**1.** Building codes generally require that the bottom of a foundation be placed at a level below the deepest level to which the ground freezes during a severe winter; consult the applicable building code to find out how deep this is. Exceptions to this general pattern are made only when there is no water below the foundation, such as when building upon solid rock, or upon permafrost, both of which are very rare. In locations not subject to freezing temperatures, building codes require that foundations must simply be at least 12 in. below finish grade (see A).  ▷

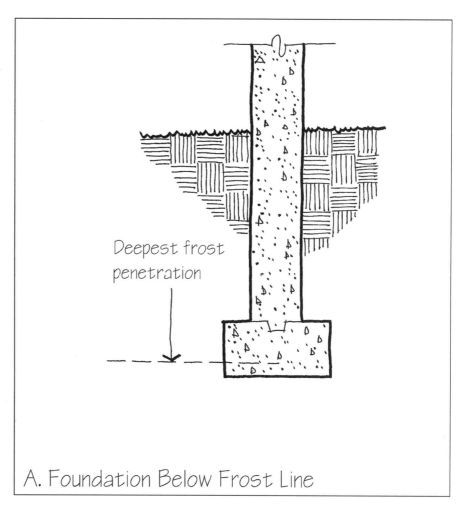

Deepest frost penetration

A. Foundation Below Frost Line

**2.** Isolated pier foundations are economical and effective for decks, fences, light poles, signs, and small wooden structures. A post-hole digger or auger is used to excavate for each pier. The concrete should not be cast directly against the rough sides of the hole, however, because frost can heave upward against the rough sides of the pier. A smooth fiber tube form should be used to cast piers whose sides are smooth above the frost line. Similarly, a foundation wall should be cast in smooth forms, not directly against the walls of the trench (see B).

**3.** It is not practical to support outdoor paving, such as roads, patios, and walks, on foundations that go below the frost line; they must be supported at a much shallower level. Most frost heaving can be prevented, however, by placing the paving (concrete, asphalt, brick, or stone) on a thick, well-drained layer of open graded (without fines) aggregate. The spaces between the stones drain water away from the underside of the paving and also furnish expansion space for water that freezes in the soil below. For brick and stone paving, a sand setting bed above the crushed stone also gives the mason a precise means of regulating the height of the masonry units (see C).

**4.** In monolithic paving systems, the surface is designed to shed water to maintain a consistent soil moisture and strength in the subsoil that supports the paving section. A crack in the pavement or failure in a joint allows water to penetrate into the lower layers of the section causing a saturating and weakening of the underlying soil and can cause ice to form below the paving, creating a void below the top surface. This is the classic recipe for a pothole. The potential problem can be avoided by maintaining the paving surface so that water is shed as intended. Secondly, the base material can be free draining to remove the water from the section.

**5.** Short, dry-laid stone walls are often built on a base of open graded aggregate that extends below the frost line. In addition, a slab is often poured on this base under the wall. The concrete keeps the base of the wall together and allows the wall to rise and fall as a unit, minimizing damage if frost heave occurs. ■

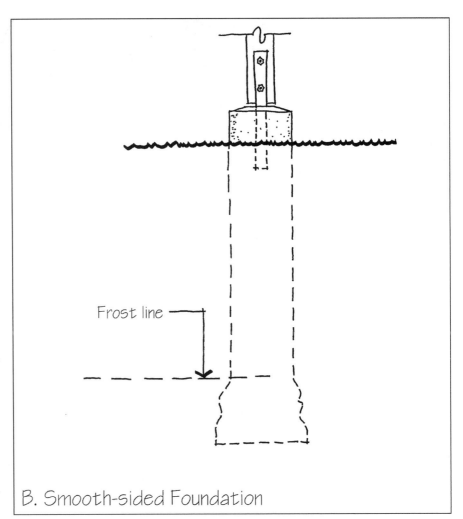

Frost line

B. Smooth-sided Foundation

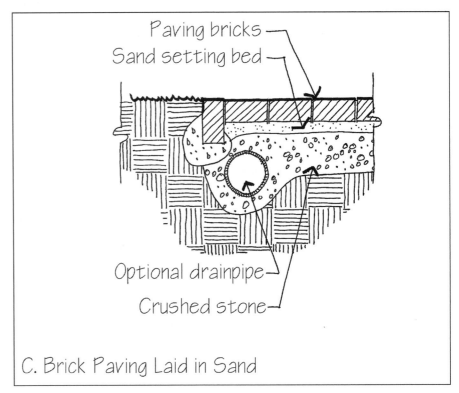

Paving bricks
Sand setting bed
Optional drainpipe
Crushed stone

C. Brick Paving Laid in Sand

In unit paving systems such as brick or concrete and asphalt pavers, it is also important to include an edge restraint such as a concrete or stone curb; or a metal, wood, or plastic edging to keep the joints from opening up and allowing fine soil particles into the joints.

The sand used between the units allows for water in the joints to drain into the subbase below and not freeze within the joint. As windborne fines fill any gaps at the surface, the sand in the lower portion of the joint will remain dry and frost free. If the edges are not restrained, the fines can infiltrate into the joints, absorb and hold water. The moist joint freezes and further opens the joint to more movement, eventually causing failure. The edge restraint must be securely anchored and set on a frost-resistant base to prevent heaving over time. The forces exerted on the edge are small, but are enough to lift an edge becoming a tripping hazard over time (see A).

**2.** When unit pavers abut a structure on a foundation that extends below frost such as a building or a light pole, the edge restraint is unnecessary and no additional expansion joint is usually required. ■

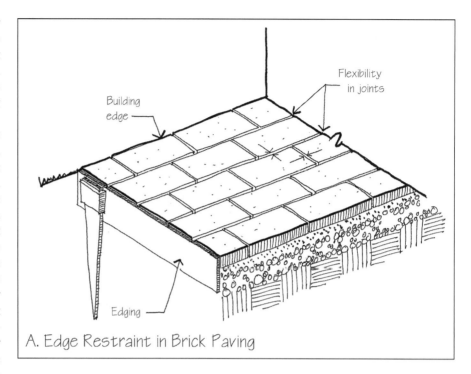

A. Edge Restraint in Brick Paving

In dry laid walls and in flexible paving systems, the wall or pavement is held together by the friction between individual stones or pavers. Each system is weakest at the joints between stones. By staggering or offsetting the joints, each unit is in contact with several adjacent units and there are no planes of weakness caused by aligned joints.

**1.** The stone mason's saying of "one over two and two over one" assures that each joint between two stones is supported by an adjacent solid stone. This assures that each joint is covered by a stone and no joint will be duplicated in adjacent courses of stone.

**2.** Similarly, the four-corner rule in paving systems assures that pavements are also supported at every joint. This assures that every joint is supported by an adjacent paver and with compacted material below the stone, so that a person's foot will not upturn the paver (see A). ■

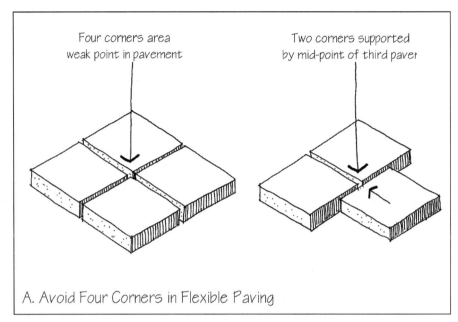

Four corners area weak point in pavement

Two corners supported by mid-point of third paver

A. Avoid Four Corners in Flexible Paving

# Structure Joint

The framework of a structure and the pavements, fences, or walls attached to it moves in different ways and has different structural capabilities. They must be joined in ways that recognize these differences.

**1.** A building foundation wall usually supports the weight of the building above. An adjacent slab on grade does not. If the slab were rigidly connected to the wall, any slight settlement in the wall foundation would bend the slab and cause it to crack near the connection. A simple movement joint between the two isolates the slab from any movement in the structural wall. A similar joint should be detailed around light pole foundations, where they intersect a rigid pavement. This type of joint is often called an isolation joint (see A). ■

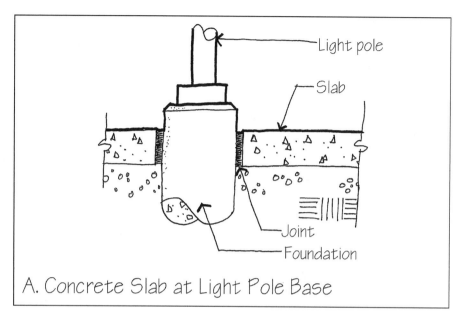

A. Concrete Slab at Light Pole Base

Abutment joints allow for movement between dissimilar materials, or between old and new construction. Dissimilar materials tend to move at different rates and in different patterns. Old construction has already undergone foundation settlement, long-term structural movements, and initial moisture movements, while new construction has not. In either case, an abutment joint should be provided to allow for differential movement between the two parts of the construction.

**1.** New and old masonry should not be interleaved but should be separated cleanly and connected by a flexible abutment joint. This is easier for masons to lay and avoids the cracking that might be caused by the shrinkage of the new mortar (see A).

**2.** A stone pier adjacent to a stuccoed wall is separated by a joint that allows for differential movement of the two materials (see B). ∎

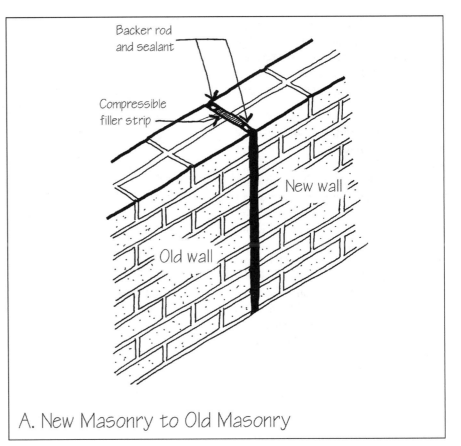

A. New Masonry to Old Masonry

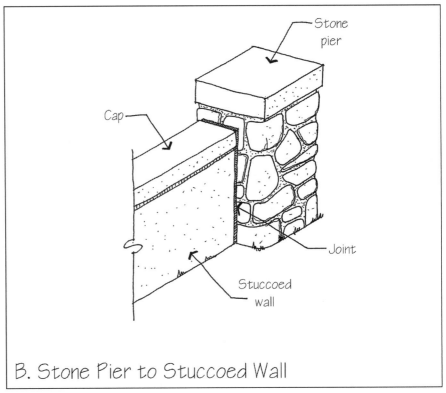

B. Stone Pier to Stuccoed Wall

# Expansion Joint

Large surfaces of materials that tend to expand after installation should be divided into smaller surfaces by a regular pattern of expansion joints. Expansion joints also accommodate shrinkage and minor differential movement between structure and enclosure. Expansion joints also can double as isolation joints.

**1.** Expansion joints in slabs should occur at the edge of the slab where it is confined by a structure on a foundation (building, light pole base, wall, and so forth). If the slab is confined only on one edge, a joint is not needed; if it is confined on two sides, at least one is needed; if confined on three sides, three joints are needed; and on four sides, four joints should be used. If it is important to maintain a level surface across the joint, smooth, greased steel dowels can be inserted. These allow for in-plane movement while preventing out-of-plane movement. As an alternate to the dowels, a shelf can be cast in adjacent structures to keep the slab from settling as it moves (see A).    ▷

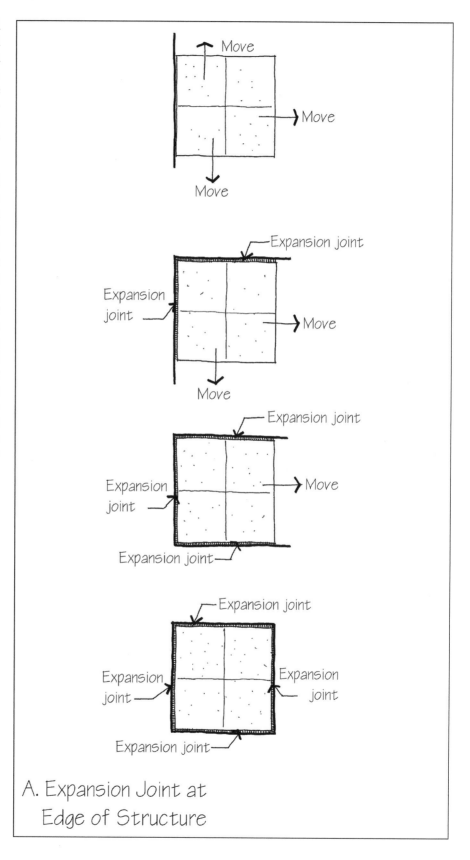

A. Expansion Joint at Edge of Structure

**2.** This expansion joint accessory for plaster allows for the slight expansion in the curing plaster, as well as for subsequent moisture movement and movement in the underlying wall structure. The metal lath must be discontinuous along the line of the joint to allow for free movement. The expansion joint accessory is a simple metal or plastic bellows shape. At the time it is installed, it is closed with a plastic tape that prevents it from becoming clogged with plaster, which would be unsightly and would destroy its function. After the plaster has been applied, the tape is stripped away, creating a straight, clean, dark shadow line in the plaster surface. As with any joint, the pattern created by the expansion joints should be worked out and described to the contractor in elevation view (see B).

**3.** Long walls of brick masonry are subject to expansion as the bricks absorb moisture and require periodic expansion joints to relieve the pressure that this otherwise would cause. Dark brick walls on sunny exposures may require expansion joints at more frequent intervals to accommodate thermal expansion. Any reinforcing in the brickwork should be discontinued across the joint. In masonry expansion joints, it is often important that a spline or tongue-and-groove feature be provided that will maintain the alignment of the wall while allowing for the necessary in-plane movement (see C).

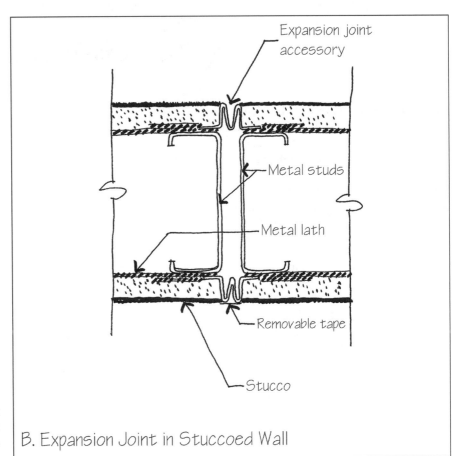

B. Expansion Joint in Stuccoed Wall

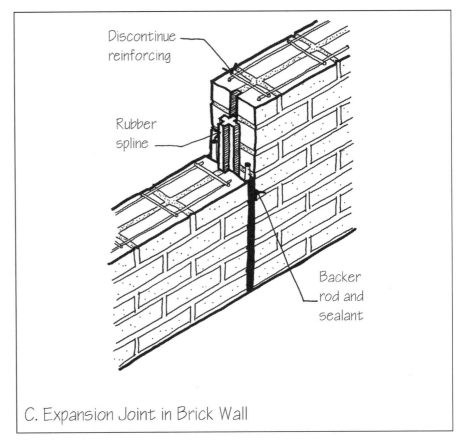

C. Expansion Joint in Brick Wall

**4.** Expansion joints in any material should be located at lines of structural weakness in the surface, where cracking or crushing would tend to occur if no joints were provided. Any openings in a wall or slab on grade weaken a planar surface, so expansion joints are often placed to align with the edges of these elements vertically, horizontally, or both (see D).

**5.** Suggested maximum expansion joint spacings for exterior concrete slabs on grade are a function of slab thickness, aggregate size, reinforcement, and slump of concrete. Thicker slab, larger aggregate, more reinforcement, and lower slumps result in greater joint spacing. See *Table* 4-2 for suggested joint spacing.

**6.** Suggested maximum vertical expansion joint spacings are 30 ft (9.1 m) for plaster, up to 125 ft (38 m) intervals for solid brick masonry, and 25 ft (7.6 m) for brick veneers. Expected movement of these materials can be quantified by using the procedure shown in *Determining Widths of Sealant Joints*, p. 49.   ▷

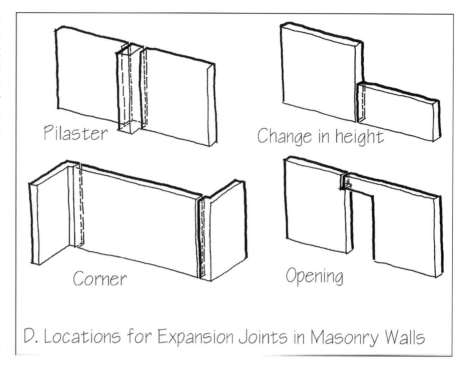

Pilaster

Change in height

Corner

Opening

D. Locations for Expansion Joints in Masonry Walls

**7.** When laying out expansion joints in one system, such as concrete paving, care must be taken to align joints in any system that bridges over those joints such as a handrail (see E).

**8.** Metal components such as handrails are subject to large amounts of expansion and contraction caused by daily and seasonal differences in air temperatures and by direct solar heating of the metal. Both horizontal and vertical expansion joints must be provided at appropriate intervals. Each joint must be designed to maintain the alignment of the components and to keep out weather while allowing for movement. In this example, horizontal movement is accommodated by a sliding connection in the handrail run (see F). ∎

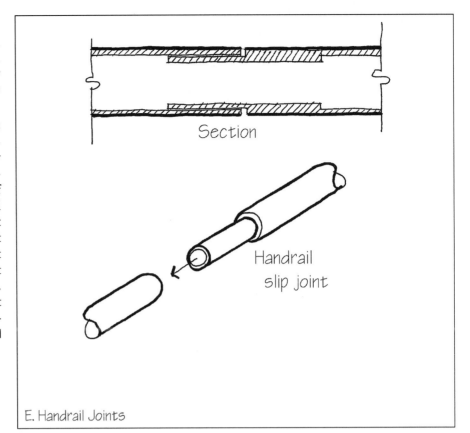

Section

Handrail slip joint

E. Handrail Joints

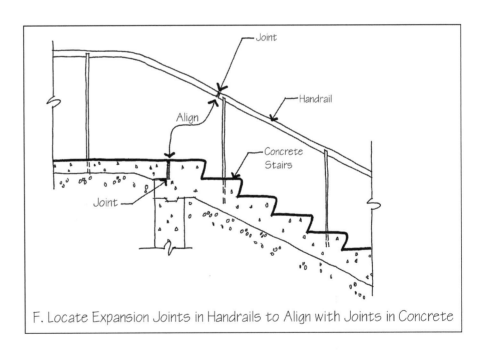

Joint

Handrail

Align

Concrete Stairs

Joint

F. Locate Expansion Joints in Handrails to Align with Joints in Concrete

# Control Joint

A control joint is an intentional line of weakness that is created in the surface of a rigid material that tends to shrink. Its role is to encourage any shrinkage cracking to occur within itself, to avoid random cracking of the surface around it. Control joints allow cracking to occur within a designed module and not mar the design with random lines.

**1.** A concrete sidewalk tends to crack roughly perpendicular to the centerline of the walk. A sidewalk control joint is formed by tooling a deep crack into the wet concrete. When the sidewalk shrinks, cracking is channeled to the tooled crack. The sidewalk remains as a group of large, stable rectangular units, rather than as a weak array of irregular concrete fragments. The tooled joint must be deep enough to create a groove in the slab that is substantially weaker than the surrounding surfaces (1 in. deep for a 4-in.-deep slab [25 mm in 100 mm]). If it is not deep enough, cracking will not be confined to the joint. The joints are usually evenly spaced and interspersed with expansion joints (see A).

**2.** A concrete slab on grade tends to crack in all directions so it should be divided by control joints into smaller rectangles that can be expected to stay crack free. The joints can be created by tooling the wet concrete, installing a premolded strip, or by sawing it during the early stages of its curing. With any method, the depth of the joint should be at least 25 percent slab depth. Any reinforcing in the slab should be discontinued across the line of the joint. If it is important to maintain a level surface across the joint, smooth, greased steel dowels can be inserted. These allow for in-plane movement while preventing out-of-plane movement (see B).    ▷

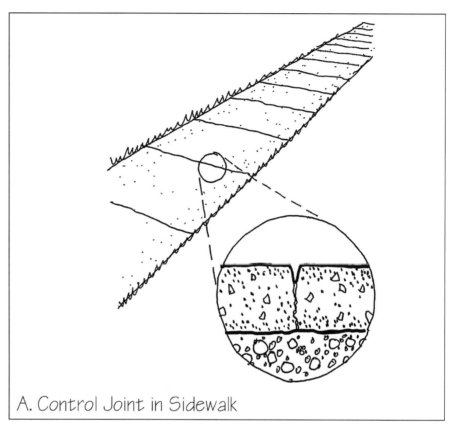

A. Control Joint in Sidewalk

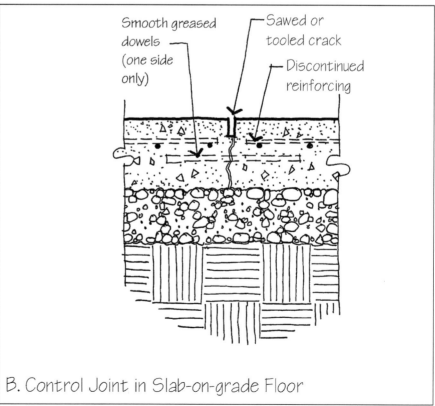

Smooth greased dowels (one side only)

Sawed or tooled crack

Discontinued reinforcing

B. Control Joint in Slab-on-grade Floor

**3.** As seen in this plan view, ground slabs should be divided in a way that avoids oddly shaped panels, because they are prone to cracking. A rectangular panel whose length is greater than 1.5 times its width is likely to crack across its middle. Control joints around pier or light pole foundations and around pilasters should be cut on a diagonal or cast in a circle, as shown, to avoid inside corners that foster cracks (see C).

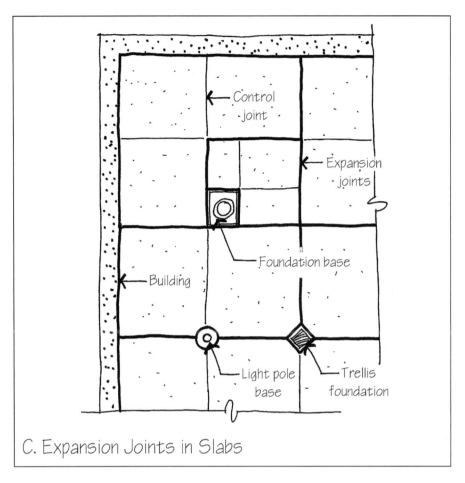

C. Expansion Joints in Slabs

**TABLE 4-2 Maximum Spacing of Control Joints**

| Slab Thickness in. (mm) | Maximum-size aggregate less than 3/4″ (19mm) | Maximum-size aggregate 3/4″ (19 mm) and larger |
| --- | --- | --- |
| 5 in (125mm) | 10 ft.(3.0m) | 13 ft.(3.75m) |
| 6 in. (150mm) | 12 ft.(3.75m) | 15 ft. (4.5m ) |
| 7 in. (175mm) | 14 ft.4.25m | 18 ft. (5.25m)** |
| 8 in. (200mm) | 16 ft. (5.0m)** | 20 ft. (6.0m)** |
| 9 in. (225mm) | 18 ft. (5.5m )** | 23 ft. (6.75m)** |
| 10 in. (250mm) | 20 ft. (6.0m )** | 25 ft. (7.5m)** |

*If concrete cools at an early age, shorter spacing may be needed to control random cracking. A temperature difference of only 10 degree F (6 degrees C) may be critical. For slump less than 4 in. (100mm), join spacing can be increased by 20%.

**When spacings exceed 15ft. (4.5m), transfer by aggregate interlock decreases markedly. If shrinkage is high or unknown, joints should not exceed 15ft. (4.5m).

Table based on *Concrete Floors on Ground* by the Portland Cement Association (see Detailer's Reference Shelf).

**4.** Poured concrete walls are also subject to shrinkage cracking. Control joints are usually created by inserting strips into the formwork to create linear slots along which cracking will occur. The slots should reduce the wall thickness by at least 25 percent. Every second reinforcing bar should be discontinued to encourage cracking forces to concentrate at the line of the joint. Alternatively, all horizontal reinforcing bars may be discontinued and a greased steel dowel used to align the walls and offer shear resistance (see D).

**5.** Concrete masonry walls need control joints, of which two examples are shown here. Both of these details interlock in a way that allows in-plane but not out-of-plane movement. As in concrete walls, a greased steel dowel can be placed in a bond beam unit to provide shear transfer between abutting masonry walls (see E).    ▷

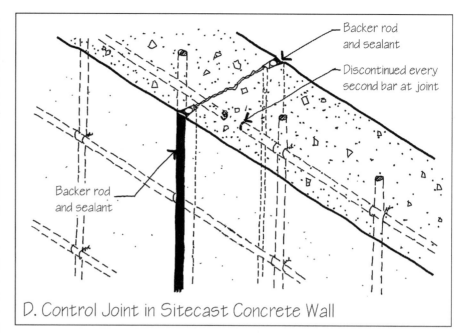

Backer rod and sealant

Discontinued every second bar at joint

Backer rod and sealant

D. Control Joint in Sitecast Concrete Wall

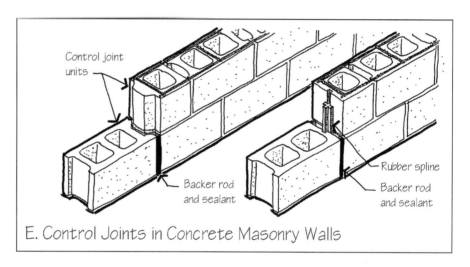

Control joint units

Backer rod and sealant

Rubber spline

Backer rod and sealant

E. Control Joints in Concrete Masonry Walls

**6.** Stucco control joints are formed with a specific accessory. The lath should be cut completely along the line of the control joint to create a line of weakness. Expansion joint assemblies can also serve as a control joint to limit cracking (see F). ■

**7.** Recommended control joint spacings for various materials are as follows:

**TABLE 4-3 Maximum Control Joint Spacing**

| Material | |
| --- | --- |
| Concrete slabs on grade | 24 times slab thickness |
| Concrete exterior walls | 20 ft (6.1 m) |
| Concrete masonry walls, joint reinforcing every second course | 25 ft (7.6 m) or 1.5 times the height of the wall, whichever is less |
| Stucco walls | 18 ft (5.5 m), 144 ft² in area (13.4 m²), or 2.5 times the height of the wall, whichever is less |

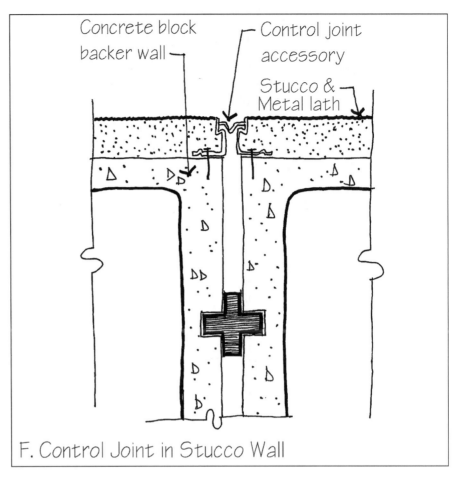

F. Control Joint in Stucco Wall

# Sliding Joint

Several traditional wood details rely on joints that allow components to slide past one another as they expand and contract with changing moisture content.

**1.** Wood siding is subject to relatively large amounts of moisture movement because it is exposed to rain and snow, as well as to the drying effects of sunlight and wind. Overlapping horizontal siding should be nailed to a wall or fence in the pattern shown here, which allows each piece to slide beneath the piece above as it moves, thus relieving potential stresses (see A).

**2.** Board-and-batten fencing should be nailed in the pattern shown here in plan view; this provides sliding joints for moisture movement (see B).  ▷

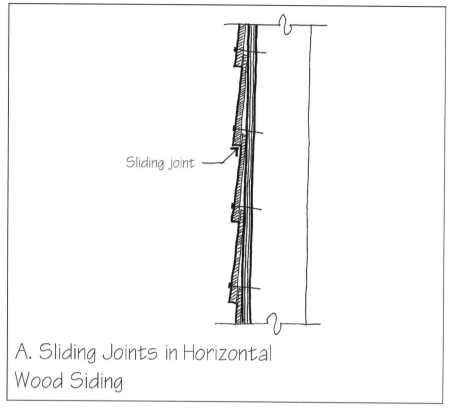

Sliding joint

A. Sliding Joints in Horizontal Wood Siding

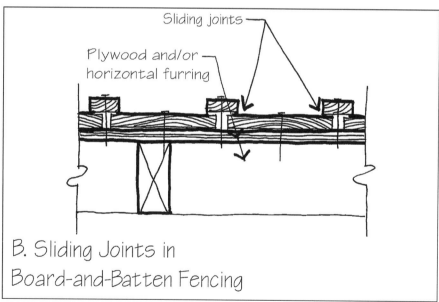

Sliding joints

Plywood and/or horizontal furring

B. Sliding Joints in Board-and-Batten Fencing

**3.** Covers over bridge expansion joints are designed to slide with the expansion of the deck. One side of the assembly is fixed and the other is allowed to slide (see C). ■

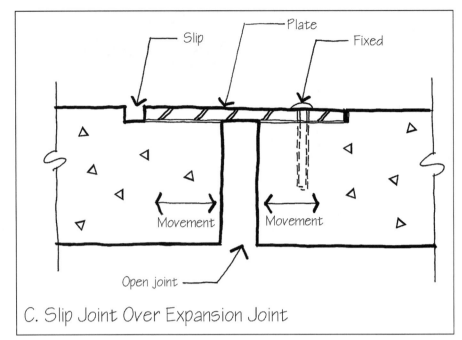

C. Slip Joint Over Expansion Joint

# Hinge Joint

The zone directly adjacent to a foundation is the most difficult to achieve proper compaction and is subject to movement by settlement. It is often an area where tolerances in grade are also critical. Thresholds need to be minimal to be accessible via wheelchair, and a change in elevation can render an entrance unusable. A hinge slab is utilized below the finished pavement to alleviate the impact of settlement in the foundation backfill.

1. A hinge slab is a technique used to maintain critical elevations at building entrances or stairs with a flexible pavement. A slab is poured over a haunch cast into the foundation. The slab is not attached to the haunch and is allowed to swing down like a hinge, maintaining a flush condition at the foundation while bridging the area of settlement (see A).

2. A post and panel fence system with mortise and tenon joints allows an installer to rack each panel to accommodate a sloping grade, but also allows for the joint to act as a hinge taking up any movement due to settlement of individual posts (see B). ■

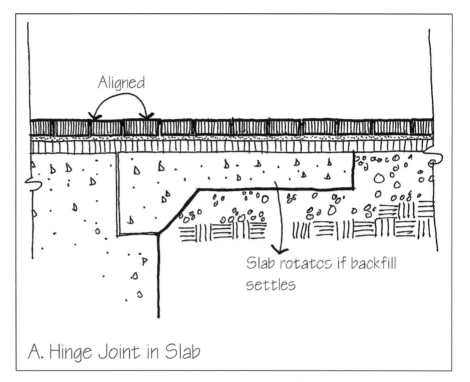

Aligned

Slab rotates if backfill settles

A. Hinge Joint in Slab

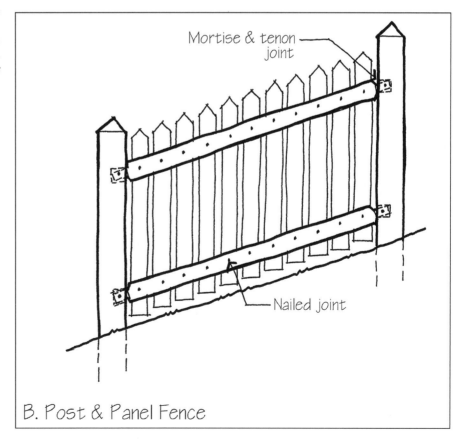

Mortise & tenon joint

Nailed joint

B. Post & Panel Fence

Buildings that are large in horizontal extent should be divided into separate structural entities, each of which is compact enough so that it can react as a rigid unit to foundation settlement and other movements, thereby avoiding damage.

**1.** This drawing shows how building separation joints should be located at points of geometric weakness, where cracking would otherwise be likely to occur. Notice how the joints divide the building into compact rectilinear volumes. At each joint plane, the structure of the building is cut completely through, with independent structural support on each side of the joint. Building separation joints are often referred to as "expansion joints," but they are really intended to separate a large building into a set of smaller buildings so that the building can deal effectively with not only thermal expansion but also soil settlement, materials shrinkage, and seismic deflections. Building separation joint locations, spacing, detailing, structural support, and foundation should be designed in consultation with the structural and foundation engineers. Thermal and moisture movement, foundation settlement, and the relative seismic motions of the adjoining parts of the building all must be dealt with adequately. Consultants responsible for plumbing and mechanical systems must detail any service lines that cross these joints to accommodate anticipated movement. As a general guide, spacings between building separation joints should not exceed 150 to 200 ft (45 to 60 m) (see A).

**2.** Building separation joints must be covered to keep out the weather and to provide continuity to interior surfaces. This is a typical design for a separation joint cover for a low-slope roof. A flexible bellows keeps water and air from leaking through the joint but adjusts

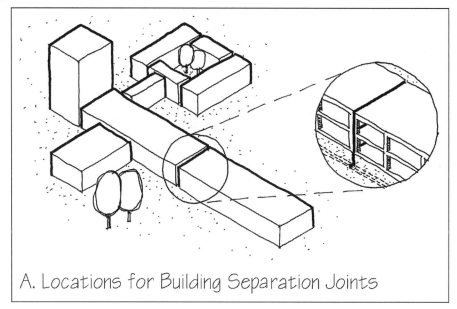

A. Locations for Building Separation Joints

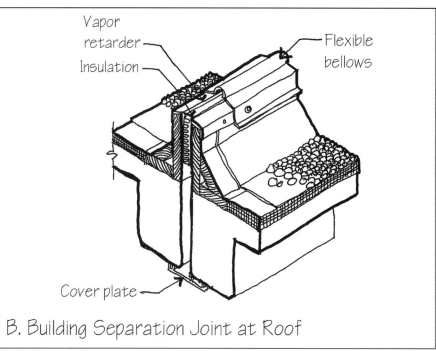

Vapor retarder
Insulation
Flexible bellows
Cover plate

B. Building Separation Joint at Roof

readily to movement between the two sections of the building. A high curb on either side keeps the bellows from being submerged in water. The joint is filled with thermal insulation and a vapor retarder. The ceiling below is provided with a gasketed metal coverplate that

can adjust to movement while retaining a reasonably attractive appearance. The bellows and the interior coverplate are common off-the-shelf components, typical of dozens of designs offered by a number of manufacturers (see B).

**3.** Rooftop landscapes that span over building separation joints must be able to accommodate the range of movement of the underlying joints. If hard surfaces are carried on a flexible base above a separation joint, the movement can be spread over a number of smaller joints (see C). ■

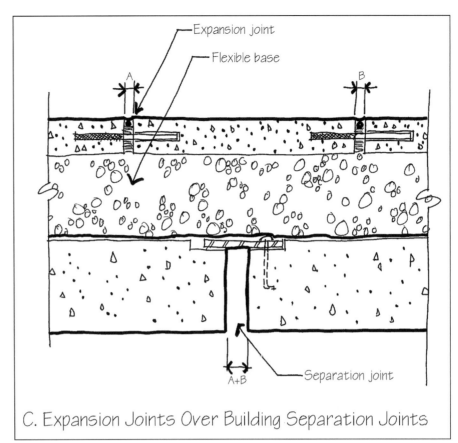

C. Expansion Joints Over Building Separation Joints

CHAPTER

# 5 Accommodating Growth

Plants grow and details involving plants must be able to accommodate that growth. In order to detail hardscape elements that support or are comingled with plant material, the detailer must have a good working knowledge of plant growth in general and the specifics of the species that is being used in a particular application.

Plants are fed by their roots and those roots need room to grow and expand with the growth of the plant. The majority of the roots grow close to the surface where there is abundant moisture, air, and nutrients. Roots are opportunistic and if their expansion is blocked and soil volume is limited, they will find their way into nearby zones of available space. This can be seen in uplifted sidewalks where roots from a nearby narrow parkway will follow a crack in the sidewalk to find sufficient soil volume in adjacent yards. This same tendency can be exploited by the detailer by designing routes for root growth that will provide sufficient soil to support plant growth over time without compromising nearby utilities, pavements, and other improvements. Trees and other woody plants expand in diameter as they grow. Trunks and branches get thicker and expand at their edges with new branches. Older branches die back or are removed. Branches do not move farther from the ground as they age (see A). Turf areas steadily increase in elevation as they trap air-borne par-

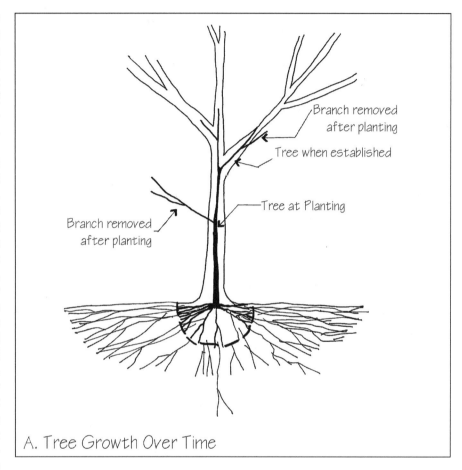

A. Tree Growth Over Time

ticles and new rhizomes grow on top of old. As plants grow, they change the microclimate around them. Maturing trees restrict the amount of light and moisture that makes it to the ground. Understory plants that may have started in full sun and no competition die as

trees shade them out and crowd out their root system. All of these growth characteristics are reflected in detailing patterns to support growth over time. Plant maintenance practices also influence detail patterns.

Roots grow and expand as the tree ages both in length and in girth. They do not grow uniformly because the medium they grow in is never uniform. They are opportunistic, extending into areas where there is physical volume and available moisture and nutrients. They also grow in a symbiotic relationship with many microorganisms. These microorganisms include fungi, bacteria, nematodes, protozoa, mites, and amoebae, which assist plants in absorbing nutrients. The growing media usually consists of inorganic particles (sand, silt, and clay), organic material, trace elements, moisture, and pore space between the particles. The roots require sufficient pore space in the soil to have room to grow. Large inorganic particle soils (sands) by themselves have a lot of pore space, but hold little moisture. Small particle soil (silts and clays) and soils with a mix of particle sizes (loams), where the small particles fill the voids between the large particles, tend not to have much void space and hold moisture. In evaluating or designing soil mixes, the specifier must balance the pore space and drainage capacity of the soil against its water-holding capacity. Detailing tree pits, planters, greenroof sections, and other conditions that include root zones use these patterns to provide for a healthy environment for root growth.

**1.** Tree roots must have a growing medium with sufficient pore space to

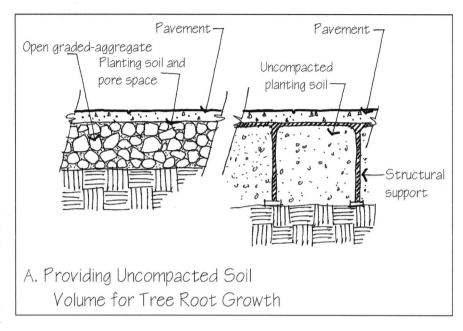

A. Providing Uncompacted Soil Volume for Tree Root Growth

be usable and must also have enough volume of that soil to allow for its growth. There has been much research in recent years into the volumes of soil needed to support an urban tree. Insufficient tree root volumes can limit tree growth and life span. Very generous tree pits with upwards of 400 cubic feet (11.5 cubic meters) of soil will limit tree growth in less than two decades and eventually lead to a premature death. The detailer should be including alternate paths to available soil volume in the detailing of tree pits and planting areas. Structural planting mixes that use large gravels or stone to supply structural support for pavers and large pore spaces to facilitate plant growth. Similarly, structural support systems that allow for uncompacted soil below structural paving systems can be used to provide additional soil volume under pavements. To be successful, both methods must have adequate soil volume, enough moisture but not be saturated and sufficient aeration for roots to grow. The detailer should include site-specific accommodations for root growth for each tree planting (see A).

**2.** Tree roots generally grow in a radial pattern when they are young. This can be altered in the nursery if a small tree is twisted when it's planted, but in general that radial tendency should be reflected in the plant pit detail. A tree pit with its roots confined along one edge will grow faster than a tree with roots confined in two or more. Ideally, the available soil should be as balanced on all sides of the tree to provide for good root growth (see B).

**3.** Tree roots can be manipulated and kept away from susceptible pavements, curbs, and walls by the use of root barriers. In warm climates root barriers are sometimes required to prevent roots from lifting sidewalks. These barriers are usually heavy plastic sheets sometimes impregnated with herbacide that can be effective in preventing root growth where expanding roots will cause future damage. However, root barriers can be detrimental to the long-term health of the tree, by limiting its available space for root growth, and encouraging girdling roots.

**4.** Walls built on a continuous foundation wall will effectively stop root growth and prevent tree roots from accessing soil beyond the wall. If the wall is detailed like a fence with piers and a structural grade beam, then roots can extend beyond the wall (see C). ∎

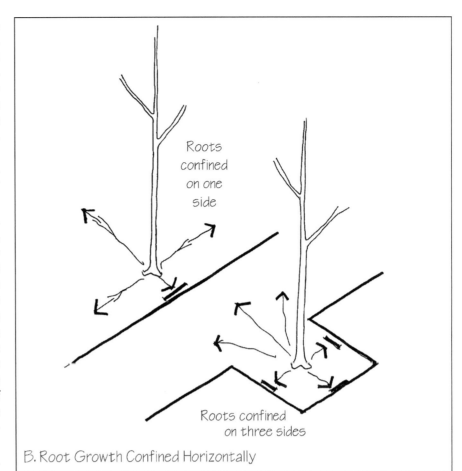

Roots confined on one side

Roots confined on three sides

B. Root Growth Confined Horizontally

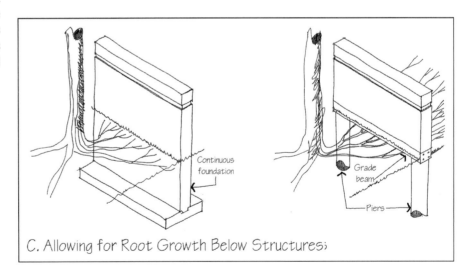

Continuous foundation

Grade beam

Piers

C. Allowing for Root Growth Below Structures

The actively growing cells in a plant are on the outside layers just under the bark. These cells carry nutrients from the roots to the leaves and sugars back to the roots. Tree trunks expand as they grow, putting on new rings of growth each year with living cells growing on the outside as the old interior cells die. In years with adequate nutrients and moisture, they put on wide annual growth rings. The rings are narrower in leaner years. As they mature, many species develop a flare at the point where the tree trunk meets the ground. Details that place solid impediments close to the trunk will eventually be in conflict with the tree's growth. When an expanding trunk comes in contact with an impediment, it continues to put on growth and exerts a pressure against the object. If the object is small (such as a nail or glancing wire) the tree may be able to grow around it, encase the object, and continue to grow. If it is too large to grow around, the tree may push the object out of alignment. In extreme cases where the tree is completely enclosed the tree can be girdled, cutting off the flow of nutrients and killing the tree.

**1.** Tree grates are often designed with concentric structural rings that allow portions of the grate to be removed as the tree grows and expands in girth. Care must be taken to plant the tree deep enough to also allow room for the expanding root flare as well as just the girth of the tree (see A).

**2.** Attachments to trees for tree identification tags, lights, junction boxes, and signage must take into account this growth. Any penetrating attachment to a tree provides a route through the tree's natural defense in its bark that can allow pathogens and pests to attack. When it is necessary to attach something to a trunk or branch, it should be detailed to minimize the potential for damage. A light that

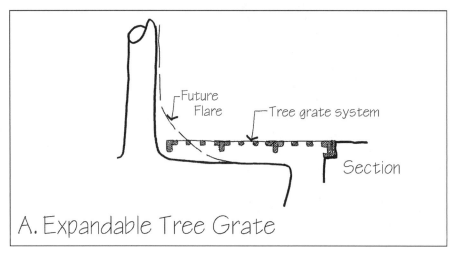

A. Expandable Tree Grate

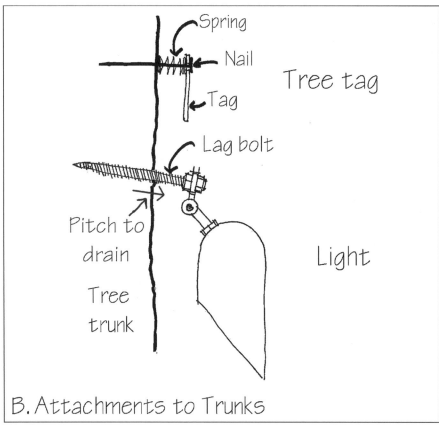

B. Attachments to Trunks

is fastened tightly to the tree trunk will be engulfed by the tree over time. Care must be taken with the fasteners as well. The fasteners should be stainless steel to minimize reactions and the detail of the attachment must be sufficiently deep into the trunk (or through-bolted) to prevent the fastener from moving which would prevent the tree from sealing the wound. Care should also be taken to allow all penetrations to a branch or trunk to drain to prevent rot (see B). ∎

# Branch Growth

Branches grow in patterns characteristic to their species, modified by pruning and other horticultural practices. Some grow with a strong central leader and branching at right angles to the trunk and form the classic lollypop shape; some grow with multiple stems directly from the ground. As the branches grow they will seek out light and grow toward the source of light. Trees planted on the south side of an urban street will lean out to the north seeking sunlight. As they grow into new spaces there may be conflicts with other elements such as lights and buildings. Vines are a special case; supports for vine growth should match the growth habit of the species. Species selection is very important in detailing for branch growth. Right plant/right place (using plants that will thrive in the site that they are planted) is an important principle, but *Small Structures* p. 103 and *Building Armor* p. 145 can reduce potential future conflicts.

1. Branch growth extends from the initial planted form and continues over the life of the tree. As the branches grow, they will seek light. Trees planted in shaded areas will tend to grow more vertically than horizontally or will grow away from shaded areas toward the light. The detailer must keep this growth in mind and be mindful of the consequences of future special conflicts as the branches grow. Conflicts with lights,

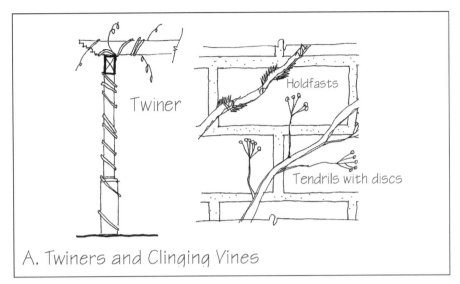

A. Twiners and Clinging Vines

building faces, canopies, and sight lines to signage and security cameras are all foreseeable and preventable.

2. Vines are a special case for the detailer. The species and expected growth habit and mature size must be matched with an appropriate support system. Vines vary in their techniques for climbing. Vines can be destructive to the surfaces or frameworks that support them. Small branches may become established in tiny crevices or gaps, then grow in size, fracturing substrates, filling small openings around windows, and pulling downspouts off of building walls.

a. Twining vines such as Akebia, Celastrus, Loniceria, and Wisteria grow in a spiral manner and twine around support structures both vertical and horizontal. As they grow they tighten their grip on the supports. Larger vines, such as Wisteria, can exert great weight and forces on the structures they grow upon and will require a substantial structure to withstand the increasing stress and weight over time.

b. Clinging vines that hold onto structures with rootlets, holdfasts, or tendrils with discs, such as Campsis, Euonymus, Ficus, Hedera, Hydrangea, and some Parthenocissus, connect themselves to masonry or wood structures and chemically bond themselves to those structures. These rootlets, holdfasts, and tendrils with discs can damage surfaces and must be removed to repoint or repaint those surfaces (see A). ▷

**c.** Clinging vines with tendrils such as Clematis, some Parthenosissis, and Vitus reach out from their stems with twining tendrils to support themselves. The growth habit of these vines is best supported with a fine textured structure or wire framework.

**d.** Climbing roses and similar shrubs that can grow very long on single stems are not true climbers in that they do not support themselves, but need to be physically supported by their support structure. Such roses and similar shrubs should be secured to the frame with corrosion-resistant ties or supported between two parallel structures. In either case, they will require continued maintenance to stay in place (see B). ■

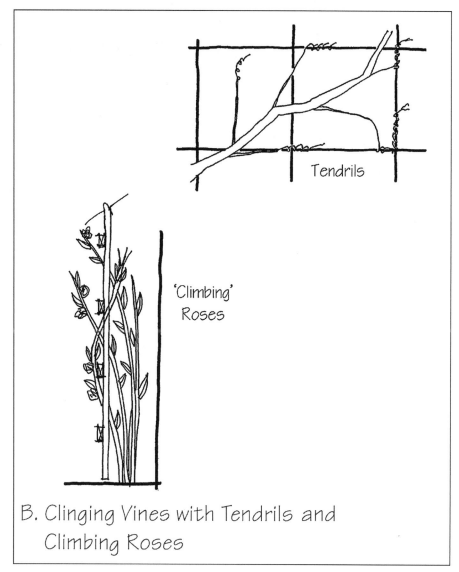

Tendrils

'Climbing' Roses

B. Clinging Vines with Tendrils and Climbing Roses

# Succession

As plants grow they modify the environment in which they grow. They fill soil pore space with roots; they get bigger and crowd out or shade out other plants. This natural succession of plants with shade-tolerant plants out-competing more sun-loving ones is a continual process in every landscape. Details for supporting plants at installation must also work in different situations in the future, or be readily adaptable to new conditions.

**1.** Plants are rarely installed at a mature size. Plants are installed to fill a space in the short run and as they grow in size the number of plants decreases through attrition but the area each plant covers increases. Shrubs may be installed 3 ft-0 in. (1 m) apart at the time of planting and evolve into a much smaller number of plants several times that width. Details for supporting systems such as irrigation and underdrainage should be adaptable to this dynamic (see A).

**2.** As trees grow in size they also grow in spread. This extended spread casts shade on plants at the ground level. Turf and other sun-loving species will not do well in the low light levels under a dense tree canopy. The details of support for trees and lawn must be adjustable to accommodate alternate shade-tolerant plantings in the future (see B). ■

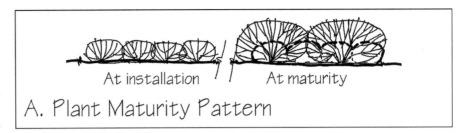

At installation     At maturity

## A. Plant Maturity Pattern

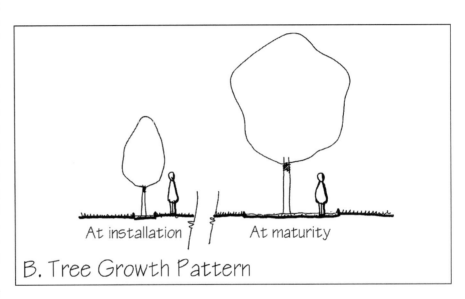

At installation     At maturity

## B. Tree Growth Pattern

As plants mature they require different maintenance practices than are needed when they are first established. Maintenance practices in the first few seasons after planting encourage growth. The plant roots and microorganisms expand out into the growing medium and the plants increase in size. After establishment, the emphasis slowly changes from encouraging rapid growth to sustaining moderate or slow growth and reacting to changes. As turf areas are walked upon, they will require aeration to remain viable, and water tables will need to be monitored in planting areas with minimal drainage. Branches will be pruned to shape plants for functional or aesthetic reasons. All these future practices should be considered when detailing a site.

**1.** Turf aeration is a very beneficial technique for increasing aeration, drainage, and nutrient uptake for soil. In order to accommodate the aeration machinery, irrigation and drainage lines must be installed deep enough to be beyond the reach of the tines. Similarly, the width of the turf area that will need aeration must accept the dimension of the machinery used.

**2.** Interior planters and planting beds over structures may require occasional flooding to dissolve accumulated salt

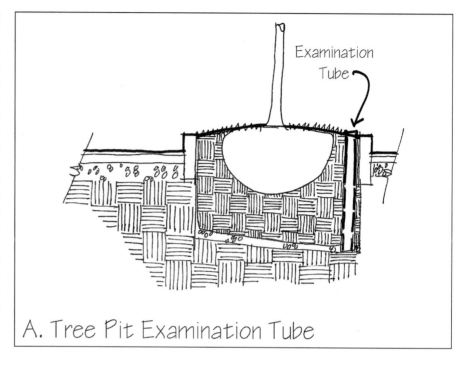

A. Tree Pit Examination Tube

layers in the growing media. To accommodate this task, the planters should have a lip at the edge that will contain the water and a large enough internal drain or access port to allow for removal of the salt-laden water.

**3.** For roof planting and streetscape planting on compacted sites, an examination tube should be included in the planting details to allow for monitoring

of the water levels within the growing media (see A).

**4.** As trees grow, they can conflict with buildings and overhead utility lines. The pruning required to accommodate this growth can work with the form of the tree or completely disfigure it. Correct pruning early in the plants life can help ensure that disfigurement will not be needed later. ■

# 6 Providing Structural Support

## Small Structures

It is obviously important that a large structure in the landscape have a structural frame that has been carefully laid out, calculated, and detailed so that it is stable and will not deflect excessively. Less obvious is the need to engineer smaller but still very important structures that are component parts of the landscape. Even light structural loads such as trellises and lights should not be placed on exterior enclosure materials without proper analysis.

Primary structural systems (such as reinforced concrete walls, steel and wood deck framing, and the like) are normally detailed and constructed with the most stringent quality control of any part of the project. Secondary and tertiary structures are the connective tissues that hold the supplemental structures (railings, canopies, benches, and so forth) and finish materials (veneers and wall panel systems) to the primary structure.

Some of these small structures are within larger assemblies, such as metal ties within a masonry wall, or lath below stucco. These elements are seldom tested in the field to verify their structural effectiveness, and many are not readily observable by anyone other than the crew installing them. Details, therefore, need to be explicit and reliable to assure that the installation will meet performance expectations.

Veneers and systems attached to primary structures in some cases become an armature for a variety of elements such as light fixtures, railings, signage, and so forth. Some of these elements may

Uniformly distributed loads of 50 lbs./linear foot (75 kg/m) applied in any direction to top, and 50 lbs./square foot (244 kg/m²) applied to handrail or guard assembly

Concentrated load of 200 lbs. (90 kg) applied in any direction to top of handrail or guard

A. Loads on Handrails and Guards

be unforeseen at the time the project is designed and constructed. Responsibility for the design of these elements may be initiated by a variety of design professionals, including the consulting engineers, architects, and manufacturers of building components, but the landscape architect oversees their integration into the project. This pattern becomes especially critical when the project is composed of a large number of elements that are layered in complex assemblies.

There are many small, seemingly trivial structural problems that the detailer must recognize and solve through standard engineering design procedures, working alone or with the help of a structural engineer:

1. A guardrail at the top of a wall, edge of a deck, or stair must meet building code requirements for resistance to lateral force. This requires a full-scale engineering analysis that includes meticulous attention to designing attachment details (see A). ▷

**2.** Masonry ties need to be checked for strength and rigidity to prevent deflection and cracking of the face veneer under wind loads.

**3.** Backup walls of concrete masonry need to be designed to carry wind loads and to transmit them to the foundation; this often requires steel reinforcing and special attachment details for the top of the wall. Steel stud backup walls must be engineered carefully to control lateral deflection so as to prevent cracking of exterior masonry veneers.

**4.** Large, heavy gates need frames, frame-to-wall attachments, hinges, latches, and closers with commensurate structural strength. Sometimes the wall or fence itself must be strengthened around a heavy gate (see B).

**5.** Fences should be designed to withstand wind loads as described in ASCE

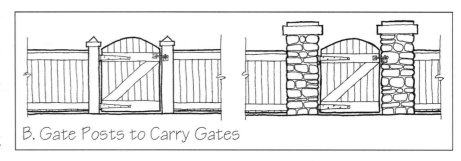

B. Gate Posts to Carry Gates

7-02. The design of fence posts should reflect this loading. Fence post details are influenced by the prevailing depth to frost, see *Foundation Below Frost*, p.75, and the potential for rot or corrosion at the point that the posts meet the ground, see *Capillary Break*, p. 43; *Wash*, p. 33; and *Dry Wood*, p. 137. A rule of thumb for post depths is ⅓ the height of the fence (without consideration of frost). These depths resist overturning due to wind gusts for most applications, but in windy areas (exposed sites, areas prone to hurricanes or tornados, etc.) additional measures should be taken. The detail of the post can increase the resistance to overturning by widening the cross section of the post perpendicular to the expected wind direction. Fences are most susceptible to wind forces perpendicular to their faces, so posts should be widened parallel to the fence panels. Similar techniques can be employed at end posts, corner posts, and at gate posts.

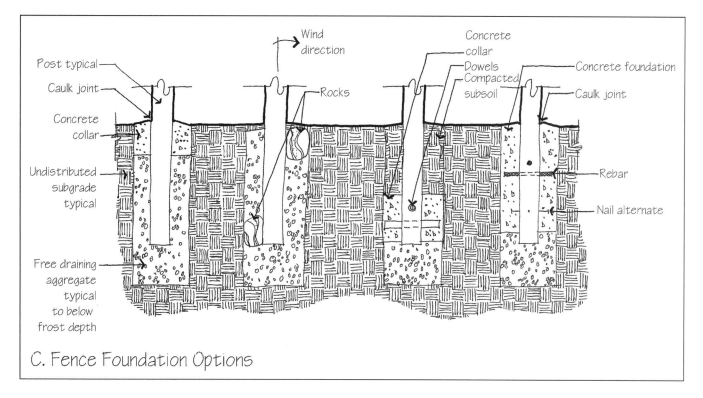

**C. Fence Foundation Options**

In these four examples all are set on a bed of free draining aggregate that will shed water from the bottom of the post and prevent frost from lifting or shifting the post.

- The first option sets the post in a compacted aggregate with a concrete collar to resist movement. The joint between the collar and the post is caulked to remain water tight as the post and concrete shrink with age.
- The second option is a traditional New England gate post detail that utilizes rocks from on-site (which are in abundance in New England) to stabilize the top and bottom of the post. It is one directional.
- The third option secures the base of the post with a subterranean concrete collar. The post has two heavy rot resistant wooden dowels or rebars run through the post to

engage the collar and prevent future movement.

- The last option is a full concrete foundation. The foundation extends from just above the bottom of the post to just above the surface. The top of the foundation has a wash to shed water from the post and foundation joint. The joint is sealed similar to the first option. The post has rebars or nails protruding from the surface to facilitate the long term connection to the foundation (see C).

**6.** Signage and other items that are added after the project is completed may need to be carefully engineered.

**7.** The selection of glass thickness and mullion section requires engineering analysis. The depth of the mullion "bite" on the glass also needs to be carefully worked out. Too shallow a bite may

allow the glass to pop out under wind load; too deep a bite may restrict excessively the wind-induced bending of the glass. Literature from glass and mullion manufacturers usually offers guidance in these matters, provided that you know the magnitudes of the expected wind pressures on the railing.

**8.** Cable rail systems are subject to the same loads as other rails, but the end posts must also be designed to resist the pull of the cables as they are tightened and contract in cold weather.

**9.** Lighting fixtures often require special attachments that are designed to bear their weight safely

It is frequently left up to the detailer to recognize such smaller-scale structural problems as these and to see that they are fully engineered and detailed. ∎

CHAPTER

# 7 Providing Passages for Pipes and Wires

Every site is laced with a three-dimensional web of pipes and wires—sanitary sewer, water, storm drainage, irrigation, gas, steam, electricity, telephone, communications, and lighting systems. Almost every existing site has been retrofitted with distribution lines for which it was not originally designed, making it a safe bet that every project that is on the drawing boards today will be called upon in the future to accommodate services that we cannot even imagine. In detailing a site, it is important to work with the designers of the irrigation, drainage, plumbing, electrical, and communications systems to furnish passages for the service distribution lines, both present and future, that will run through the site. In most cases, these lines should be comfortably concealed; if they are exposed to view, it should be by design, not by default. Trenching for future lines can cause tremendous damage to finish pavement and plant roots as well as to existing pipes and wires. Sleeves or conduit banks are provided for future lines with sufficient worker access points and workable interconnections from one plane of distribution to another in ecologically sensitive areas and areas that would be expensive to repair. This will allow

economical installation, maintenance, and future change of the services. It will also avoid having the appearance of the landscape and its details spoiled by the improvised installation of service systems that its designer and detailer did not anticipate.

Buildings are often detailed with separate structure and finish panel creating gaps between them that can be used for connecting pipes and wires without having to rip out finished walls or ceilings for the entire run. Site elements such as walls and pavements are usually detailed without that gap, so the detailer must make allowances for future utilities in their detailing.

As services onsite become more dense and complex, design professionals must collaborate to provide an efficient arrangement of compatible services. Water pipes are typically kept distant from power lines, and telecommunication wires must be isolated by distance or shielding from power distribution wires to avoid interference. Drain lines that flow via gravity take precedence over wires and pressurized lines. Care should be taken in combining various lines in the same trench. Shallow lines in the same zone can make deeper ones difficult to access. In shallow soil sections

such as rooftop gardens, and narrow sections such as urban streetscapes, root zones must compete with utilities for space over the life of the project. Protocols based on the technical requirements of each system should guide the initial design as well as the ongoing maintenance of these services.

To provide a fully three-dimensional network of passages, two detail patterns must be combined:

*Vertical Chase* (p. 108)

*Horizontal Distribution Ways* (p. 110)

At each point of intersection between vertical chase and horizontal distribution ways, the various services must have space to make the transition from vertical to horizontal.

Piping and conduits may be exposed on the surface rather than concealed, but this will not necessarily lead to more economical construction. Vertical and horizontal spaces will still have to be reserved for these services, and funds must be allocated for additional design time to lay out neat arrangements of lines, additional installation time to permit a high standard of workmanship, and the cost of painting and finishing the lines.

# Vertical Chase

A vertical chase is a concealed passage in which services can run from below ground to above grade. A hollow wall that serves as a vertical chase can often perform some horizontal distribution functions as well.

**1.** The hollow vertical spaces between wood or steel studs in a stud wall or built up posts furnish convenient passages for small-diameter services, usually without further attention from the detailer. Vertical runs of electrical wiring or irrigation lines fit easily into these spaces. Steel studs with their prepunched holes also make horizontal runs of wiring easy. Horizontal runs of wiring through wood studs require that the studs be drilled, which is easy and acceptable if the holes are not too large. Long horizontal runs of piping are generally difficult to thread through holes in studs. Drain lines, with their larger diameters, often require deeper studs, a double row of studs, generous horizontal furring, or a dedicated chase. Deep horizontal furring over studs offers chases both ways, minimizing interference between studs and service lines. In fence panels that are framed with horizontal rails and vertical slats or siding, wires or pipes are easily run in the space between the rails (see A).

**2.** Solid walls must be detailed with conduits, chases, or sleeves to provide access for pipes and wires through finished work. Lights can be connected via conduit to nonpaved areas that are easily repairable to allow for updating and replacement of wiring. Oversized conduit can be built into columns of shade structure and can accommodate wiring and drip irrigation lines (see B).

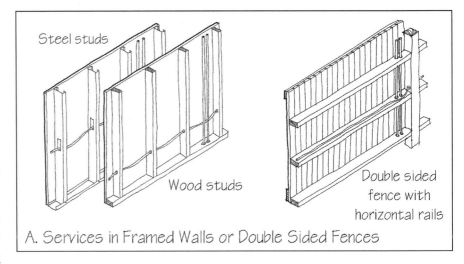

A. Services in Framed Walls or Double Sided Fences

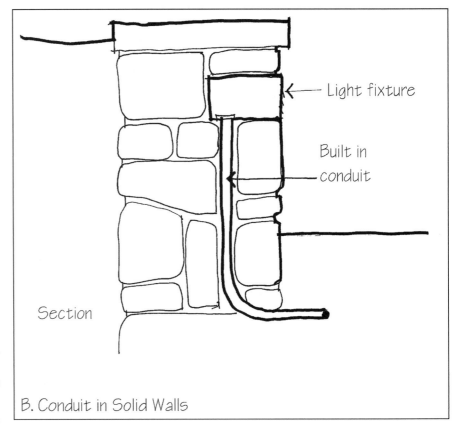

B. Conduit in Solid Walls

**3.** There are some general precautions that relate to any type of vertical chase or shaft. Access panels must be provided at points specified by the designers of the various systems (such as to gas shut-off valves for grills and heaters). Remember that new service lines may occupy these spaces in the future (see *Accessible Connections*, Chapter 10, p. 161). Conduits for wiring should turn corners with a curved section or sweep to allow wires to be pulled through the conduit. Angular turns should be wide enough to accommodate connections and fittings for wires or pipes (see C). ∎

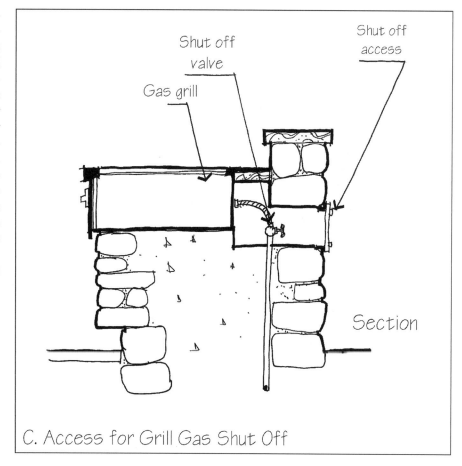

Shut off valve

Shut off access

Gas grill

Section

C. Access for Grill Gas Shut Off

**1.** Most horizontal distributions of services in the landscape are buried below grade. Wiring and irrigation laterals are buried in shallow trenches with drain lines and water services buried deeper. Drain lines that flow by gravity must be installed with exacting pitches or they will not function, so in the event of conflict, other line locations are modified to go above or below gravity drain lines. Potable water lines must be code conforming, separated from sanitary sewer lines and also from electric lines. Water lines are buried below frost depths. Any or all of these services can conflict with tree roots. In projects where the concentration of services is low, such as a park or residence, there may be ample space to run all the needed services without the attention of the detailer. But in densely packed service areas such as urban streetscapes, each service must be located in three dimensions to allow space for all others and for future plant growth.

**2.** While new lines can be buried in many planted areas with minimal damage there is a notable exception. If new services require trenching through the root zone of mature trees, would kill the roots that are cut by the trench. In these locations, it may be desirable to bore under the majority of the roots to preserve the tree root system. Trenching can also be located at the edge of a tree root zone and a root barrier such as an existing wall or pavement with minimal impact to the tree. Many plans describing new service are often diagrammatic in nature. If trenching in existing root zones is to be avoided, it is wise to specifically locate services where they are not in conflict with root zones (see A).

**3.** Finished pavement set on a rigid base, such as concrete or asphalt, is dif-

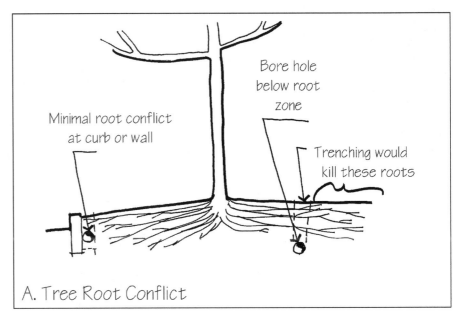

A. Tree Root Conflict

Minimal root conflict at curb or wall

Bore hole below root zone

Trenching would kill these roots

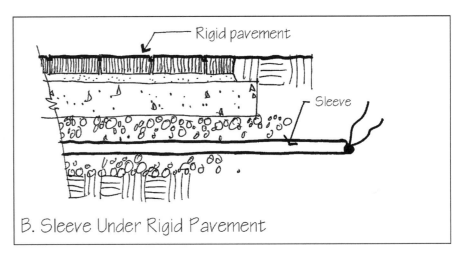

Rigid pavement

Sleeve

B. Sleeve Under Rigid Pavement

ficult and expensive to repair if it has to be removed to repair or replace a pipe or wire. It is good practice to enclose pipes and wires in sleeves. The sleeves serve to protect the pipes and wires during construction as well as act as a corridor for installing new lines without removing the finished pavement. Extra (spare) sleeves are often placed beneath pavements to accommodate future services. These sleeves are usually placed to supply access to every planting bed and should be big enough to accommodate irrigation piping and in separate sleeves. Additional sleeves may be required to separate communications and power to prevent interference in the sound or video feeds (see B).

**4.** When building on a roof, many times it is advantageous to use a pedestal system to support a raised surface of pavers. This raised system is less weight than comparable aggregate bases, allows for a level surface with drainage through the paver joints to the roof surface, and also provides a zone for pipes and wires below the pavement surface. This system also allows for easy inspection and alteration to the services below (see C).

**5.** Similarly, services can be attached to the structural members of decks or bridges using clamps or hangers. When running services to lights, speakers, or hanging planters in a structure with an exposed structure such as a fence or trellis, careful placement of the pipe or wire relative to the eye level of the user can serve as an alternate to a dedicated space for horizontal runs inside of rails, rafters, or beams. Lower fence rails can be notched to hide services and the tops of beams in trellises can serve as wire races (see D). ■

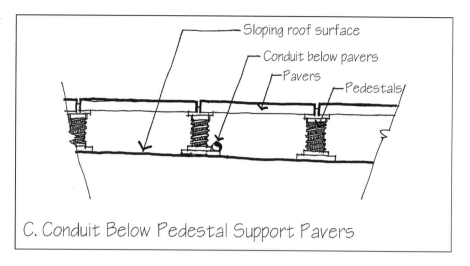

C. Conduit Below Pedestal Support Pavers

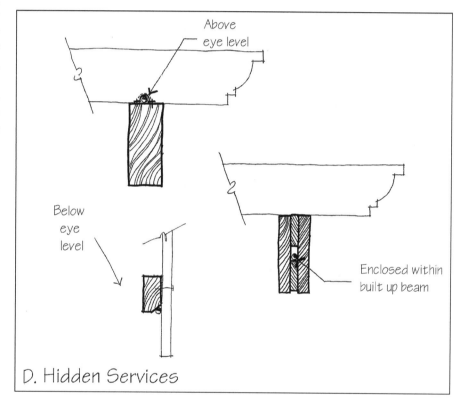

D. Hidden Services

CHAPTER **8** Health and Safety

A tremendous number of people are injured needlessly each year on unsafe sites. People trip and fall on uneven pavements and poorly constructed stairs. They cut, scrape, and gouge themselves on rough surfaces, sharp edges, and broken glass. People who are ill, aged, or otherwise disabled may find themselves unable to reach whole areas of a project because of physical barriers that have been incorporated into the design. Most health and safety issues in detailing are regulated by accessibility and building codes; others are merely based on common sense.

When particular materials or construction assemblies are found to be fundamentally unsafe, building codes or other regulations are often revised to exclude them. Innovation with construction materials and details is encouraged, provided public health and safety are not jeopardized. Detailers are expected to assess a new material or a new detail to thoroughly investigate its health and safety implications. Manufacturers will often provide needed information about materials and proprietary assemblies, and may assist in further testing if needed.

Detailers rely on many organizations that produce and disseminate information about materials and methods of construction. National codes and standards organizations, professional and trade associations, master specifications, and manufacturers are parts of this information base. References that appear in The Detailer's Reference Shelf (p. 241) and Internet Web searches are used daily by the detailer to remain current.

Detail patterns relating to health and safety are the following:

*Safe Footing* (p. 114)

*Fall Protection* (p. 116)

*Safe Edges* (p. 119)

*Safe Glazing* (p. 122)

*User-Appropriate Features* (p. 123)

*Nontoxic Materials* (p. 124)

*Site-Specific Hazards* (p. 125)

*Barrier-Free Design* (p. 126)

Tripping and slipping are two occurrences that the detailer must guard against in pavement and stair details.

**1.** Tripping on pavements can be caused by abrupt changes in level or material. Individual paver surfaces should be no more than ¼ in. (6.4 mm) difference than adjacent pavers with a maximum of ⅛ in. (3.2 mm) preferred  Changes in elevation of up to ½ in. (12.7 mm) are allowed with a leveled transition of no more than 2:1, or 50 percent slope for any transition beyond ¼ in. (6.4 mm). Beveled edges on pavers reduce the potential for tripping as well as reduce the potential for surface spalling (see A).

**2.** Tripping on stairs can be avoided by careful compliance with building code provisions and accessibility standards. Proportion treads and risers as the codes require, and take care when inspecting construction that excessive variations do not creep into tread and riser dimensions, especially at the beginning or end of a run of stairs.  Users find exterior stairs are more comfortable in a shallower pitch than is used for interior stairs. A good working ratio is two times riser height (in inches) plus the length of the tread (in inches) should be between 24 and 26 in. Do not design stairs that have only one or two risers; people tend not to see them until they have fallen on them. Always comply exactly with building and disability code handrail requirements. When combining ramps and stairs, make the distance between the steps an even module of three comfortable strides (about 5 ft; 1525 m).

**3.** Use abrasive tread inserts to prevent slipping on stairs that are made of polished materials such as stone, precast

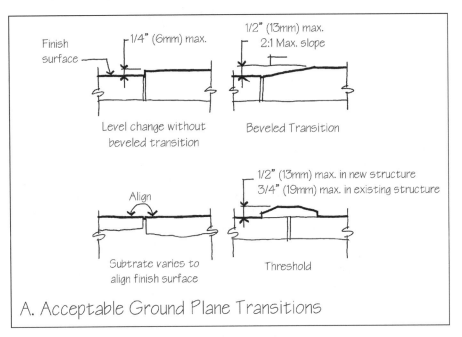

**A. Acceptable Ground Plane Transitions**

concrete, or metal. Use contrasting colors at tread nosings to enhance visibility and safety.

**4.** Steps should be lit at night. Lighting sources should light the nosing and forward portion of the tread. A shadow cast on the riser and rear of the tread increases the visibility of the stairs.

**5.** Pay particular attention to the slipperiness of materials when wet. On pavements of stone and/or tile, use a slightly rough surface finish rather than a highly polished one. Pavement materials that absorb water or are covered with water can become glazed when frozen. These should be more coarsely textured to provide traction slightly above the plane of the water. Although there are no legal guidelines for the coefficients of friction of floor materials, such coefficients are published by many paving manufacturers. In general, avoid

paving materials with a coefficient of friction less than 0.5. Use higher values for ramps and stairs and areas that are chronically wet, such as pool decks and pavement around fountains and near water bodies.

**6.** Drainage should be diverted away from circulation routes. Drains are not always maintained and sometimes more water flows to the drain than can be accommodated through the grates. The puddles formed over these drain structures will be avoided by pedestrians in wet weather whenever possible, causing them to walk over grass areas and other unsuitable walking surfaces. In cold weather, the puddles and flowing water can freeze and create a very dangerous condition. Drainage should be diverted from doors, stairs, and ramps to avoid potential icing conditions.

**7.** Metal gratings give good traction underfoot, but openings must be small to allow passage of people with strollers, in wheelchairs, or wearing shoes with small or pointy heels. Gratings should have spaces no wider than ½ in. (13 mm) in one direction, and elongated openings must be oriented perpendicular to the dominant direction of travel. In street similar consideration should be given to bicycle traffic with openings no wider than ¾ in. (19 mm) in grates or between grates and frames parallel to the flow of traffic. Honeycomb, wave, or grid patterns are preferred to bars for drainage grates in bikeways (see B).

**8.** Passenger transit platforms without guardrails, such as a train platform, are required to have a 24-in.- (610-mm-) wide detectable warning at the edge. This tactile signal is made using a specific pattern of raised truncated domes that are recognized by people who are visually impaired. Similar provisions for visibility should be given at any abrupt edge such as at a seawall or loading dock that operates without guardrails. ■

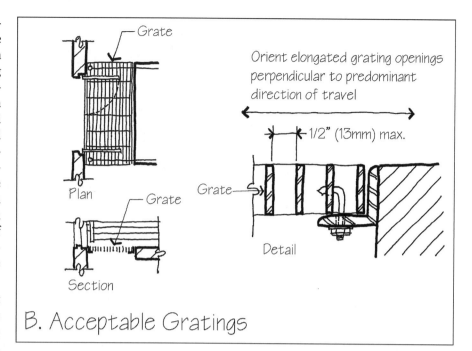

Orient elongated grating openings perpendicular to predominant direction of travel

1/2" (13mm) max.

Grate

Grate

Grate

Plan

Section

Detail

B. Acceptable Gratings

# Fall Protection

Handrails are required by code to help prevent falling on stairs and ramps, and guardrails are required at open vertical drops of over 30 in. (762 mm).

**1.** Building codes and accessibility standards are very explicit in their requirements for detailing handrails and guardrails. Stairs are required to have handrails on each side, except on aisle stairs where a center rail is provided. Ramps of over 5 percent slope with a vertical drop of 6 in. (152 mm) or more are required to have handrails on both sides. If the vertical drop of a ramp, landing, or floor level is 30 in. (762 mm) or more, guardrails are required.

**2.** Handrails are provided on stairs and ramps to help steady the users and to prevent them from falling. Such handrails must be of such size and shape in a cross section configuration that a human hand can grip at least three-quarters of the perimeter of the rail. Generally, an uninterrupted round piece of metal pipe or wood is best. Rectangular pieces of wood are hard to grip and are illegal under most codes. Every handrail must be set away from the wall by a specified distance and must be mounted a specified distance above the floor or ramp. The wall behind the handrail must be smooth to prevent scraping of knuckles, and the edges of the handrail must have a minimum radius of 1/8 in. (3 mm) (see A).

**3.** At the top and bottom of each flight of stairs, a handrail must run out horizontally at least 12 in. (300 mm) beyond the end of the stair, and it must be turned into the wall or curved down and attached to a vertical support so that it will not snag clothing. Handrail mountings must be engineered carefully to keep the rail rigid and to hold it tightly to the wall or securely to a foundation against any expected push or pull. The center handrail in

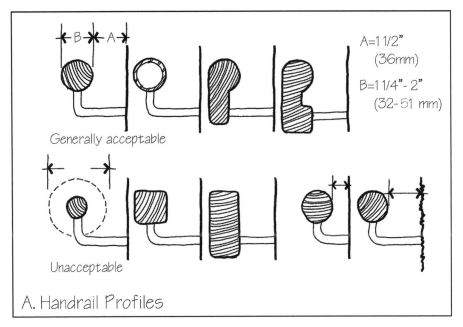

A. Handrail Profiles

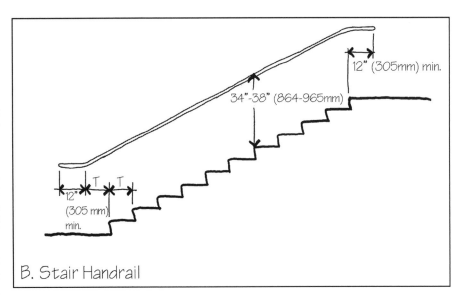

B. Stair Handrail

a switchback stairway must be continuous from one flight to the next. If there is no center wall in a switchback stairway, the center handrail is also a guardrail and must be provided with balusters, as described in the following paragraphs. Free-standing rails must not extend into connecting pathways at the top or bottom of a stair or ramp (see B).

**4.** Guardrails must be provided to prevent people from falling over the edge of any abrupt change in elevation (of more than 30″, 226 mm per most building codes). Exceptions are permitted at edges of seawalls, stages, service pits, or loading docks or when pathways are not directly adjacent to the edge and another alternate barrier such as a planting is present. Minimum guardrail heights are specified in the building codes, but it is often desirable to make the guardrail higher to avoid unpleasant psychological feelings of danger. A guardrail at a scenic overlook should be at a height that is comfortable to lean on with the elbows (see C).

The balusters, safety glazing panels, or other infill between the guardrail and the edge of the floor must be spaced closely enough so that an unsupervised small child cannot slip through. Research has shown that the maximum clear opening within a guardrail should not pass a ball more than 4 in. (102 mm) in diameter. Building codes use this figure for guardrails up to 34 in. (864 mm) above grade; above that height the pattern can be more open, allowing a sphere of up to 8 in. (203 mm) in diameter to pass. Even if the applicable code allows for some openings larger than 4 in. (102 mm), it would be wise to stick to the smaller figure, because larger dimensions are demonstrably unsafe. Horizontal balusters are generally legal, but if balusters are vertical, it is very difficult for a child to climb over the guardrail.

Building codes sometimes require that there be a solid kick strip or curb several inches high at the base of a

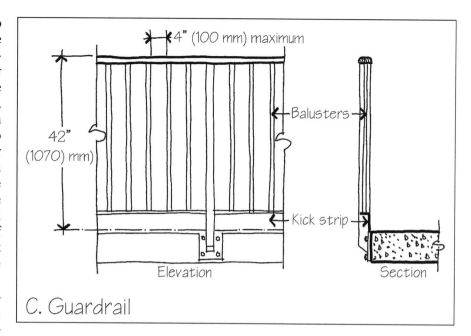

**C. Guardrail**

guardrail. Its function is to prevent debris on the floor from accidentally being kicked through the guardrail and onto people below.

**5.** Building codes specify structural requirements for guardrails, handrails, and grab bars to prevent them from collapsing under the forces that people apply to them. This means that the rails, posts, and particularly the attachments of the posts to the wall and deck edges must be engineered with great care to resist large lateral loadings. They must be designed to carry a concentrated load of 200 lbs. (91 kg) pushing or pulling, horizontally or vertically, and a distributed load of 50 lbs. per linear foot (75 kg/m) (see *Providing Structural Support*, p. 103).

**6.** Fall protection in playground design is of specific concern to designers. Most injuries in playgrounds are due to falls. Requirements for guardrails are different for various age groups. Toddlers require full barriers, but they can be relatively low. Preschoolers can also make use of guardrails that allow for them to duck under the rail and jump off low platforms, but require somewhat taller rails. School-age children use full barriers and guardrails with rail heights over 38 in. and platforms up to 48 in. tall (see D).  ▷

**7.** Playground surfaces are designed to absorb some of the shock of a fall. Surfaces are either a loose-fill material (sand, pea stone, wood chips/mulch, or shredded rubber), or a unitary surface (mats, tiles, or poured-in-place rubber or synthetic material). A unitary surface is more expensive than a loose-fill material and not all unitary surfaces are porous, but they do not require the same level of maintenance and inspection that loose-fill materials require. Loose material will compress after installation and will shift from areas of heavy use to areas of low use over time. The material must be maintained at a minimum thickness to be effective. If drainage is not provided and maintained, the surface can compact, freeze, or decompose reducing its effectiveness. The surfaces should also be evaluated for accessibility, toxicity, and the presence of sharp impurities such as wire strands in recycled tire products. Regular inspection and maintenance will be necessary to assure that effectiveness of the playground surfaces are not compromised.

Each play component requires a protective surface around it that is deep enough to protect the users from a fall known as a fall zone. These fall zones should be free of potential fall hazards such as benches, curbs, fences, and the like as well as other components and main circulation routes. Some fall zones for nonmoving equipment can overlap with the fall zones of other components. The depth of material required is a function of the height of the potential fall. Overlapping fall zones should accommodate the greatest depth of material required. ■

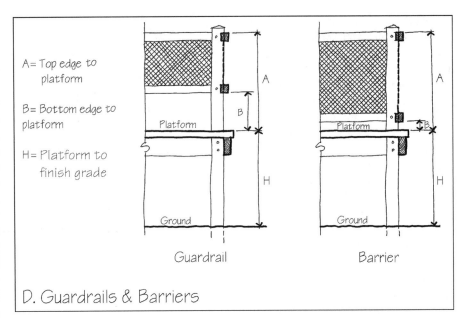

A= Top edge to platform

B= Bottom edge to platform

H= Platform to finish grade

Guardrail                    Barrier

D. Guardrails & Barriers

**TABLE 8-1: Guardrail and Barrier**

|  | Guardrail | Barrier |
|---|---|---|
| **Toddlers** | | |
| A | Not recommended | 24" (610 mm) or higher |
| B | Not recommended | less than 3" (76 mm) |
| H | Not recommended | 18" (457 mm)* or higher |
| **Pre-Schoolers** | | |
| A | 29" (736 mm) or higher | 29" (736 mm) or higher |
| B | > 9" (229 mm) and < or = 23" (584 mm) | < 3.5" (89 mm) |
| H | > 20" (508 mm)* and < or = 30" (762 mm) | >30" (762 mm) |
| **School-age** | | |
| A | 38" (965 mm) or higher | 38" (965 mm) or higher |
| B | > 9" (229 mm) and < or = 28" (711 mm) | < 3.5" (89 mm) |
| H | > 30" (762 mm)* and < or = 48" (1,219 mm) | >48" (1,219 mm) |

* Note: guardrail or barrier is not required below these heights

Barriers protect against accidental falls from the platform and against climbing through in addition to climbing over, while the guardrails just protect against accidental falls.

**TABLE 8-2: Play Surface and Depths Material**

| Depth Of (inches/mm) | Loose-Fill Material | Protects to Fall Height (feet/mm) |
|---|---|---|
| 9 (229) | Shredded/recycled rubber | 10 (3048) |
| 9 (229) | Sand | 4 (1219) |
| 9 (229) | Pea Gravel | 5 (1524) |
| 9 (229) | Wood mulch (non-CCA) | 7 (2134) |
| 9 (229) | Wood chips | 10 (3048) |

# Safe Edges

Although not generally covered by building codes and accessibility standards, an important safety concern of the detailer is to provide safe edges and surfaces wherever people come into contact with a structure.

**1.** Avoid splinters from wooden components by using vertical-grain wood and chamfering or rounding all corners.

**2.** Do not place rough surfaces of masonry, plaster, stucco, or concrete or thorny plants along stairs, walkways, and entrance areas where people are likely to brush against them. Avoid sharp edges and corners, especially in handrails and guardrails.

**3.** Be sure that doorknobs, latches, and handles are set back sufficiently from the frame of the door or gate so that knuckles will not be skinned accidentally.

**4.** Avoid protruding hardware. Nuts, protruding threaded ends of screws and bolts, and other hardware can catch skin or clothing if protruding beyond the surface.

**5.** Be particularly careful about elements and structures in the path of travel. Bollards and other street furniture, door swings, handrail extensions, and other elements that are below eye level can be a hazard. They should be located out of main travel ways, be contrasting in color or hue to their surroundings, and/or detailed without sharp edges.

**6.** Tree branches can also be hazardous to pedestrians. Trees along streets or paths should be specified with a standard height above most pedestrians and should be maintained to stay clear of pedestrian ways. If cyclists travel the street or path, then the clear height should be increased.

**7.** Play equipment and pool copings should be rounded to prevent injury during use.

**8.** Playgrounds require an elevated level of care in detailing safe edges. The illustrations are based upon the *Handbook for Playground Safety* by the U.S.

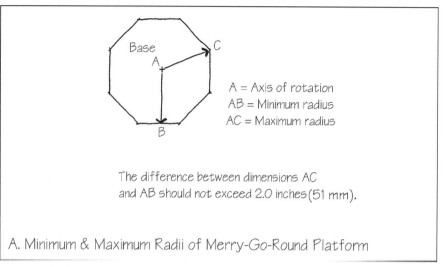

The difference between dimensions AC and AB should not exceed 2.0 inches (51 mm).

A = Axis of rotation
AB = Minimum radius
AC = Maximum radius

A. Minimum & Maximum Radii of Merry-Go-Round Platform

(From *Handbook for Playground Safety*)

Consumer Product Safety Commission. The standards are continually updated, so the current standards should be verified when detailing playgrounds. These recommendations are of particular importance in playground design, but may be applicable in other settings where active children are expected.

**9.** Anything that could crush or shear limbs should not be accessible to children.

Rotating play apparatus such as merry-go-rounds should not vary more than 2" (51 mm) from widest to narrowest dimension (see A).

**10.** Hardware projection should not be able to entangle children's clothing or be deep enough to impale them if they should fall. Nuts and other fasteners should be smaller than the washers and fasteners below them. Threaded ends should    ▷

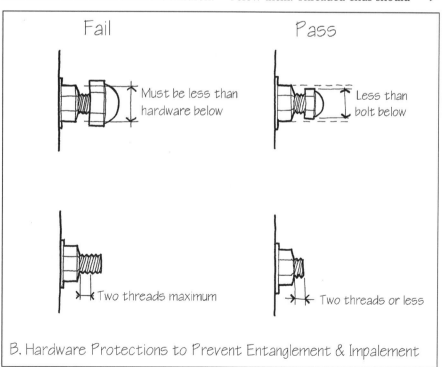

B. Hardware Protections to Prevent Entanglement & Impalement

(From *Handbook for Playground Safety*)

not protrude more than 2 threads beyond the nut. All hooks should be closed and completely filled to prevent the snagging of clothing during use (see B).

**11.** Avoid equipment with ropes that are not secured at both ends.

**12.** Avoid dangerous gaps between vertical or horizontal rails, between horizontal rails and the ground or platforms, or between open stair risers where users can entrap their head or feet (see C).

**13.** To avoid entrapment, avoid angles of less than 55 degrees when joining 2 members or notching top surfaces such as the top of a fence or edge of a barrier (see D).

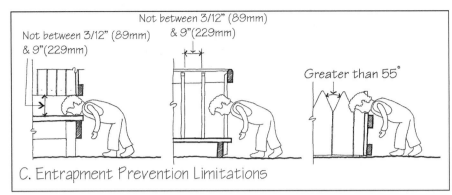

C. Entrapment Prevention Limitations

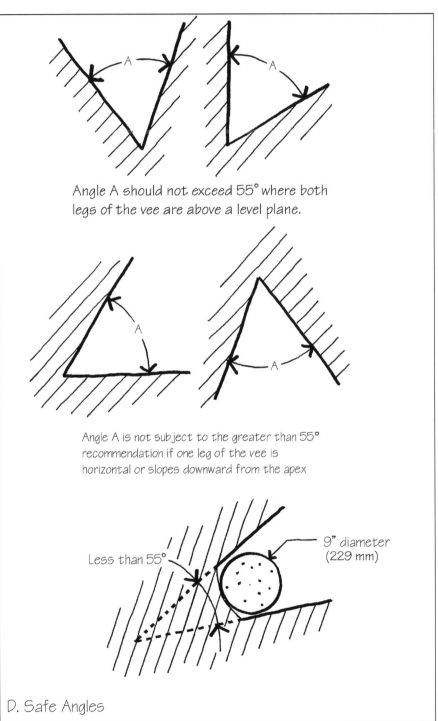

Angle A should not exceed 55° where both legs of the vee are above a level plane.

Angle A is not subject to the greater than 55° recommendation if one leg of the vee is horizontal or slopes downward from the apex

D. Safe Angles

**14.** Avoid suspended ropes, wires, cables, or nets that may catch users as they pass by. Climbing nets should have a combined opening perimeter of between 17" (432 mm) and 28" (711 mm) (see E).

**15.** Avoid tripping hazards (protruding footings, containment edges, tree roots, and the like). This issue can develop over time as the site ages and materials settle. ■

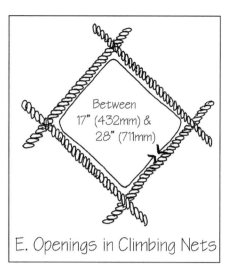

Between 17" (432mm) & 28" (711mm)

E. Openings in Climbing Nets

## Safe Glazing

Glass usage in landscapes is often code regulated to prevent several types of glass-related injuries.

**1.** Avoid using glass in such a way that it does not seem to be there. Many early landscapes in the modern style featured glass railings that were purposely detailed to be virtually invisible. People tended to run into these transparent walls, sometimes shattering the glass and injuring themselves badly, even fatally, on the sharp spikes of glass. Using safety glazing alone does not solve the safety problem with floor-to-ceiling glass. People can be injured just by the impact of running into a large, invisible, unbreakable sheet of glass. It is wise to install a horizontal mullion or a guardrail at railing height across the glass to warn of its presence, or use glass that is etched or printed to make it more readily seen. These precautions also make the glass surfaces more visible

to birds and other animals, reducing the likelihood of impact.

**2.** Building codes require that all-glass guardrails or balcony fronts must be made of safety glass.

**3.** Safety glazing is made of tempered glass, laminated glass, wired glass, or impact-resistant plastic. Check codes to determine which of these products is permitted for a specific location. These products are much stronger than ordinary annealed glass and are much less likely to break. If tempered glass does break, it disintegrates into small, blunt granules rather than large, sharp spears.

**4.** Safe glazing is dependent upon firm support in a frame. Excessive deflection of the glass, or gradual lateral movement of the glass in its frame, may cause the edge of the glass to come free of its frame. The detailer should provide support for glass at all edges, and limit glass deflection to less than

$\frac{1}{175}$ of the glass edge length, or $\frac{3}{4}$ in. (19 mm), whichever is less. See *Joints and Gaskets*, p. 45, for typical glazing details.

**5.** Light-transmitting plastics, such as polycarbonate and acrylic, are impact-resistant, lightweight, and are often less costly than glass. They are often less durable than glass and unfortunately less resistant to combustion, and may give off toxic gases when burned. Codes usually prohibit their use in large assembly buildings, institutional buildings, and exit passageways unless the building is fully sprinklered. Refer to relevant codes for additional detailing factors associated with plastic glazing.

**6.** When using glass for exterior railings, it may be necessary to etch or apply a pattern to the surface to make it detectable to birds. ∎

# User-Appropriate Features

Landscape improvements should be matched to the needs of its intended users. The standards for a toddler playground are different than a playground for older children. An assisted care facility has different requirements for lighting, flatness of walking surfaces, and so forth than a site for general use.

**1.** Site improvements such as stairs and railings for children should be scaled to their use. These child-scaled features are provided in addition to the normal features provided for adults, such as their caregivers.

**2.** Elderly users also require special considerations. Stairs and steep inclines are difficult to negotiate with a cane, walker, or wheelchair. Edges should have a strong visual contrast so they are perceivable to users with impaired vision.

**3.** Special populations, such as the visually impaired, may require additional detail analysis. Pavements should be examined for how they sound as well as how they look. Edges should be distinguishable by touch with recognizably different textures as well as colors. ■

# Nontoxic Materials

Some elements of the landscape can make people ill unless great care is taken to select and detail materials so as to avoid toxic effects.

**1.** The toxicity of materials used in construction is coming under increasing regulation, and it is a significant concern of any sustainable design initiative. Specific laws relate to lead paint, asbestos in all its forms, preservatives such as creosote, pentachloro-phenol, and copper arsenate, formaldehyde emissions from insulating foam and wood panel products, and hydrocarbon solvents that evaporate from coatings and adhesives.

Usually, the primary responsibility for avoiding toxic substances in construction rests with the specifier, but the detailer should also take care especially to avoid using materials that may contribute to poisoning of a site's users. This is of particular importance in the detailing of playgrounds. Airborne toxicity is rarely a prime concern in detailing, but contact with lead, toxic preservatives, pesticides/ herbicides, and fertilizers should be prevented.

**2.** Toxic plants must be kept away from places where they may harm people or animals.

**3.** Special care should be taken by the detailer when working with toxic sites such as brownfields. Soil conditions can interact with common building materials and release toxic elements into the air or water. ■

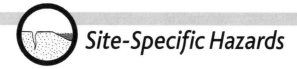

# Site-Specific Hazards

Many sites contain inherent hazards due to their location, geology, hydrology, or history. The nature of these site-specific hazards must be reflected in a project's details.

**1.** In wildfire-prone sites, defensible zones may be required around all buildings. Structures such as decks, fences, and trellises must be constructed of fire-resistant materials. Planting must be low in profile and replace potential fuel with water-rich plants such as sedum and irrigated lawn.

**2.** In earthquake-prone areas drainage and grading can be regulated to prevent the oversaturation of soils that are prone to liquefaction as well as the creation of unstable slopes. Clearing existing vegetation from potentially unstable slopes can also be prohibited. Detailing of fill slopes can include geogrid reinforcement to maintain stability.

**3.** Projects adjacent to bodies of water carry inherent hazards as well as beauty. The edge sections of deep water bodies should provide for a shelf below the surface to allow someone that inadvertently falls in to retain their footing before they slide into deep water.

Building codes require fencing around pools to prevent unsupervised access and accidental drowning. Pool covers can give another level of protection against accidental drowning while saving energy. Building codes also mandate pool drain standards that should prevent entrapment by suction in the drain lines. Drains can be modified at the intake grate to prevent suction, install multiple intakes, or other techniques to be safe.

**4.** There are many man-made hazards on sites that should be considered by the detailer. Many of them are related to transportation and utilities. Airports have many layers of security that must be considered for travelers and employees. Highways and railroads also have requirements that limit access to hazardous traveled ways. Electrical switching yards, water pump stations, and gas storage are often restricted to protect the public from potential hazards. ∎

# Barrier-Free Design

Projects that are open to the public must be planned and detailed in specified ways that make them accessible to all members of the population, including those who are in wheelchairs or strollers or on crutches; the aged, blind, or deaf; and those in ill health or otherwise incapacitated. Nearly everyone is disabled at some point in life. Wherever possible, landscapes should be designed to be universally accessible.

In multifamily housing projects, a small percentage of the dwelling units must conform to barrier-free standards so that they may be occupied by people with disabilities. The legal requirements for barrier-free design of buildings and sites are detailed in the Americans with Disabilities Act, or ADA, in various building codes and state laws, and in the American National Standards Institute (ANSI) National Standard A117.1, Accessible and Useable Buildings and Facilities. *Landscape Architectural Graphic Standards* and *Time-Saver Standards for Landscape Architecture* also give extensive information on barrier-free design (see Appendix A). Building codes may not include all provisions of ANSI A117.1 or of the ADA Accessibility Guidelines. Features outside of buildings may be governed by the Architectural Barriers Act (ABA) Accessibility Guidelines. Therefore, designers and detailers should not rely solely on building codes to determine compliance with all accessibility requirements. This detail pattern can list only a few of the ways in which provisions of these documents affect the detailing of a site.

**1.** The most prominently visible result of barrier-free regulations is that there must be accessible routes into and through the site. This can involve accessible parking spaces nearby building entrances, curb ramps, and specified types of ground surfaces. Ramps may be required to reach the main entrances of public buildings. The dimensions and gradients of ramps, the provision of landings, and the details of ramp

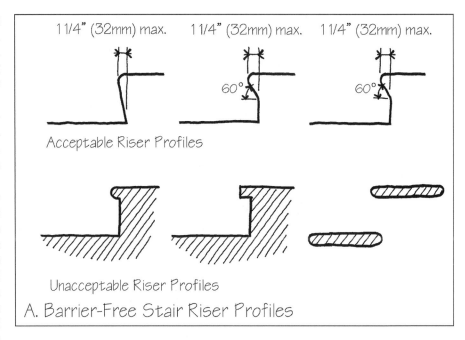

A. Barrier-Free Stair Riser Profiles

handrails are all closely specified, as are elevator dimensions and controls.

**2.** Stairs must be profiled so that people on crutches can climb them easily. This rules out abruptly projecting nosings that can catch the toes of a person on crutches as they slide up a riser. Open-riser stairs are also prohibited. Instead, a smoothly profiled riser is required (see A).

**3.** Drinking fountains must be of specified types that allow a wheelchair occupant access to the stream of water, and the valve must be operable by persons with impaired hand and arm dexterity. Public telephones must meet accessibility requirements.

**4.** To aid persons with visual disabilities, surface materials and colors of important site features may be differentiated from their surroundings using contrast. This is especially important to avoid danger, such as at stair nosings, vehicular crossings, or pool edges.

**5.** Playground surfaces need to be soft enough to limit injury in the case of a fall, while being firm, stable, and slip-resistant for wheelchair access. ASTM F1292-99 sets a standard for

impact-attenuating surfaces and ASTM F1951-99 sets the standard for wheelchair accessible surfaces. Standard sidewalk material easily meets the wheelchair accessibility requirements, but not the impact attenuation, while loose material does just the reverse. In areas of handicapped access, surfaces should be an approved synthetic interlocking tile, or poured surface.

**6.** Guidelines for access to play components are proscribed by the US Access Board and further supplemented by state boards. In general, play components are classified into two types: ground level play components (swings, spring rockers, standalone climbers, and the like) and elevated play components (composite structures). Not all of the components in a playground are required to be accessible. The number required is a function of the total number of components and inaccessibility to high platforms can be offset by additional access to ground level components.

Elevated structures are rendered accessible with wheelchair accessible ramps and transfer stations and platforms that allow for users to transfer from a wheelchair to the structure. ∎

# 9 Providing for the Life Cycles of the Landscape

When we design and build a landscape we hope that it will last a very long time. Many landscapes do. As the months and years go by, every landscape changes. Weathering and natural succession takes place. For instance, some plants may thrive while others die out as trees mature, and the ground beneath them becomes shadier. Hard surfaces wear, weather, and gather dirt as well as undergo chemical changes such as fading and corrosion. Components of the landscape such as lights and benches wear out or fail and are replaced. While some landscapes grow in character and become more beautiful over time, sometimes a beautiful landscape grows less so as these changes take place. Some landscapes last only a short time; others last for centuries. There are many reasons for these differences. Most have to do with materials and detailing.

Many of the detail patterns throughout this book have a profound effect on the rate at which a particular landscape ages, but there are three categories of detail patterns that relate specifically to managing the life cycle of a landscape.

The first category contains patterns about designing a landscape with a perspective toward its entire lifetime:

The second category relates to the need to maintain a landscape:

The third category includes five patterns that have to do with preventing hardscape deterioration:

## Seasonal Cycle

All site construction takes place outside in the elements. The extremes of yearly weather cycles affect construction schedules as well as the details and specifications of all site elements. Landscape architects routinely deal with growing seasons. The cycles of cold and hot and wet and dry determine the most desirable time to install new plantings. Planting survival rates in areas with severe winters and hot summers are highest in spring and fall.

1. Planting details and specifications can be modified to extend the planting season into the summer and winter. Bare root stock is the most seasonally dependent, followed by balled and burlapped stock, leaving container-grown material the most resilient. Grasses and other plants grown from seed are most successful in wet seasons (generally spring and fall in temperate areas) while sods, plugs, or sprigs may be needed to extend the season into hotter or cooler periods.

2. Excavation is limited in freezing or wet weather. Compaction may require the addition of water in dry weather to achieve optimum results. Frozen subsoil may need to be removed prior to paving or the instruction of foundations. Pavement finish materials may also be temperature dependent. Both concrete and asphalt require additional steps during

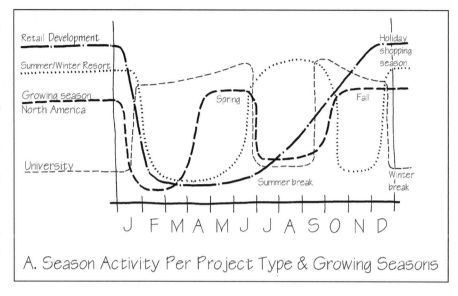

A. Season Activity Per Project Type & Growing Seasons

installation in extremes of temperature. Concrete, mortar, waterproofing, and other hardscape components are similarly restricted. Construction schedules that are limited to a single season can greatly influence the detail design of project components.

3. Additional seasonal cycles are specific to site locations. Sites in floodplains can only be worked on outside of the flood season and must be detailed to withstand scouring, inundation, and cleanup of silt deposits. Sites with a large accumulation of snow may not be workable for an extended period of time in the spring due to snow melt during that season.

4. Individual project types may also vary seasonally. School vacations and graduations often dictate construction schedules and indirectly the details of those projects. Retail developments have their highest sales volume in November and December and must function under the highest use at that time. Resort operations may have multiple high-use seasons. These cycles need to be overlayed over the seasonal cycles of the locale to create a scheme of construction (see A). ■

Landscape architects use materials that, by their nature, will change. Plants grow and get bigger, spreading beyond their area of initial installation, or decline and die. The process of change where some plants succeed and others do not is called succession.

New construction sites usually have poor quality compacted soils that are missing many of the components that allow plants to thrive. Trees and shrubs are installed well below their mature size. Groundcovers and other herbaceous plants are spaced far apart. But over time, the plants grow and modify their environment. The soils become richer biologically, freeze-thaw cycles and root growth can reduce soil compaction, and conditions tend to become shadier as tree canopies mature and there is competition between the root zones of the plants for resources. Plants compete for water, light, nutrients, and space with their roots and canopies zones. They crowd and shade each other out in the competition. The smallest, most sun-loving plants die out and are replaced by the expansion of larger more shade-tolerant plants. Shrubs are thinned out so a single plant in a mature landscape can take the place of many in one newly planted. Grasses and other smaller plants reproduce themselves via rhizomes, underground roots that parent plants send out to extend new growth into adjacent open areas. These new plants make a lawn or groundcover bed self-repairing in the proper environment and allow the colony of plants to live long beyond the life of a single plant (see A).

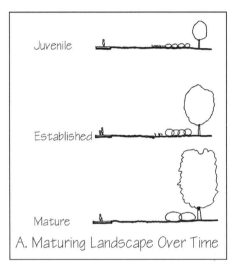

A. Maturing Landscape Over Time

**TABLE 9-1: Life Cycles of Plant Material**

| | |
|---|---|
| Oaks, Maples, Beech | 100+ years |
| Ash | 50 to 100 years |
| Willows, Apples | Up to 50 years |
| Yews, Rhododendrons | 20 to 50 years |
| Spireas, Forsythias | Up to 20 years |
| Turfgrass | 2 to 3 years |

1. The initial planting process and replacement of plants that have died is followed by selective removal. As the size of plants increases in a given area, their number tends to decrease. Irrigation systems that served an initial installation must be modified to reflect the moving lines of turf and other planting beds. Designers should have this dynamic in mind when designing details around planting. Plant beds should be accessible for plant replacement over time.

2. Maintenance practices can control growth and extend the life cycles of plants. Most gardening activities such as mowing, pruning, watering, and fertilizing were developed to manipulate the natural growth of plants allowing them to live longer in more productive forms than in nature. Mowing removes seed heads and encourages vegetative growth for thicker lawns. Pruning changes the size and forms of plants, increasing their usefulness and life span. ∎

Landscape architects understandably focus chiefly on the initial conditions of the landscape. We must also consider the impact on conditions "upstream" and "downstream" of the project itself. Building materials come from someplace, are used in the landscape, then they go someplace else. The project's distant and long-term impacts on the environment are important if advances in design and construction are to be sustainable.

**1.** Construction by its nature transforms raw natural materials into useful building elements, each of which has its own life cycle. At varying rates these materials expire physically, or they become functionally obsolete as im-proved products become available.

**2.** Owners and regulatory bodies may require that specific environmental impact objectives be met in order for a project to be built. No single aspect of life cycle assessment dominates all others, and a given project may give priority to one aspect over others. The detailer should look creatively at various options to find the strategy most appropriate for a particular project. Many computer models are available to examine options and document results.

**3.** The priorities for some elements may be different than others due to differences in their service lives. For instance, use of recyclable materials is a higher priority for decking materials and asphalt roadways that must be replaced periodically during the life of the project. Durability is the highest priority when designing foundations, retaining walls, and other elements that ensure the long-term safety of the site. Recyclability is of greatest concern when the service life of the element is

## LIFE CYCLE OF A BUILDING MATERIAL WITH ASSOCIATED ENVIRONMENTAL IMPACT AT EACH STAGE

1. Source of material: Extraction of renewable or nonrenewable material from nature; recycled from previous use; or some combination

2. Transport: Means, distance, and type of fuel

3. Industrial processes: Refinement of raw material; fabrication of finished product; energy types and quantities consumed; generation of byproducts

4. Construction and maintenance processes: energy types and quantities consumed; generation and reuse of byproducts, maintenance or repair during life of the landscape

5. Site operation: energy types and quantities consumed for illumination, water and fertilizer usage, impact on air quality and water quality and quantity, etc.

6. Deconstruction or demolition: energy types and quantities consumed; generation of byproducts

7. Reuse of serviceable components and recycling of salvageable materials: energy types and quantities consumed; generation of byproducts

8. Disposal of waste: Air and water quality impact; transport means, distance and type of fuel

short, and is less important when the service life is very long.

**4.** Renewable resources such as wood should be used at rates less than the rate at which they are replenished by nature. Many manufacturers offer information about the origins of their products, making it easier for designers to choose low-impact products. Labels on materials and certificates of authenticity document the claims.

**5.** Nonrenewable resources should be used efficiently and durably, and they should be reused or recycled at the end of the initial service life.

**6.** Embodied energy is the energy needed to extract, refine, process, transport, install, and reuse or dispose of a material. It is very difficult to measure, but generally materials that require a great deal of energy to extract or manufacture, or which are transported a great distance, will have highest embodied energy. Materials of local origin that are not energy intensive in their manufacturing process will likely have the lowest embodied energy. Embodied energy constitutes only a small percent of all energy consumed in the life of the project, a tiny fraction compared to the energy used to maintain the site.  ■

# Expected Life

How long should a material or detail last? The durability of a specific building material or detail must be proportional to its intended useful life.

**1.** The useful life of a material or an assembly is determined by how its intrinsic physical properties resist deterioration caused by conditions of its environment, use, and errors of workmanship at the time of installation. The life span is also affected by nonphysical factors such as economic forces, aesthetic trends, and functional obsolescence, but these are beyond the scope of this book.

**2.** Decisions regarding materials and details are based on a premise about the anticipated life span of the landscape. We should always build well, but materials and details appropriate on a site meant to serve for a few years may be different than those for a landscape meant to serve for 100 years or more. For instance, stainless steel flashing and pressure-treated wood is less appropriate in a temporary exposition that will be used for two years than it is in a city park that has an unlimited life expectancy. Conversely, it would not be appropriate for the stone walls that have an unlimited life expectancy to use PVC flashing, which has a service life of only about ten years.

Premature failure of a building material may result in damage to adjoining materials and will require costly and disruptive repair. Premature failure is especially disruptive when an otherwise durable assembly fails because of one weak link. Ideally, the detailer should anticipate the forces acting on an assembly and design the details so that the components of an assembly expire uniformly or in manageable segments.

Predicting the service life of a detail or an assembly is difficult because there is insufficient knowledge about the actual performance of specific materials and details. Therefore, detailers and owners should establish durability criteria for materials and details based on past experience.

**3.** Establish a premise about the service life of the project in general, for instance, 1 year, 25 years, 50 years, or 100 years. There are no legal standards for this, but precedents for the type of project are a good indication. Recognize that it is not essential that all elements of an entire project expire at the same time. Establish service-life tiers or categories, within which the elements should last about the same length of time. The hardscape elements of a landscape need to be balanced in life cycle with the planting elements.

**4.** To lower initial construction costs, elements of a detail are sometimes eliminated, or less durable alternative elements are chosen, often with disastrous results. Many expensive rehabilitation projects are the result of hastily made cost-trimming decisions that saved a small proportion of the eventually needed repair costs. Lower-quality execution during initial construction often results in higher maintenance costs and/or shorter service life. Detailers are well informed and should assist in making optimum choices regarding substitutions of materials and details.

**5.** Just as we have an operating manual for our automobile, landscape architects may offer to provide owners with a guide summarizing the maintenance and replacement cycles anticipated for each tier of the landscape. Owners and maintenance staff are collaborators in determining the project's life span; maintenance procedures need to be followed if the predicted service life is to be realized.

**6.** Details for all elements and assemblies should be designed to be accessible for maintenance in proportion with their longevity. Site elements that are to be replaced at the most frequent intervals, such as light bulbs and water filters, should be detailed to make routine maintenance easy. See *Maintenance Access,* p. 136. ∎

## TABLE 9-2: Service Life Tiers

| Primary structures | Pavements, landforms, long-lived trees and drainage | Long life: As long as the intended life of the project |
| Service systems | Irrigation, fountains and electrical/lighting systems, wood components (decking, fences) | Medium Life: Should last over 20 years |
| Furnishing and finishes | Site furniture, sealants and finishes | Temporary: Should last up to 20 years |

*Surfaces That Age Gracefully*

Some materials take on added visual interest as they age; others look progressively worse with the passing years. Exposure to sun, acid rain, sea and road salt, as well as the biological deterioration of mold and mildew all contribute to the aging of materials in the landscape.

**1.** Most species of wood deteriorate rapidly outdoors unless they are stained or painted. A few species are naturally resistant to decay, however., if left uncoated, they weather gradually to attractive shades of brown and gray. These species include Cypress, Redwood, Black Locust, White and Red Cedars, Teak, Mahogany, and various tropical hardwoods. Heartwood is inherently more resistant to deterioration than sapwood. Weather will slowly erode the surfaces of these woods, requiring eventual replacement. Tropical hardwoods have come under some scrutiny in recent years and some species have become scarce or prohibited due to unsustainable forestry practices. Repairs of projects that used these scarce or prohibited species may become difficult in the future. A plan for stockpiling some additional material to age in place as "attic stock" may be prudent.

**2.** Bright paint colors fade quickly outdoors to unattractive, streaky pastel shades. Clear coatings, such as some types of varnish, allow sunlight to attack the wood beneath, and they peel off in a year or two. Clear coatings containing ultraviolet (UV) filters are much more durable and are slow to yellow. White paint, through an intentional chalking process, renews itself continually and tends to remain attractive. Earth color pigments and soft grays tend to hold their colors longer in sunlight than do brighter hues.

**3.** Among the metals, ordinary steel rusts away, unless it has been painted. Stainless steel, especially in a brushed finish, retains its good looks indefinitely without painting. Aluminum forms a self-protecting oxide coating

and does not corrode further, but this coating is thin, easily damaged, and looks splotchy. Through the process of anodizing, aluminum can be manufactured with a thick, durable coating of oxide that contains integral color of the designer's choice, and it will look good for decades. Copper forms a self-protecting oxide coating that is usually an attractive blue-green or black in color, depending on the pollutants in the atmosphere, and it is a traditional choice for a metal that ages gracefully outdoors. Lead protects itself with a white oxide coating. A steel alloy is available that forms a tenacious, self-protecting coating of red-brown oxide, and it needs no painting. Weathering steel, lead, and copper tend to shed some of their oxide coatings, staining surfaces below and effecting soil chemistry, so care should be taken in detailing them to catch and drain all rain water that has flowed over them before it can run onto such stainable surfaces as stone, concrete, wood, and glass. The presence of salt from ocean spray or deicing can further accelerate the natural deterioration.

**4.** In general, matte surfaces age more gracefully than glossy surfaces, which tend to weather rapidly to a matte finish on most materials. A mirror finish stainless steel panel, for example, soon grows dirty, obscuring its luster, whereas a matte finish stainless steel surface changes relatively little in appearance as it accumulates the same amount of dirt. Glossy paints lose their luster quickly in sunlight, chalking to a matte texture. The exceptions are glass, glazed ceramic tiles, and polished stone. These lose some of their sheen as they grow dirty, but when washed they regain their lustrous surfaces and bright colors.

**5.** Smooth concrete surfaces—those formed against steel, plastic, or overlaid plywood—have a tendency to feature every small flaw in the concrete. They also change appearance rapidly as

they weather, becoming rougher and attracting more grime. The concrete surfaces that are more tolerant of flaws and that weather more gracefully are those formed with heavy textures, such as exposed aggregate and sand-blasted, bush-hammered, board-formed, or ribbed composite finishes.

**6.** Glass is one of the few materials that is not altered significantly by exposure, although the frames, clips, fasteners, and sealants used to secure it are vulnerable.

**7.** Plastics such as polycarbonate and acrylic are sometimes used in glazing applications. They are lighter in weight and may be less costly than glass, but their surfaces are much less hard, so they may become scratched or dulled more readily than glass and can change color over time.

**8.** Sealants are available in a wide variety of colors, making it possible to select initial colors that match surrounding materials. However, they may weather differently than adjoining materials, causing the sealant to become more prominent over time. Chemicals in adjoining materials or used in building maintenance may also cause sealant color to change. Detailers are urged to review manufacturers' technical information to select the best products.

**9.** How water will flow over all exterior surfaces is another important consideration. Not only can water itself harm materials and assemblies, but also it can carry eroded soil, atmospheric debris, and water-soluble chemicals that will stain or otherwise harm materials in their path. Be especially thorough in addressing water flow at transitions. Areas of greatest concentrated water flow, such as a gutter, will be scoured clean and may even be eroded as the water removes material in its path. Where flow is less rapid, particles and chemicals will be deposited onto surfaces, often darkening them. When these two conditions are in close proximity, as they often are, a contrast of clean and soiled surfaces may result.

**10.** Textured exterior wall surfaces will darken over time, especially where most exposed to airborne particles or where minor biological growth can occur. Surfaces become more place-specific as this happens such as moss growing on shaded pavements. The change is a subtle index of what and where the surface is, and it may not threaten the integrity of the assembly.

**11.** Porous materials that people touch will generally darken over time, as the oils from fingertips lend color and sheen to the surface. Cast-in-place concrete benches and walls are subject to staining. ■

Detailers cannot prevent wear, but they can assemble materials and details so that surfaces wear evenly and slowly. It is wise to anticipate the inevitable need to repair the surfaces and to use materials that can be repaired easily and inconspicuously.

**1.** The appropriate method of repair varies according to the type of installation.

**a.** Some materials are monolithic or seamlessly whole when installed; examples include asphalt, cast-in-place concrete, and stucco.

**b.** Others are discrete pieces that are imbedded in a monolithic base, such as stone, masonry, or tile.

**c.** A third category includes discrete pieces that are fastened or anchored to a structural substrate.

**2.** Blemishes in monolithic surfaces are generally patched or repaired to blend with the surrounding surface, sometimes with mixed results. Most landscape materials are unfinished, so a patch usually cannot be covered with a coating to blend in. Roadway patches in a street is a prime example. Planted areas, though, can be self-repairing. Damage to turf or groundcover can be regraded and planted to match and as the plants grow, the seam will disappear.

**3.** Damaged pieces embedded in a monolithic base must be carefully extracted, then replaced. A terrace or wall of polished stone or ceramic tile, while inherently durable and attractive, can be very difficult to repair if a unit of material is damaged. The individual brick, stone, or tile can be troublesome to remove, and replacement materials often do not match the surrounding material in color or pattern. The matching problem can be minimized by using a blend of colors, or a varied pattern in the original installation: a mix of several colors of tiles, for example, or of a highly variegated blend of stone, in which a slight color mismatch created by a later repair will not be noticeable.

**4.** Discrete pieces that are individually installed may each be replaced with a matching item. A surface made up of a large number of small, individually installed units, such as a plaza with precast pavers, does not tend to look bad if one or two units are damaged. It is easily and unobtrusively repaired by replacing the damaged units.

**5.** Future availability of a specific color, texture, or shape is not assured, especially if a product is unique or custom made for the project. In those cases, the owner may be well advised to acquire a small quantity of the special items for future use. Alternatively, portions of the project that are most vulnerable to deterioration may be made of standard materials and assemblies in the hope that they will remain available in future years. ∎

Detailing decisions often affect the ease and expense of keeping landscape surfaces clean. All landscape surfaces need to be waterproof, but also need to be able to withstand the removal of debris, leaves, and snow in cold climates.

**1.** Surface finishes need to be matched carefully to the areas in which they are used. Exterior fireplaces, kitchens, dining, and work areas should be finished in materials that can be cleaned by washing in place. Grease-resistant materials with smooth, dense surfaces are best: stainless steel, polished stone, glazed ceramic tiles, glazed concrete masonry, terrazzo, and porcelain. The best detailing of these materials features rounded, crack-free junctions, such as integral cove interior corners and bullnose exterior corners.

**2.** Pools and fountains often use a strip of tile at the waterline to facilitate scrubbing the residue that accumulates at the edge of the water. Copings and pool edges are also best detailed with rounded edges (see A).

**3.** Detail installations that will withstand the cleaning process. Exterior pavements are often cleaned with a power-washer or industrial power brushes. Both of these methods can detach small pieces of aggregate from an exposed aggregate or undermine soft joints between bricks or stone.

**4.** Avoid installations that complicate the cleaning process. Most large exterior spaces are kept free of debris and leaves with blowers. Tight interior corners and areas between fences and

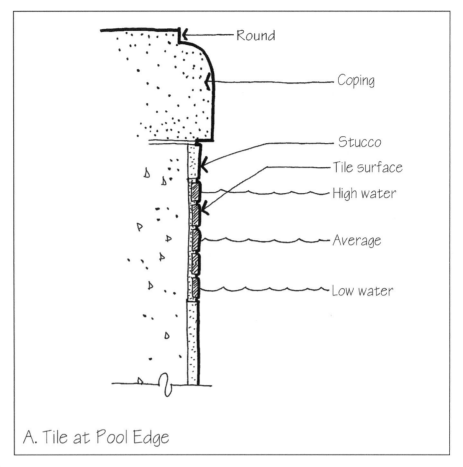

A. Tile at Pool Edge

walls are particularly difficult to clean with a blower.

**5.** Curbs and the edges of walks should be able to withstand the impact of a snow plow or snow blower. Areas off the pavement that are used for snow storage should be durable enough to withstand the weight of snow and any loose material scraped up by plows as well as the effects of salt and other deicers. They should provide drainage for the melt water when temperatures rise. Areas behind curbs can be reinforced with a strip of pavement, or planted with salt-resistant perennials to withstand the effects of piled snow.

**6.** Salt and other deicers can react with cement in concrete and mortar. Pavements and walls in areas prone to icing and the application of salt should avoid exposed cement finishes. ∎

Many components need to be detailed to allow for maintenance and inspection access throughout the life of the landscape.

**1.** Components that may require adjustment or replacement during the life of the building should be attached with screws or bolts so that they can be removed and replaced, rather than welded, glued, or nailed permanently in place. This is why we use screws and bolts rather than nails to attach hardware to gates, and fence panels, and to attach lighting fixtures to walls and foundations.

**2.** Concealed mechanical and electrical components that require inspection and maintenance should be placed behind snap-off covers, hinged access panels, manholes, handholes, or access ports of appropriate sizes and shapes. Never seal off permanently any component that moves, that connects electrical wires, that may need cleaning, or that may deteriorate or go out of adjustment prematurely. Examples include gate hinges and latches, irrigation valves, pumps, plumbing cleanouts, electric junction boxes, lighting ballasts, transformers, gas connections for grills and firepits, and telephone wiring junctions. Work continually with electrical, mechanical, and structural consultants to see that all necessary access devices are provided.

**3.** Maintenance access generally requires floor space on site in a building or vault. A fountain pump, filter, or similar piece of equipment requires space for servicing and storage for supplies. Electrical transformers, generators, and switch-gears need free frontal access and room to remove and replace components. Air conditioner condensers need open space for air exchange. Lay out spaces for mechanical, plumbing, electrical, and communications equipment in close cooperation with engineering consultants to be sure that these concerns are met. ■

Wood must be detailed so that it will stay dry; otherwise, it will decay in only a few years.

**1.** A covered bridge is durable because it is covered to keep water off the joints in the wood trusses. Joints between pieces of wood that are exposed to the weather absorb and hold moisture by capillary action. This encourages decay. Uncovered constructions made of ordinary wood seldom last as long as a decade before their joints rot beyond repair. Exposed exterior wood constructions with many joints, such as fences, decks, sunshades, railings, benches, gates, and doors, should be made of decay-resistant wood. It is not enough merely to paint them, because the paint cracks at the joints due to normal seasonal moisture movement in the wood, allowing water to enter and slowing evaporation of moisture from the wood (see A).

**2.** Wood must be kept well away from the ground so that it will remain dry and therefore free from decay. In the sill detail of a wood frame building, all wood is kept at least 6 in. (150 mm) above the surface of the soil. As a further precaution, it is wise to use pressure-treated or naturally decay-resistant wood for the sill plate that rests on a concrete or masonry foundation, because moisture may rise from the ground through the porous material of the

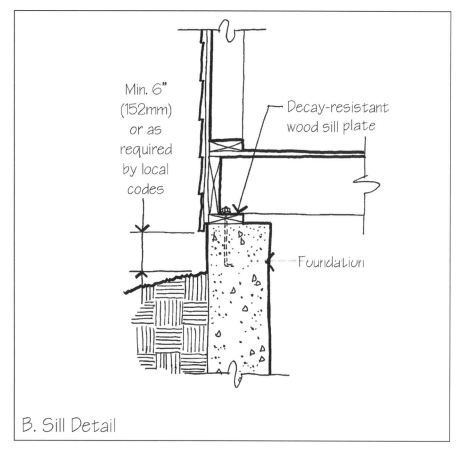

Min. 6" (152mm) or as required by local codes

Decay-resistant wood sill plate

Foundation

B. Sill Detail

Weather tight skin

Wood trusses

A. Covered Bridge

foundation and wet the underside of the sill. On wet sites or in very damp climates, a continuous flashing should be installed between the sill and the foundation as a barrier against capillary moisture rising from the soil. The bottom edge of fence panels, pergola posts, and the cladding of outbuilding walls are similarly kept above the ground, detailed using under-tolerant materials near the ground (see B).

**3.** The microorganisms that cause decay in wood need three things to survive: air (oxygen), wood for food, and small amounts of moisture. Usually decay is discouraged either by treating the wood with chemicals that make it unfit for food, by selecting a wood species that is unappetizing to the microorganisms, or by keeping wood completely dry. Paradoxically, wood that is completely and permanently submerged in water will not decay. This is because water does not allow the organisms in the wood access

to air. Thus, we sometimes use untreated wood for foundation pilings in soils that are completely saturated with water. This works well as long as the water level in the soil does not drop. In cases where the water level has fallen, piles have rotted off at the level where the saturated soil joins the drier soil above, the one location where air, water, and wood are all available to the decay organisms.

**4.** All wood-destroying insects require moisture. Many species can live only in damp wood and are easily discouraged by details that keep wood dry. The most common species of termites are subterranean, but they can attack dry wood if they have access to damp soil. These species are dealt with by keeping wood well above the soil line and by installing a continuous flashing with projecting edges between the exposed wood and the foundation. This will require that the tubes built by these termites to ▷

make contact with the ground are easily spotted and destroyed. Soil poisons are also used against this type of termite to create a chemical barrier, but the safety of these poisons is coming under increasing scrutiny. To avoid chemicals, a fine stainless steel mesh can be installed prior to construction across the soil adjacent to the structures. A few species of termites that thrive only in very warm, damp climates can live in dry wood without soil contact, taking their moisture from the air or the wood itself; these are dealt with by poisoning them through fumigation. Treatment with very hot or cold temperatures is also possible.

**5.** When detailing wooden fences and structures, the tops of vertical boards should be covered with a horizontal board or flashing to keep water from entering the end grain of the wood (see C).

**6.** In decks with open joints, the joints should be wide enough to maintain a gap when the boards swell or warp. ■

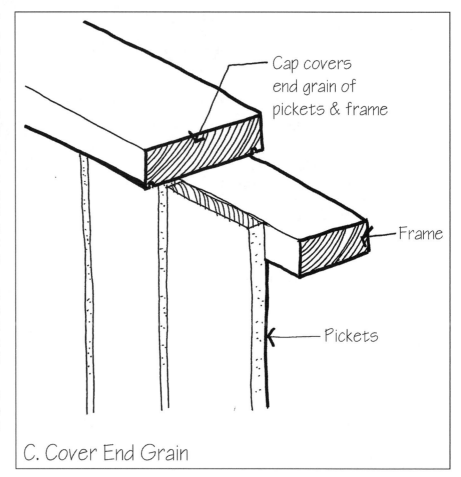

Cap covers end grain of pickets & frame

Frame

Pickets

C. Cover End Grain

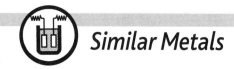

# Similar Metals

Avoid details in which two different metals are attached directly to one another.

**1.** Simple corrosion is oxidation that occurs when air and moisture are present simultaneously on the surface of a metal. Most nonferrous metals (such as aluminum, zinc, brass, bronze, lead, and copper) quickly form stable, self-protecting oxide coatings that prevent further corrosion. Stainless steels and certain weathering steels are also self-protecting.

**2.** Ordinary steel (carbon steel), wrought iron, and cast iron need protective coatings to avoid destruction by oxidation (rusting) if they are used outdoors or in wet interior environments. These may take the form of paint, various factory-applied organic coatings, or metallic coatings.

**3.** The most common metal used for protective coating of steel is zinc. Zinc coating is known as galvanizing. Galvanizing works because the zinc slowly sacrifices itself through oxidation to protect the underlying steel. A galvanized surface even heals small scratches in the coating with its own oxide. Eventually, the zinc weathers away, leaving the steel to rust. This can take from 5 to 40 years, depending on the thickness of the coating and the presence of salt and industrial/urban pollutants in the air. For the longest possible life, use the heaviest available zinc coating. This is usually applied by means of traditional hot-dip galvanizing. There are many other methods of galvanizing including color treatments, some of which result in only thin coatings that have a short life. It is important to do careful research in order to determine the degree of protection that is required in a given situation and to specify the galvanizing process and thickness of coating that will best satisfy this need.

**4.** Because of contaminants that are always present, both rain water and groundwater are electrolytes. When rain water or groundwater comes in contact with an assembly that includes two different metals, a galvanic reaction can occur, generating an electrical current that will corrode one of the metals with astonishing rapidity. The safest approach in detailing to avoid bimetallic corrosion is to use the same metal in all of the components of a detail: steel anchor bolts for steel street furniture frames, and copper nails with copper fence flashing.

**5.** It is often necessary, however, to confront such problems as attaching bronze light fixtures to a steel frame or an aluminum railing to a galvanized anchor bolt. To solve these problems, we must look more deeply into the nature of the galvanic reaction between dissimilar metals. Metals vary in their chemical activity. When two different metals are brought together and bathed with an electrolyte such as (acid) rain water, an exchange of electrons takes place that protects the less active metal while corroding the more active one. The greater the difference is between the activities of the two metals, the greater the potential for corrosion.

**6.** In the accompanying table, the metals commonly used in construction are ranked with respect to their relative activity: the most active metals are at the top and the least active are at the bottom. Metals with similar levels of activity are grouped together. In general, it is safe to combine metals that are in the same group.

### TABLE 9-3: Galvanic Series of Unweathered Metals

| | |
|---|---|
| **Most Active** | Magnesium and its alloys |
| | Zinc |
| | Galvanized steel and iron |
| | Aluminum |
| | Steel |
| | Wrought iron |
| | Cast iron |
| | Active stainless steel [a] |
| | Lead-tin solder |
| | Lead |
| | Tin |
| | Brass |
| | Bronze |
| | Copper |
| | Silver solder |
| | Nickel |
| | Passive stainless steel [a] |
| | Silver |
| Least Active | Gold |

[a] Whether stainless steel is considered "active" or "passive" depends on its surface finish. Stainless steel normally forms a self-protecting coating of chromium oxide and is considered passive. The electropolished surfaces used on some architectural hardware and trim are also passive. But if the coating of chromium oxide is disturbed by grinding, machining, or wire brushing, the finish becomes active. Most stainless steel fasteners are active. Active stainless steel can be made passive by treatment with acids. The detailer should work closely with the manufacturer of the stainless steel product if these distinctions become important in preparing a detail. ▷

**7.** If a metal from one group is used with a metal from another group, the potential for galvanic corrosion is roughly proportional to the distance between the two groups in the galvanic series. For example, a detail that used zinc or galvanized screws in copper light fixture housing would combine a metal from the most active group with one from the next-to-least active group; the zinc screws would virtually disappear after only a few rainfalls.

**8.** The rate of corrosion is also affected by the relative surface areas of the two metals. If the area of the less active metal is very large in relation to the area of the more active one, corrosion will be very rapid. This would be the case with zinc nails in a copper fence flashing. If copper bolts were used in a zinc (galvanized) railing, however, the area of the less active metal would be very small when compared with the area of the more active one, and corrosion would be very slow. Nevertheless, one would be foolish to detail a galvanized railing with copper bolts, because of the extreme difference in activity between the two metals. But this area effect is useful in combining metals that lie more closely together on the galvanic series, such as stainless steel screws (which have an "active" finish) in an aluminum railing. Aluminum screws in a stainless steel railing, on the other hand, would be at great risk because of the very large surface area of the less active metal compared with the more active one.

**9.** Taking all these factors into account, and relying also upon data from actual installations, the American Architectural Manufacturers Association has developed the accompanying table that suggests the best fasteners to use with different combinations of metals.

**TABLE 9-4: Compatibility of Fasteners with Metal Roof and Wall Panels***

A. Painted and Unpainted Galvanized Steel
  1. Zinc-plated steel
  2. Organic Coated Steel
  3. Hot-dipped galvanized
  4. Zinc Alloy Steel
  5. Stainless Steel
  6. Aluminum
  7. 300 Series Stainless Steel
  8. 400 Series Stainless Steel

B. Unpainted Galvalume Steel
  1. Organic Coated Steel
  2. Hot-dipped galvanized
  3. Zinc Alloy Steel
  4. Stainless Steel
  5. Aluminum
  6. 300 Series Stainless Steel
  7. 400 Series Stainless Steel

C. Painted Galvalume Steel
  1. Zinc-plated steel
  2. Organic Coated Steel
  3. Hot-dipped galvanized
  4. Zinc Alloy Steel
  5. Stainless Steel
  6. Aluminum
  7. 300 Series Stainless Steel
  8. 400 Series Stainless Steel

D. Aluminum
  1. Aluminum

E. Copper and Copper Alloys
  1. Copper and Copper Alloys
  2. 300 Series Stainless Steel
  3. 400 Series Stainless Steel

F. Stainless Steel
  1. Zinc Alloy Steel
  2. Stainless Steel
  3. 300 Series Stainless Steel
  4. 400 Series Stainless Steel

G. Zinc Alloy
  1. 300 Series Stainless Steel
  2. 300 Series Stainless Steel

This table is intended as a general guideline for fasteners used with metal roofing systems where the performance of the fasteners matches the expected life of the panels. In highly corrosive environments such as heavy industrial areas, heavily polluted or areas of heavy salt use, marine sites, or details with preserved wood components, the performance of the fasteners can be compromised. In addition damage or scratches to the coatings can also affect the integrity of the coatings and life of the details.

\* *From the Technical Bulletin #80-001, Compatibility of Fasteners with Metal Roof and Wall Panels*, Reproduced by permission of the Metal Construction Association.

**10.** In many cases, it is possible to avoid corrosion between dissimilar metals by separating the metals with an electrical insulating material. The insulation might take the form of a plastic or synthetic rubber washer, gasket, shim, sleeve, or bushing that is placed between the materials. It might be a nonconductive coating on one or both of the materials. It might be a plastic or plastic-headed screw or bolt. A municipal water supply pipe made of steel can be safely joined to copper pipes inside the building using a plastic coupler that isolates the two metals electrically. Obviously the insulating material should be durable, because if it disintegrates, the metals will come into contact and corrode. Insulating washers made of many plastics and rubber are vulnerable to ultraviolet light, so they should be capped with a metal washer to prevent exposure to sunlight. Insulating materials would be the best answer to attaching an aluminum mast to a copper roof, because the two metals are too reactive with one another to join in any other way.

**11.** There are also damaging chemical reactions that can occur between metals and certain nonmetallic materials. Steel will not corrode in concrete that is free of acidic admixtures, as long as it is completely surrounded by concrete and outside water cannot penetrate. Aluminum, however, is chemically incompatible with concrete, especially when the concrete is fresh, and the two materials should never be used in direct contact. Lead flashings tend to corrode in mortar and are not recommended for use with masonry. Naturally decay-resistant woods contain acids that can react chemically to cause corrosion of some metals, and some chemicals used in pressure treating of wood can cause similar problems. It is best to consult literature from the trade organizations and manufacturers that promote these woods for recommendations on fasteners and flashings.

**12.** In this detail for anchoring stone facing panels to a wall, stainless steel is chosen for the anchor because it will not rust. This avoids staining of the stone and corrosion failure of the anchor. It avoids the spalling of the stone that could occur from the expansion of steel as it rusts. Stainless steel is also resistant to the acid chemistry of such stones as granite. The stainless steel anchor is fastened to its support angle with a stainless steel bolt, nut, and washer. A plastic shim and sleeve are used to isolate the stainless steel components from the galvanized steel support angle. A galvanized steel washer is used against the back of the galvanized angle, isolated from the stainless steel bolt head by a plastic washer. ■

The whole detail could be executed in stainless steel, of course, but the support angles would be almost prohibitively expensive in this material (see A).

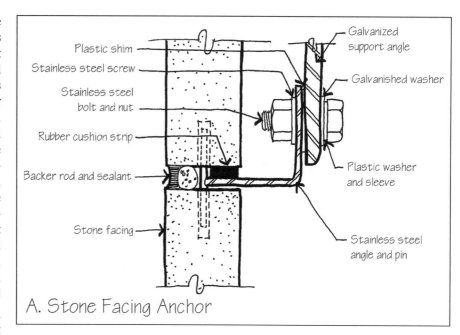

Plastic shim
Stainless steel screw
Stainless steel bolt and nut
Rubber cushion strip
Backer rod and sealant
Stone facing
Galvanized support angle
Galvanished washer
Plastic washer and sleeve
Stainless steel angle and pin

A. Stone Facing Anchor

Exterior surfaces should be made of materials that absorb as little water as possible.

1. Porous materials are often vulnerable to water, or they may convey moisture to vulnerable adjoining materials.

2. In climates with cold, wet winters, hard materials such as concrete, stone, and brick are subject to spalling and flaking of the surface, caused by water soaking into the material and then freezing. The expansion of the freezing water exerts pressure from within the material and forces flakes from the surface. This effect can be minimized by using materials that absorb as little water as possible.

3. Concrete that is formulated with a low water-cement ratio has fewer pores created by the escape of excess water and is less susceptible to freeze-thaw damage than more watery concretes. Concrete that will be exposed to cold winter weather should also be formulated with an air-entraining admixture. During the mixing process, this admixture causes the formation of microscopic air bubbles that make up 2 to 8 percent of the volume of the concrete. The resulting voids in the concrete reduce freeze-thaw damage by acting as expansion chambers for the freezing water.

4. Denser stones, such as granite, absorb less water and hold up better in wet locations in cold climates than more porous stones, such as limestone and sandstone. Sedimentary stones should be laid with their natural bedding horizontal. Traditional stone buildings often have granite foundations and then change to limestone or marble above ground level.

5. Clay bricks for exterior wall use in cold, wet climates should be Grade SW (severe weathering, ASTM C62), which comprises bricks that do not absorb very much water. Even Grade SW bricks must absorb some water; otherwise they would not bond to mortar. Bricks for paving are especially vulnerable to freeze-thaw deterioration; in severe climates, only Class SX clay bricks, as defined by ASTM C902, should be used. Similarly, concrete paving bricks should have a water absorption rate of 5 percent or less.

6. Glazed masonry products such as terra cotta, clay bricks, and concrete masonry units have much lower surface absorbency than unglazed units. However, moisture may enter the wall through other avenues, such as mortar joints, and then enter the masonry units through their unglazed surfaces that are in contact with the mortar. This sometimes causes the glazed surface to spall. When using glazed masonry units, check with manufacturers for mortar joint specifications; a chemical may be added to the mortar mix to reduce water absorption.

7. Mortar joints in masonry are tooled to create a finished profile. But the tooling is more than cosmetic: It also helps the mortar joint shed water, and it compresses the mortar at the face of the joint, making it denser and less absorptive of water, and sealing it more tightly against the masonry units on either side. In climates with cold winters, noncompressed joints, such as the flush, raked, stripped, and extruded joints, should be avoided, because they are too absorptive. The raked and stripped joints are also undesirable, because they tend to trap water. The concave and vee pro-

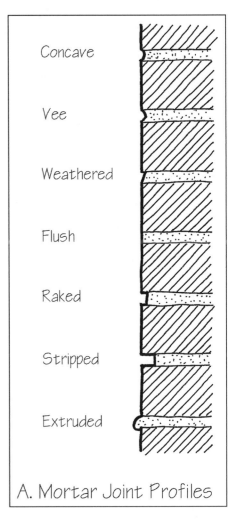

## A. Mortar Joint Profiles

*Concave*

*Vee*

*Weathered*

*Flush*

*Raked*

*Stripped*

*Extruded*

files are the best from the standpoint of weathering (see A).

8. Like the mortar joints shown here, walls built using porous materials such as wood, masonry, concrete, and stucco should have profiles that shed water quickly. Corbels and reveals are interesting visually, but they may present small shelves on which water can puddle to be absorbed into mortar or other wall materials (see B).

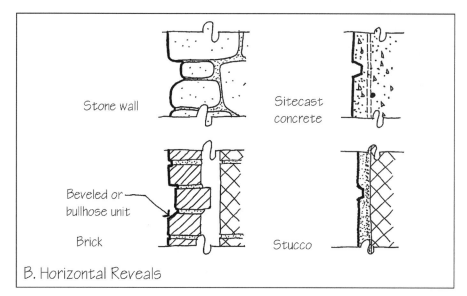

Stone wall

Sitecast concrete

Beveled or bullhose unit

Brick

Stucco

B. Horizontal Reveals

sedimentary sandstone are more porous than the surfaces parallel to those layers. Detailers should cap exposed end grain on wood pickets, or they should cut the picket back at an angle to minimize exposure of the end grain to the weather (see C).

**13.** Premanufactured steel column bases are used to secure posts for trellises or pergolas while keeping moisture away from the bottoms of the post. Often the base of the columns is trimmed out to hide the steel base. The trim can be replaced without replacing the column or it can be constructed of a synthetic, nonabsorbent material (see D). ■

**9.** The more absorbent the material, the steeper the *wash* (p. 33) should be to shed water quickly. Even small surfaces that face skyward should be impermeable, very steeply sloped, or detailed for easy replacement as they deteriorate. This principle applies to steps, copings, pier caps, and many other elements.

**10.** Less absorbent materials are also more resistant to graffiti or environmental staining and are generally more tolerant of aggressive cleaning methods, making them good choices where graffiti and environmental staining are expected.

**11.** The useful life of absorbent materials can be extended by reducing their absorbency. Porous wood becomes less absorbent when sealed, painted, or stained. Concrete masonry units can be manufactured with an additive in the mix that reduces their absorption rate. After construction, walls made of concrete, masonry, and stucco can be treated with various clear penetrating compounds to reduce their absorbency, while still allowing vapor to escape. These compounds need to be reapplied periodically during the life of the project.

**12.** Some materials have a microscopic grain or pore structure that makes some surfaces more absorbent than others. The end grain of a piece of wood, for instance, is much more porous than its broad face. Exposed strata edges of

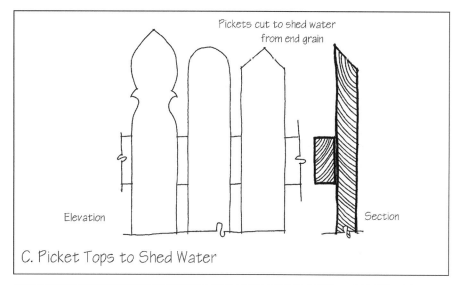

Pickets cut to shed water from end grain

Elevation

Section

C. Picket Tops to Shed Water

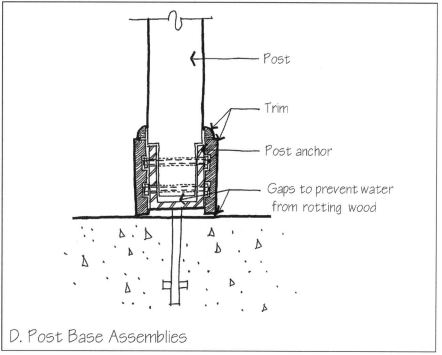

Post

Trim

Post anchor

Gaps to prevent water from rotting wood

D. Post Base Assemblies

The rate of aging of a project is often determined by the level of redundancy or ability of the assemblies to resist deterioration.

**1.** Most landscape walls should be constructed of solid material without cavities. Cavities are used in building walls to control heat and moisture flow through the building envelope. Walls in the landscape do not have a need for temperature control and are less sensitive to moisture than building walls. Moisture should be repelled at the surface and additional moisture barriers are unnecessary and may be counterproductive. A solid wall is much more durable than a cavity wall. It is more resistant to impact and to wind and other forces that could cause structural damage.

**2.** There are, however, several cases where a cavity wall should be used in the landscape. If a wall is intended to match a building wall, if the masons are unfamiliar with landscape walls, or if free-standing walls need to be built cheaply, a cavity wall may be the best solution (see A).

**3.** For maximum life, a masonry cavity wall not only has a well-crafted veneer to repel most water but also a clear cavity with flashing and weeps to direct water out. Metal ties between the veneer and the backup wythe of masonry should be

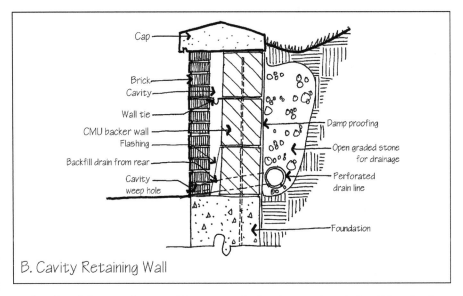

B. Cavity Retaining Wall

made of stainless steel to avoid corrosion. They also should have drips built into them to release water before it can bridge across the cavity to the inner wythe. The cavity could be compartmented to use pressure equalization to resist wind-driven rain penetration. It should allow air to convect through it to carry water vapor out. This wall has redundant layers and multiple strategies to resist water, the chief agent of deterioration in this case (see B).

**4.** Guardrails need to be substantial enough to function for their intended use without any additional sway. Wood

decks also need to feel solid underfoot. The higher the deck, the stiffer it needs to be with a heavier structure to feel secure and comfortable.

**5.** Materials may not be perfect. Workmanship during installation may not be perfect. Maintenance may not be perfect. Details and assemblies can still work if they have some tolerance for imperfection. Assemblies or details that are thin, one-layer barriers lack redundancy. If used, extreme care must be taken to be sure they are detailed, installed, and maintained flawlessly.

**6.** Well-detailed landscapes have a better chance of being well-maintained. They often outlive their initial program manyfold, and in them new functions or technical improvements are more likely to be introduced with care, not as violent intrusions. A landscape that is made with consideration to fundamental principles of design, crafted of materials appropriate for the task, will offer value to its future stewards. A poorly detailed landscape is more likely to become unsightly as surfaces and joints deteriorate, discouraging users and provoking owners to avoid making difficult or costly repairs. Landscape architects enhance a site's useful life through competent technical detailing and with deliberate thought to future maintenance. ∎

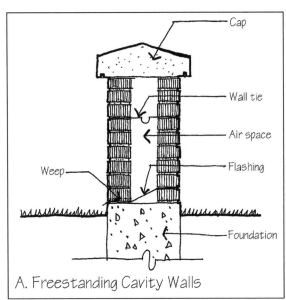

A. Freestanding Cavity Walls

# Building and Landscape Armor

A built element needs to be armored where it is likely to get kicked or scuffed, pushed or punched, bumped into, or splashed.

**1.** Forms of building armor include curbs and bollards to confine vehicles to roads and drives, and corner guards, protective posts, and dock bumpers where vehicles are allowed to come close to the building (see A).

**2.** It is best to avoid superficial colors and finishes in high-traffic areas where surfaces are likely to be damaged. Wear and chipped surfaces will reveal inner colors or textures that are different than those on the outside, making the blemish all the more apparent. Sand-finished brick, surface-pigmented concrete, and asphalt are all materials that are superficially coated; they should be avoided in high-traffic areas.

**3.** Skateboards and roller blades can damage benches, rails, walls, and stairs if the users are present and the surfaces are conducive to sliding. The edges most susceptible to abuse can be detailed with integral ribs, grooves, ridges, or applied premanufactured guards to eliminate long continuous slides (see B).

**4.** Turf that is subject to excessive use can be reinforced with a composite system of plastic grids, stones, or pavers

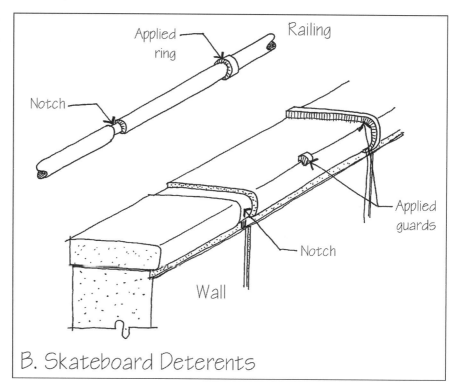

B. Skateboard Deterents

that keep heavy loads from compacting the grass, roots, or the soil itself can be reinforces reinforced with fibers or grids to spread out the loads and discourage compaction.

5. Mowers and string trimmers can damage hard surfaces as well as plantings. A mow edge at the face of a

building prevents the need for a string trimmer. Other areas can be detailed in a durable stone such as granite that can take the repeated nicks of the string. In turf areas that cannot be accessed via a ramp, mowers can chip and discolor the nosings of steps. A higher strength concrete or stone can be used to armor the nosing from damage. ∎

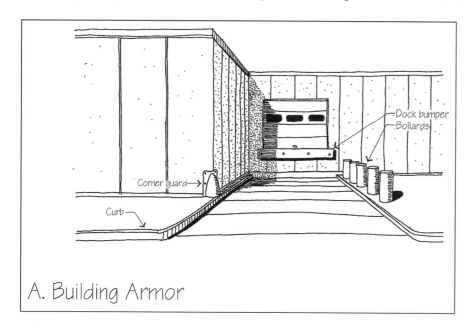

A. Building Armor

# SECTION
## 3
# CONSTRUCTIBILITY

Adetail may work perfectly with respect to water, sediment or structural movement, accommodating growth, expansion and contraction, and every other functional requirement, but if it is troublesome or unnecessarily expensive to make, it is not a good detail. The owner of a project has a right to expect construction to proceed smoothly, swiftly, and economically. The contractor and workers who construct the project have a right to expect it to go together with no more than the normal degree of difficulty. From the designer's point of view, a smooth construction process generally produces a project with fewer defects and fewer disputes among the participants. Constructible details are essential to a smooth construction process.

By understanding the construction process and creating details that can be efficiently crafted, the detailer can save substantial amounts of time, material, and energy, contributing to the sustainability of the project. Well constructed details also require less maintenance and have a longer useful life than those that are not.

As a bonus, the effort to design constructible details can lead the designer into explorations of building craft that may yield substantial aesthetic rewards: Much of what we admire and enjoy most about great landscapes can be traced to a deep understanding of the craft that is evident in their details.

Consider the classic Italian gardens, whose ornate fountains, walls, and stairs sprang from the craft of stone masonry. Think also of the California gardens of the mid-twentieth century with curving concrete planes and redwood fences and decks. Both landscape styles evolved from similar site conditions, but the forms that are the hallmark of the respective styles were an outgrowth of the craft prevalent at each particular time and place.

Many contemporary landscapes derive visual impact from precise concrete forms and sleek constructions in steel and glass that make knowledgeable use of the craft disciplines of these modern technologies. A contemporary construction site may combine hand-crafting and machine production side by side.

Constructibility can be summarized in three general guidelines:

1. A detail should be easy to assemble.
2. A detail should be forgiving of small inaccuracies and minor mistakes.
3. A detail should be based on efficient use of construction facilities, tools, materials, and labor.

The logic of these three guidelines may be summarized in a single sentence: A project ought to go together easily and efficiently, and it should do so even though many little things can be expected to go wrong during the construction process.

CHAPTER **10** Ease of Assembly

Ease of assembly is important because a detail that is a struggle to build is likely to be expensive and will often be executed poorly. A detail that goes together in an easy, relaxed manner is economical with regard to labor and will generally be done well. There are nine detail patterns that concern ease of assembly. Their names are almost self-explanatory, because these patterns deal with common-sense issues of simplification, reduction of effort, and provision of sufficient spaces for workers to do their work.

It is generally easier to assemble elements that share common features. Choose a family of materials or components that either share similar physical properties, such as brick and concrete block, or are designed to be joined readily, such as steel edging and precast concrete pavers. These are compatible because they come from common sources or have been refined through use in previous projects.

The scale of the project may affect how you apply these patterns. In a small project such as a residential garden, the contractor may have diverse skills and may install everything from rough to finished elements. In such projects, custom features executed by a broadly skilled craftsperson may be more feasible. In a larger project, it is more likely that each subsystem will be installed by a different crew of specialized workers.

No matter what the project scale or the level of uniqueness of its features, the details should represent the easiest means through which the intended finished condition can be achieved. The patterns in this group will help the detailer anticipate the challenges faced by those who build the project.

With certain materials, it saves time and money to detail in such a way that few, if any, units of material need to be cut.

**1.** Off-the-shelf products, such as lumber, plywood, pipe, and masonry units, are all manufactured to standard dimensions that designers must take into account. Other products, such as site-cast concrete formwork, and machine laid pavement and curbing, also have industry standard dimensions that the detailer should respect. Working with the standard dimensions of building materials minimizes the need to cut them and saves time and money.

**2.** When materials of varying sizes are to be combined in an assembly, choose products that share a common dimensional module. The dimensions of the various materials should be whole number multiples of this module, or they should yield whole numbers when divided into the module. Often the module of the coarsest (largest) material governs building dimensions of assemblies using those materials. For instance, in a wall made of brick and concrete masonry, the governing module is the concrete block, which is larger than the brick.

**3.** Brick masonry and concrete masonry should be dimensioned and detailed so that there is little need to cut bricks and blocks. This often involves slight adjustments in the overall dimensions of the wall or pavement.

**4.** Concrete masonry should be dimensioned in multiples of 8 in. (200 mm), making small corrections for the thickness of a mortar joint where required. Over its entire length, outside corner to outside corner, a concrete block wall has one fewer mortar joints than it does blocks, so $3/8$ in. (10 mm) should be deducted from the nominal length of the wall to arrive at the actual dimension (see A).

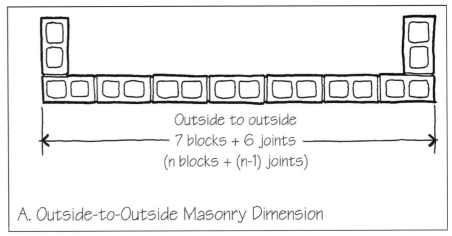

A. Outside-to-Outside Masonry Dimension

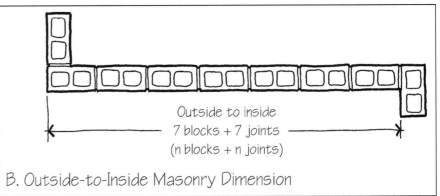

B. Outside-to-Inside Masonry Dimension

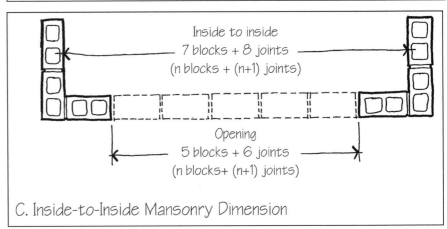

C. Inside-to-Inside Mansonry Dimension

**5.** Between an outside corner and an inside corner, a concrete masonry wall has the same number of mortar joints as blocks, so the actual length of the wall is the same as the nominal length. In other words, the length will be an exact multiple of 8 in. (200 mm) (see B).

**6.** An opening in a concrete masonry wall has one more mortar joint than it does blocks. Therefore, the nominal dimension must be increased by $3/8$ in. (10 mm) to find the actual dimension. The same principle applies to an inside dimension between masonry walls (see C).

**7.** The general dimensioning principles that have just been described also apply to brickwork, stonework, and other types of masonry. The labor required to cut such materials may increase the in-place cost of the unit as much as tenfold. Before preparing a detail, determine what type of masonry units you will be using and what their dimensions will be. Decide on the dimension of a standard joint. Then note each dimension on the drawing: both as numbers of masonry units and as feet and inches (or millimeters). This makes the work easier for the masons, and increases the likelihood that the wall will be built as intended.

**8.** Even for easily cut materials, such as plywood or lattice, it is economical to work with uncut units as much as possible. An 8 ft (2400 mm) -high fence is easily covered with two uncut horizontal sheets of plywood or lattice. An 8 ft 6 in. (2600 mm) -high wall requires the addition of a narrow strip of board or lattice that takes time to cut and is not sufficiently stiff to secure the panel. A 10 ft (3000 mm) -high wall or fence can be built without waste and with a minimum of cutting, because a sheet split lengthwise can be fully utilized to make up the extra 2 ft (600 mm) of height on two fence sections (see D).

**9.** If the deck plan can be dimensioned in 2 ft multiples (600 mm), fewer deck boards will have to be cut than off module dimensions, and there will be little waste. This dimensioning scheme also minimizes waste of joist material, which is also furnished only in lengths that are multiples of 2 ft (600 mm).  ▷

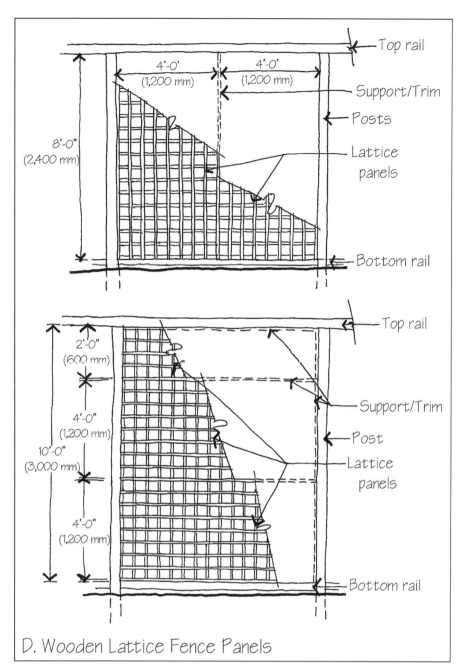

D. Wooden Lattice Fence Panels

**10.** It is almost impossible to avoid cutting in all the different materials used in a project. It is difficult to make the tiles or pavers in a patio or plaza come out to a whole number of units in all dimensions, for example. Masons and tile setters are accustomed to having to cut all the tiles around the edge of a space to meet a border or edge.

**11.** Cut edges and surfaces may not be suitable for exposure to view or to weather. Cut edges are often raw and have a different surface quality than the factory-produced condition, and they may not weather well. Concrete and brick pavers often come with a beveled edge on the finished surface. A cut surface may have a very different surface color and texture as well as casting a very different shadow pattern than whole units. Cut pavers are often limited to the edge of a field terminating in an edging or border course (see E).

**12.** Materials or products from different sources may have limited commonality regarding product dimensions. If compatible dimensions cannot be found, consider altering the design slightly to match a modular dimension. For instance, a 3 in. by 6 in. (76 × 152 mm) recessed wall light could be replaced with a 2 in. by 4 in. (50 × 100 mm) or a 4 in. by 8 in. (100 × 200 mm) unit to agree with the module of this utility-sized brick masonry. In this case, a wraparound face plate that matches the masonry opening is used. Both of these solutions are better than cutting all of the surrounding masonry units (see F). ■

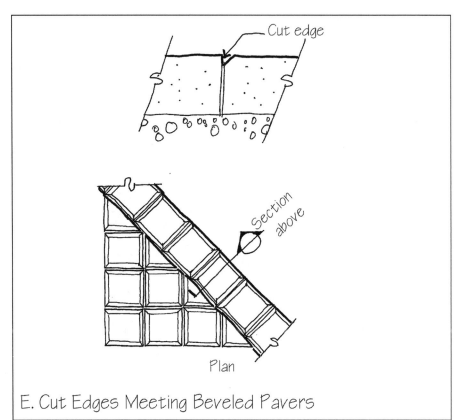

E. Cut Edges Meeting Beveled Pavers

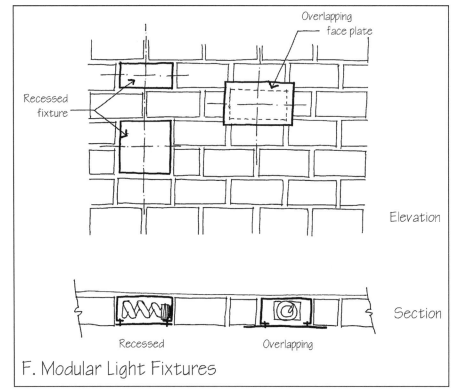

F. Modular Light Fixtures

# Minimum Number of Parts

The fewer the number of different parts a detail requires, the more efficient and trouble-free the construction process is likely to be.

**1.** A construction worker who is assembling a connection onsite needs to have all the required parts close at hand. The fewer the number of different parts there are, the less time will be spent looking for misplaced items or restocking depleted supplies and, generally, the fewer tools will be required. A carpenter erecting wooden fences needs to have at least three sizes of galvanized common nails available at all times, as well as a hammer, a tape rule, a level, square, and a pencil. All these items are carried in the pouches of a tool belt so they are always close at hand. This works out reasonably well, because the carpenter does a standardized set of operations and can rely on the tool belt as an organizer. But if a special fencing detail requires several sizes of screws as well as nails, the tool belt no longer has sufficient pouches, and the carpenter's efficiency drops off.

**2.** It is especially important to avoid parts that differ so little from one another that they can be confused easily, such as 1 in. long and 1⅛ in. long (25 and 29 mm) screws of the same diameter and head style.

**3.** A masonry wall pattern that requires three different kinds of brick and two colors of mortar would tax a mason's patience. There would not be sufficient space at the mason's workstation to keep the five different types of materials within reach, and such an elaborate pattern would present a maximum number of opportunities for errors to occur—errors that would be difficult and costly to correct.

**4.** When precast concrete panels are used to create a wall, it is better to fabricate fewer panels of larger size than to use a greater number of small panels. Large panel sizes reduce the amount of handling and coordination; the number of connections to the foundation or frame is also reduced. To avoid a monotonous appearance in elevation, the large panels can be designed with a variety of patterns or surface treatments or may incorporate fenestration systems.

**5.** A corollary to this pattern is that if there are fewer parts in a structure, then each part should perform a greater number of functions. Elements that only perform one function, unless essential, are often edited out of the design, especially when economic constraints are prominent. See *Forgiving Details* (p. 165).

**6.** One strategy to reduce the number of parts in a structure is to use prefabricated subassemblies. Construction technology is evolving toward greater use of preassembled components that are made up of smaller elements. Use of these unitized assemblies is intended to speed project completion without increasing cost or compromising quality. An example of this unitization, in its simplest form, is the shop fabrication of fence panels or fountain pump room assemblies. Using this approach, the more technically complex parts of a landscape, such as walls, rails, trellises, green wall and green roof panels, and the like may be preassembled in a shop or factory using techniques that are more specialized or precise than in the field. These parts are then transported to the site for installation. The number of parts is reduced, but each part is equipped to perform a greater range of functions (see *Factory and Site*, p. 184).

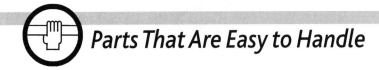
The detailer should always be conscious of the size and weight of building components, and of what will be required on the jobsite to handle them.

**1.** A standard brick takes its size, shape, and weight from the dimensions and capabilities of the human hand. A bricklayer works efficiently and comfortably by holding the trowel in one hand while lifting and placing bricks repeatedly with the other. If a substantially larger brick is specified, the bricklayer may fatigue more quickly, have muscular problems, and have difficulty in maintaining proper alignment of bricks in the wall. Many masons' unions have work rules concerning maximum weights of various kinds of bricks and blocks, and these must be taken into account.

**2.** Very small parts should be avoided, especially where the worksite might be dark, wet, windy, or cold, making it difficult to see and handle the parts. Tweezer-size parts should be avoided altogether. Finger-size parts, such as nails, screws, bolts, and nuts, are easy to handle in warm to moderate temperatures and in adequate light. Hand-size components, such as wood shingles, bricks, tiles, and groundcovers or flowers are ideal for the worker to handle. Concrete blocks, wood studs, and plywood panels, or containerized shrubs require the use of both hands, which is acceptable but less desirable because it necessitates laying down tools to lift the component. Some components take two or more people to handle: a jumbo concrete block or fieldstone, large pavers, a frame for a fence or wall, a balled and burlapped tree, or a large sheet of glass. This is reasonable in most situations. Very large sheets of glass and large plant material are challenging because of their weight

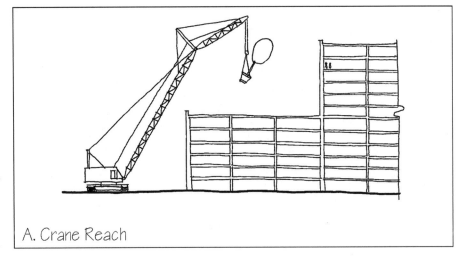

A. Crane Reach

and fragility. They may require special equipment to move safely. Components that require three or more workers are awkward and waste time. Large components can be more costly to transport. A standard trailer can only accommodate 2–3 large caliper trees, while that same trailer can accommodate dozens of smaller ones.

**3.** Hoists and cranes come in many configurations, reaches, lifting capacities, and maneuverabilities. Components requiring the use of a crane should be avoided, unless there will be a crane on the site to lift many other components as well. Sometimes, of course, it is economical or unavoidable to rent a crane to hoist a single large component into place; but such situations should be studied carefully, because crane time is expensive. In some instances, it is more economical to use a crane and large modules for a short period of time to offset smaller hand-set units over a long period of time (such as when using a large precast block retaining wall systems in lieu of smaller blocks).

**4.** Cranes and hoists must be selected and located on the site so that they are

able to lift the required components and to place them where they are wanted. This is largely the business of the contractor, but the detailer should be sure that all details that require crane lifts lie within reach of likely crane locations. Lifting materials over a lower portion of a building to reach a roof is a typical problem. Overhead power and telephone lines can also inhibit the work of a crane (see A).

**5.** Components need not be large to present material handling challenges on the jobsite. Concrete work may require the use of a pumper truck or temporary road bed for truck access. Even moving large volumes of hand-scaled components like bricks and pavers will present difficulty when site access is tight. The detailer must be aware of these challenges even when the execution of these tasks is largely the responsibility of the contractor, because access and handling impacts often lead to soil compaction and infringe upon elements the landscape architect may want to protect, such as existing trees and vegetation.

**6.** Large trees and structural components must be sized to fit available transportation modes. Highway widths and clearances govern the sizes and weights of trucks, which in turn determine the maximum sizes of trees. Oversize loads can be trucked in some situations, with accompanying cost penalties for off-hour deliveries and special police details. Barges or railroad cars can be used to carry oversize components to some waterfront and railside construction sites. Rooftop development may be accessed via elevater that can severly limit the size and weight of material to be used.

Transporting plant material may also require agricultural permits, covering to prevent drying out, or even refrigeration in very warm climates.

**7.** Ease of handling includes consideration of the possibility that parts can be inadvertently installed backward or upside down. Wedge anchor inserts that are installed in formwork before concrete is poured are useless and impossible to replace if they are installed upside down. They should be manufactured with prominent UP indications, and the detailer should make a note to pass on to the construction supervisor to check the installation of these components very carefully before concrete is poured (see B).

**8.** Where possible, detail components so that they are either symmetrical and can be installed in either direction or so that they are asymmetrical, in a way that only permits them to be installed correctly. This wall panel anchor tee cannot be installed upside down because it is symmetrical: Either way will work. If the vertical spacing between bolt holes is different from the horizontal spacing, it will also be impossible to err by installing it sideways (see C). ■

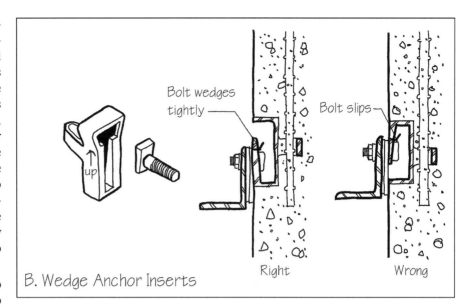

B. Wedge Anchor Inserts

Bolt wedges tightly

Bolt slips

Right

Wrong

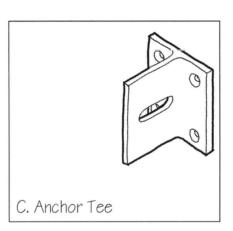

C. Anchor Tee

All other considerations being equal, details that construction workers repeat again and again are more economical and less error-prone than non-repeating details.

**1.** Special conditions often lead to errors in construction. A reinforced concrete wall in which all of the rebars are the same size, with one exception, is likely to end up with the special rebar in the wrong place. For this reason, rebars are often engineered to be all the same size, even if this means a slight diseconomy in weight of steel. The same principle applies to deck and wall framing members (see A).

**2.** It is easiest and least error-prone for bricklayers to lay continuous facings of running bond, and this is all that most walls require them to do. Unfortunately, running bond has little character, and bricklayers often enjoy a challenge to their craftsmanship more than the boredom of unrelieved repetition. When designing brickwork patterns that use corbeled, recessed, or different colored bricks, try to design patterns that are repetitious in their variety, so that the bricklayer can easily learn the pattern and keep track of what is going on. One can get variety through varying one aspect of the material. A single size brick can be used and a contrasting color can provide interest. Highly intricate or irregular patterns require that the mason refer constantly to the drawings. This takes time and can lead to errors that are difficult and expensive to correct.

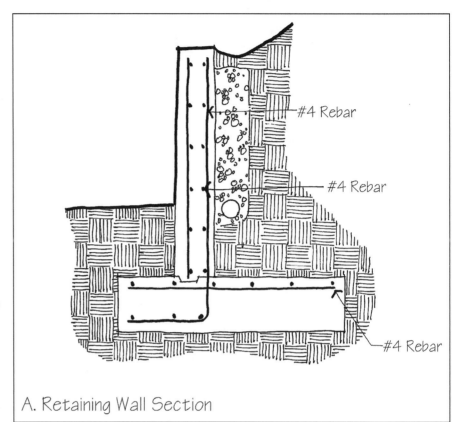

#4 Rebar

#4 Rebar

#4 Rebar

A. Retaining Wall Section

**3.** Formwork construction accounts for a very large share of the cost of site-cast concrete structures. The easiest and least expensive forms to build are level, continuous, uninterrupted surfaces of plywood. This is why gravity or cantilevered walls are usually the most economical system for most landscapes and counterfort walls are rarely used (see B).

**4.** This pattern is especially important when the project schedule or budget is constrained. It may be less important in a very small project, where almost everything is uniquely made, and where efficiency of means is not a high priority. Repetitious assembly might also be less critical in the relatively rare case in which mass-customization techniques are being used, in which digitally controlled mechanisms in a shop or factory are used to quickly and accurately produce many slightly varied products, such as custom cut steel fence panels. ■

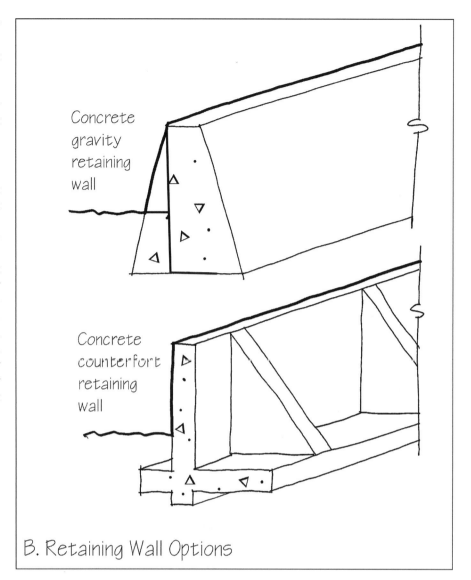

Concrete gravity retaining wall

Concrete counterfort retaining wall

B. Retaining Wall Options

# Simulated Assemblies

Build representative samples of challenging or unusual details to simulate the construction processes and to reveal the qualities of the finished product. The sample is the dress rehearsal of the intended landscape assembly.

**1.** Simulating the construction of landscape assemblies helps to avoid costly and difficult removal of unsatisfactory work, and establishes acceptable standards of appearance and workmanship. This is especially important when materials or construction techniques are innovative, unfamiliar to the builder, or dependent on a particular quality of workmanship.

**2.** Much of the flow of information in a project is from the landscape architect to the contractor. The simulated assembly allows the contractor to demonstrate what the result will be, at minimal cost. It is also a vehicle for the contractor to suggest changes to the details that can improve the constructability, durability or decrease cost. It is an excellent vehicle to bring expectations of landscape architects, contractors, and owners into convergence. Once accepted, the simulated assembly sets

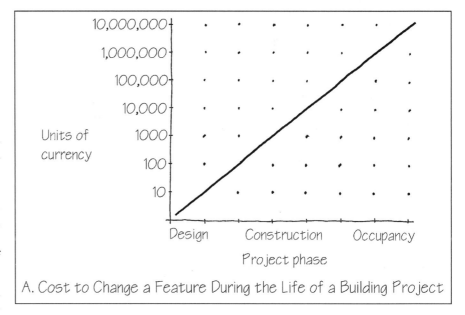

A. Cost to Change a Feature During the Life of a Building Project

the standard for quality of work and appearance. It should be left safely on the site for the duration of the project, serving as a record of many qualitative features that are difficult to describe through drawings or specifications.

**3.** Changes in a detail are easiest and least expensive to make early in the design process, and they are most

difficult and costly when part of the finished project. Costs of changes escalate steeply at each stage in the design and construction process. Erasing a sketch is much easier and cheaper than jackhammering concrete. Simulated assemblies help identify areas where changes are needed before they become part of the finished landscape (see A).

**4.** A sample panel may be used to demonstrate the exposed appearance and workmanship of the detail or assembly. Typically, a sample panel is for the appearance of the work (such as paving and wall finishes) and a mock up is a simulation of the workings of a component (such as a fountain or light fixture). The materials, colors, textures, joints, and accessories intended for the walls or pavements are used in the sample panel. It may be free-standing constructions, apart from the rest of the finished assemblies, or may be the first portion of the actual construction. Sometimes multiple free-standing samples can be prepared, each revealing a variation in material or finish, to give the best possible basis for final selection (see B).

**5.** A mockup assembly may be used for more complex details or assemblies. It demonstrates appearance and workmanship, as with the sample panel, but it also shows critical features within the construction. In integrated paving, site furniture, and lighting schemes, constructibility and ease of maintenance can be demonstrated. These features can be observed and potential technical performance can be assessed, using experimental testing if necessary. For instance, a mockup of a fountain weir can be used to test the actual flow of water to determine the optimum flow

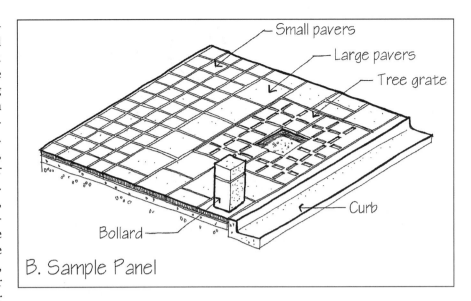

B. Sample Panel

— Small pavers
— Large pavers
— Tree grate
— Curb
Bollard —

rates, edge condition, and drip effectiveness, or a custom lighting fixture can be tested in the dark and in various weather conditions to assure that it will function as intended.

**6.** The sample panel or mockup assembly usually includes the intended finishes, such as paint, caulk, and mortar tooling profiles. These finishes should also be cleaned or power-washed, just as the actual project will be, because these processes sometimes alter their final appearance. For project additions or renovation/restoration projects, the simulated assembly allows

for accurate comparisons of new and existing conditions.

**7.** In most projects, crews composed of several tradespeople, each with different experience and skills, carry out the installation of the project. The simulated assembly establishes a common standard of workmanship; it is a reference for the workers to minimize variation due to differences in techniques. This is especially important when freehand finishing techniques are used, such as brick or stone masonry, stucco, or a textured concrete slab. ■

# Observable Assemblies

Critical details in an assembly should be observable when they are built. Subgrade materials must be verified to be uniformly compacted prior to the installation of finish pavements; irrigation systems should be observed and tested for leaks prior to backfilling; direct bury cables should be tested for electrical continuity before completion; roof decks must be tested and secured as watertight prior to building over the waterproofing.

**1.** The detailer should design assemblies that can be built from their structural substrate toward the exposed finished surfaces, so that the materials and their connections are visible at each stage of completion. A contractor can better control the quality of the work if it can be seen while being installed. This is not a problem in most construction processes, but in others it is very difficult to achieve.

**2.** It is difficult to observe fluid materials when they are incorporated into rigid assemblies. Examples include casting concrete into formwork, and the grouting of cells in concrete masonry. Is the fluid material located where it was meant to be and not elsewhere? Small openings or inspection ports in the rigid assembly could make those critical areas observable to the builder during installation. The port may be a small hole in the facing material or a void made by omitting one of the facing elements such as a masonry unit. After the assembly is substantially complete and inspection reveals no problems, the inspection port can be closed to match surrounding surfaces.

**3.** Critical details sometimes become concealed soon after they are installed, and they may be vulnerable to harm by subsequent construction activities. For example, weep holes in built-in light

fixtures must be clear so that water can drain, but they may become clogged by debris or mortar crumbs as a wall is built around them. If the fixture is installed within a housing, the weep holes can be examined and debris can be removed prior to installing the fixture within the housing. Sleeves for irrigation and lighting are often placed prior to much heavy construction and can be crushed rendering them unusable. An examination of the sleeve systems by pulling a string through the openings is a good check prior to the installation of finished paving. Electrical connections are often made within a manhole or handhole to allow for those connections to be observed and to allow for easy access if repairs are required. ■

It is important to detail in such a way that workers can reach the work easily.

**1.** For maximum comfort and productivity, a worker should be standing on a level, secure surface, working between waist height and shoulder height, within a couple of feet of the front of the body. This ideal is readily achieved in a factory, but it is more difficult to achieve on a construction site. Overhead work is fatiguing, as is work that requires stooping or squatting. Excessive reaches are bad, because they put the worker dangerously off balance. They are also likely to result in less-than-perfect workmanship.

**2.** Avoid creating apparently logical details that cannot be assembled because of accessibility problems. This innocent-looking detail for attaching cladding panels to a masonry backup wall will not work, because there is no way for a worker to insert the screws into the lower edge of a panel (see A).

**3.** Avoid connections that lie behind columns, in sharp inside corners, or in reentrant corners. These positions are difficult to reach, if they can be reached at all. In tight locations such as these, be sure that the worker can not only reach the connection but also has space for the hammer, wrench, or screwdriver that must be used to make the connection. The worker should also be able to see the connection rather than have to work by "feel".

**4.** Connections may also need to be accessible for maintenance, renovation, or deconstruction at the end of the element's useful life. This is especially important when elements are expected to have a useful life that is shorter than that of the structure they are tied to, such as lighting systems and irrigation lines.

**5.** Make critical subgrade connections accessible to workers by creating vaults or manholes at the connections, making it easier and safer for workers to install and maintain them, as well as minimizing the damage to a finished landscape if repairs are needed. ■

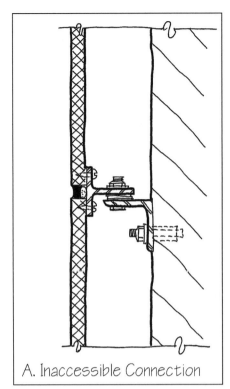

A. Inaccessible Connection

Every component needs a little extra space in addition to its own dimensions.

**1.** Any component that has to be installed between two other components needs a small amount of additional room so that it can be maneuvered into place. Cast iron drainage grates are always cast slightly smaller than the frame which they will reside; if they were not, they would bind during insertion and would be almost impossible to install or remove (see A).

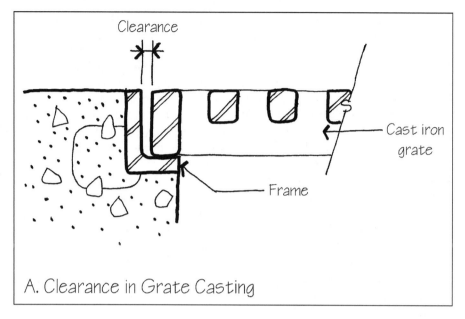

A. Clearance in Grate Casting

**2.** Recessed light fixture housings are large enough to allow for installation and adjustment. The housing is built or cast into the wall structure and the light fixture can then be adjusted within the housing to lay flush against the finished wall surface (see B).

**3.** In post and rail fences, the posts are drilled through to allow for an adjustment of the rails at each post. In addition, the holes are a little oversized to allow for racking the rail sections to accommodate for sloping terrain (see C). ∎

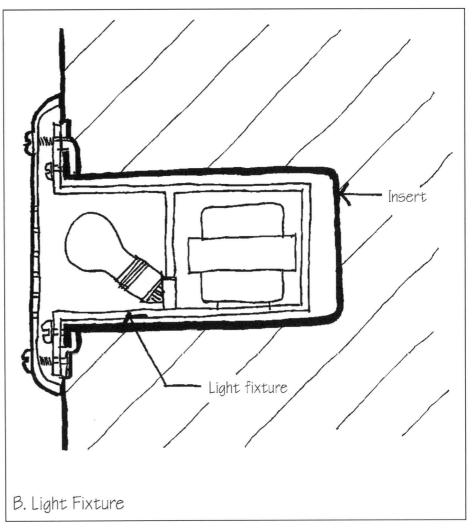

B. Light Fixture

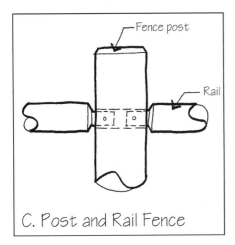

C. Post and Rail Fence

A landscape should be detailed so its various parts and systems mesh smoothly in three dimensions. This requires the detailer to create reserved zones for each of the systems.

**1.** In the usual project organization for a streetscape, the structural base is designed by one professional, the utility systems by others, and the irrigation, underdrainage planting surface finishes, and street furniture by still others. Coordination is necessary to avoid a situation in which a tree root ball, a duct bank or conduit, drainage line, irrigation pipe, and/or foundation, are all planned to occupy the same space (see *Vertical Chase*, p. 108 and *Horizontal Distribution*, p. 110).

**2.** Coordination of utilities is often difficult. Utility plans are often schematic in nature and notoriously short on detail. The sketchy nature of most utility plans leads many contractors to use the plans as general guidelines to placement and not to be taken literally. This makes coordination difficult if not impossible. Locations and elevations of utility lines and structures that are designed to accommodate future plantings or hardscape elements are often disregarded. Care must be taken at the planning stage and even more importantly during construction to assure that utilities are located in their proper places. Many cities have staff engineers that designate particular zones for each type of service line in the underground layers. This is done to minimize conflict between the service lines initially (see A).

**3.** Wall cladding or fencing that runs in its own zone outside the columns is much easier to detail and to install than cladding that is interrupted by each framing members. For example, chainlink fence fabric is easier and cheaper to stretch over a frame between end or corner posts than to install as separate panels between line posts (see B).

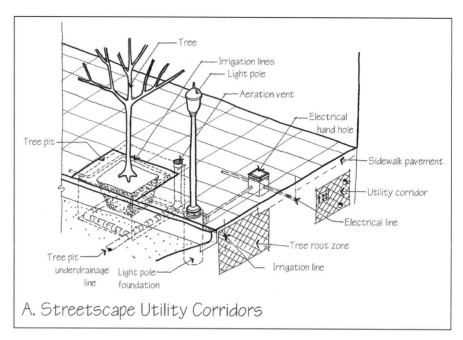

A. Streetscape Utility Corridors

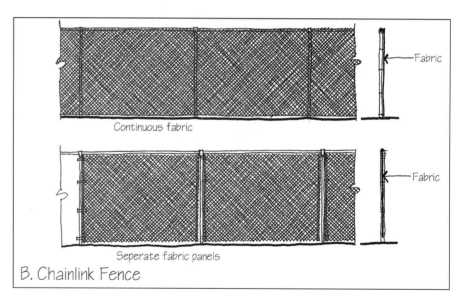

B. Chainlink Fence

**4.** Rooftop pedestal paving systems provide a similar zone between the paving surface and the structural roof deck through which power and irrigation networks can be easily distributed. This makes them easy to install and consequently less expensive. Both zones are readily accessible for maintenance or replacement. ∎

**11 Forgiving Details**

The ability to create forgiving details is among the most rewarding skills of the detailer. A forgiving detail is one that always furnishes a way for a worker to deal easily with inaccuracies or mistakes. Most traditional details are very forgiving of inaccuracies and mistakes, because they evolved over a period of many years, gradually incorporating features that made them easier and more convenient for workers.

When inventing new details, the designer should pay particular attention to avoiding features that would "trap" the worker if they are not applied perfectly. Remember that even skilled craftspeople do not work with machine-like accuracy. Also remember that if a detailer forces a design on builders whom he or she knows are not sufficiently skilled or trained to do the job, then the detailer is the one to blame for the poor result. You cannot expect A+ results from C− workers. The same principle applies to the use of industrial processes;

the detailer must know their limits and work within them. Details should be attractive and functional, but they should also be practical in the reality of the project's construction processes.

A handful of patterns for designing forgiving details can help the designer avoid these mistakes. They are as follows:

A dimensional tolerance is a maximum amount by which a dimension can be expected to vary from the intended measurement because of normal inaccuracies in manufacture and installation.

**1.** There is a tolerance associated implicitly with every dimension on a set of drawings. These tolerances have a direct effect on how details are designed. Tolerances are needed because of thermal and moisture movement, structural settlement and deflection, workmanship, and other factors. This pattern is especially important in walls or paving areas composed of large prefabricated components, where "cut to fit" methods are not used.

Tolerances are based on material properties and construction methods, not by the capacity to measure accurately. Laser and global positioning system (GPS) surveying instruments are far more accurate than most construction methods. Tolerances cannot accommodate careless measurement, nor can they be eliminated by measuring very accurately.

**2.** This base plate for a steel light pole is not attached directly to the top of a concrete footing, because, although the footing cannot be perfectly flat or very precisely located, the light pole always must be plumb and often its horizontal location can be critical. Instead, the base plate is located and leveled on shims or leveling nuts above the top of the footing, and the space between is filled with grout. This provides a tolerance vertically for the expected imprecision of the footing.

Obviously, it is important that the top of the footing not be higher than the bottom of the base plate. At least 1 in. (25 mm) of clearance must be provided for the insertion of grout. With regard to the bottom of the base plate, therefore, the top of the footing might be dimensioned to lie between 1 and 2 in. (25 and 51 mm) lower. Thus, there is a vertical dimensional tolerance of 1 in. (25 mm) within which the installers of

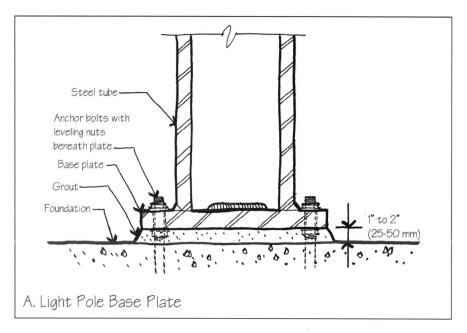

A. Light Pole Base Plate

the footing can work. This is reasonable for this type of work.

To avoid problems in the horizontal plane, a plywood template is used to position the light pole's anchor bolts in the concrete footing. This template is often made from the same shop drawing used by the steel fabricator to make the column base, virtually assuring a match (see A).

**3.** Every trade and craft has its normal level of precision. Precision inside an irrigation impact head is very high; precision in pouring a concrete footing or driving a pile into the earth is very low. Good detailing takes into account the normal tolerances for dimensional inaccuracy in each phase of construction.

Table 11-1 gives a small sampling of accepted industry standard tolerances for different materials and systems. Every detail of a landscape should respect these tolerances. From this table, we see that it is considered acceptable for a conventional concrete base slab to be out of line by as much as ¾ in. (19 mm) above or below the specified line. It is evident that we cannot mortar pavers directly to the base with a consistent 3/8 in. (10 mm) joint that is typical of joints between the side edges of pavers and set the pasess a true line. A mortar setting bed for pavers

is usually over 1 in. (25 mm) deep to allow for the imperfections in the base slab. The base slab is poured to allow 1″ (+/- ¾″) below the finish grade of the pavers. If there are sections of the base slab that are at the maximum allowable elevation, there will still be ¼″ of depth between the bottom of the paver and the slab for the mortar setting bed. Stone or precast wall cladding installed over a concrete backer wall should be installed in a plane that lies at least 1 in. (25 mm) outside the face of the concrete backer wall, and a more generous distance than this would be wise, considering that concrete backer walls are not always built to accepted tolerances. In actual practice, a cladding installer measures the faces of a wall with great precision before beginning work and establishes planes for the cladding that will clear the largest bulges on each face. The cladding attachment details must provide for a range of dimensional adjustment, using such devices as shims and slotted fastener holes that allow for these tolerance dimensions (see *Adjustable Fit*, p. 172).

If greater than normal precision is required in a particular project, then it must be clearly specified in the contract documents.

**TABLE 11-1: A Sampling of Accepted Dimensional Tolerances in U.S. Construction**

**Survey Stakes for Layout and Grading per NSPS (National Society of Professional Surveyors – Model Standards of Practice)**

| | | |
|---|---|---|
| Urban property line | ± 0.07 (⅞″)ft. + 50 PPM(Parts per million) | ± 21 mm, + 50 PPM |
| Suburban property line | ± 0.13 ft. (1 ½″)+ 100 PPM | ± 40 mm, + 100 PPM |
| Rural property line | ± 0.26 ft. (3 ⅛″)+ 200 PPM | ± 79 mm, + 200 PPM |
| Rough grade | ± 0.20 ft.(2 ⅜″) | ± 60 mm, |
| Finish grade | ± 0.05 ft. (⅝″) | ± 15 mm, |

**Asphalt**

| | | |
|---|---|---|
| Pedestrian paving variation from a straightedge perpendicular to CL | ±¼ in. in 10′ | ±6 mm, in 3000 mm |
| Pedestrian paving variation from a straightedge parallel to CL (centerline) | ±⅛ in. in 10′ | ±3 mm, in 3000 mm |
| Pedestrian paving running slope | 1% slope ±⅛ in. | 1% slope ±3 mm, |
| Pedestrian paving cross slope | 2% slope ±¼ in | 2% slope ±6 mm, |
| Thickness surface course | ±¼ in. | ±6 mm, |
| Thickness base course | ±½ in. | ±13 mm, |

**Concrete**

| | | |
|---|---|---|
| Pedestrian paving | ±¼ in, in 10′ | ±6 mm, in 3000 mm |
| Concrete steps riser or tread length | ± 3/16 in. | ±5 mm |
| Pedestrian paving running slope | 1% ±⅛ in, in 10″ | ±3 mm, in 3000 mm |
| Pedestrian paving cross slope | 2% ±¼ in., in 10′ | ±6 mm, in 3000 mm |
| Slab on grade variation from a straightedge – conventional (90% compliant) | ±½ in, in 10′ | ±13 mm, in 3000 mm |
| Slab on grade variation from a straightedge – conventional (100% compliant) | ± ¾ in, in 10′ | ±19 mm, in 3000 mm |
| Slab on grade variation from a straightedge – moderately flat (90% compliant) | ± ⅜ in, in 10′ | ±10 mm, in 3000 mm |
| Slab on grade variation from a straightedge – moderately flat (100% compliant) | ± ⅝ in, in 10′ | ±16 mm, in 3000 mm |
| Slab on grade variation from a straightedge – flat (90% compliant) | ±¼ in, in 10′ | ±6 mm, in 3000 mm |
| Slab on grade variation from a straightedge – flat (100% compliant) | ±⅜ in, in 10′ | ±10 mm, in 3000 mm |
| Construction and control joint locations | ± ¾ in. | ±19 mm |
| Vertical control joint locations 2″ or less | ± ⅛ in. | ±3 mm |
| Vertical control joint locations 2″ – 12″ | ± ¼ in. | ±6 mm |
| Expansion joint locations | ± ¾ in. | ±19 mm |
| Dimension of footing | –½ in., +2 in. | –13 mm, +51 mm |
| Anchor bolt placement | ±¼ in, vertical | ±6 mm, vertical |
| Anchor bolt placement ¾″ (19), 7/8″ (22) | ±¼ in, horizontal | ±6 mm, horizontal |
| Anchor bolt placement 1″ (25) – 1½″ (38) | ±⅜ in, horizontal | ±10 mm, horizontal |
| Anchor bolt placement 1 ¾″(44) – 2½″ (64) | ±½ in, horizontal | ±13 mm, horizontal |
| Squareness of residential foundation | ½ in. in 20 ft | 1:500 |
| Plumbness of wall | ±¼ in. in 10 ft | 1:500 |
| Variation of wall from line in plan | ±1 in. | ±25 mm |
| Variation in wall thickness | –¼ in., +½ in. | –6.35 mm, +12.7 mm ▷ |

**TABLE 11-1:** (*continued*)

**Precast Concrete Fabrication**

| | | |
|---|---|---|
| Pavers length and width | ±¹⁄₁₆ in. | ±1.6 mm |
| Pavers depth | ± ¹⁄₈ in. | ±3.2 mm |
| Pavers warping | ± ¹⁄₃₂ in. per foot | ±0.75 mm per 33 mm |
| Precast panels (ht and width up to 10′) | ± ¹⁄₈ in. | ±3.2 mm |
| Precast panels (variation from square) | ± ¹⁄₈ in. per 6′ | ±3 mm per 2000 mm |
| Precast panels (bowing) | length/360   max.1 in. | length/360   max.25 mm |
| Benches, bollards, etc. (ht. or length) | ± ¹⁄₄ in. | ±6 mm |
| Benches, bollards, etc. (dia. or width) | ± ¹⁄₄ in. | ±6 mm |
| Benches, bollards, etc. (loc of inserts) | ± ¹⁄₄ in. | ±6 mm |

**Precast Concrete Installation**

| | | |
|---|---|---|
| Architectural precast panels relative to design line or adjacent panel | ± ¹⁄₄ in. | ±6 mm |

**Structural Steel Fabrication**

Mill tolerances vary with shape and size of member. The designer should check the tolerances with the fabricator.

**Structural Steel Installation**

| | | |
|---|---|---|
| Plumbness of columns upto 20 stories tall shall not exceed 1:500 and the following | 1 in. toward or 2 in. away from structure | 25 mm toward or 50 mm away from structure line |
| Architecturally exposed structural steel beam elevations relative to design level | ⁵⁄₁₆ in. above and ³⁄₁₆ below design level | 8 mm above and 5 mm below design level |

**Granite, Marble, and Limestone Fabrication**

| | | |
|---|---|---|
| Face dimension | ±¹⁄₁₆ in. | ±1.6 mm |
| Thickness ¾″ – 1 ⁵⁄₈″ (20 – 41 mm) | ±¹⁄₈ in. | ±3 mm |
| Thickness greater than 1 ⁵⁄₈″ (41 mm) | ±¹⁄₄ in. | ±6 mm |
| Deviation from square | ±¹⁄₁₆ in. | ±1.6 mm |
| Flatness of face honed finish | ± ¹⁄₁₆ in. | ±1.6 mm |
| Flatness of face sawn finish | ± ¹⁄₈ in. | ±3.2 mm |
| Flatness of face thermal finish | ± ³⁄₁₆ in. | ±4.8 mm |

**Granite, Marble, and Limestone Wall and Column Installation**

| | | |
|---|---|---|
| Deviations from plumb | ±¹⁄₄ in. in 10' | ±6 mm in 3050mm |
| Deviations from level | ±¹⁄₂ in. in 20' | ±13 mm in 6100mm |

**Masonry Pavement and Wall Installation**

| | | |
|---|---|---|
| Brick paver dim. type PS less than 3″ | ±¹⁄₈ in. | ±3.2 mm |
| Brick paver dim. type PS over 3″ to 5″ | ±³⁄₁₆ in. | ±4.7 mm |
| Brick paver dim. type PS over 5″ to 8″ | ±¹⁄₄ in. | ±6.4 mm |
| Brick paver dim. type PS over 8″ | ±⁵⁄₁₆ in. | ±7.9 mm |
| Brick paver distortion type PS under 8″ | ±³⁄₁₆ in. | ±2.4 mm |
| Concrete block length, width and depth | ±¹⁄₈ in. | ±3.2 mm |
| Concrete block deviation from square | ±¹⁄₁₆ in. | ±1.6 mm |

**TABLE 11-1:** (*continued*)

| | | |
|---|---|---|
| Face brick dim. type FBX less than 3″ | ±$\frac{1}{16}$ in. | ±1.6 mm |
| Face brick dim. type FBX over 3″ to 4″ | ±$\frac{3}{32}$ in. | ±2.4 mm |
| Face brick dim. type FBX over 4″ to 6″ | ±$\frac{1}{8}$ in. | ±3.2 mm |
| Face brick dim. type FBX over 6″ to 8″ | ±$\frac{5}{32}$ in. | ±4.0 mm |
| Face brick dim. type FBX over 8″ to 12″ | ±$\frac{7}{32}$ in. | ±5.6 mm |
| Face brick dim. type FBX over 12″ | ±$\frac{9}{32}$ in. | ±7.1 mm |
| Face brick distortion type FBX under 8″ | ±$\frac{1}{16}$ in. | ±1.6 mm |
| **Masonry Wall Fabrication** | | |
| Out of plumb or top of wall | ±$\frac{1}{4}$ in. in 10 ft | ±6.4 in 3m |
| Column and Wall widths | +$\frac{1}{2}$ in. - $\frac{1}{4}$ in. | + 12.7 mm - 6.4 mm |
| Deviation from plan location | ±$\frac{1}{2}$ in. in 20 ft (3/4" max.) | ±1:500 |

aThese values are excerpted from a number of standard industry sources. A full display of construction industry tolerances is a book in itself; consult publications of individual industry associations for tolerances for each material. A consolidated summary of accepted industry tolerances is available in David Ballast's *Handbook of Construction Tolerances*; see *Detailer's Reference Shelf* in Appendix 241.

**4.** Where dimensional tolerances accumulate from a set of assembled components, each with its own individual tolerance, an overall tolerance can be calculated by taking the square root of the sum of the squares of the individual tolerances.

If, for example, a section of paving is made up of ten precast concrete planks, with each plank having a tolerance of ±$\frac{1}{8}$ in. (3 mm), and a drain assembly (frame and grate) with a tolerance of ±$\frac{1}{16}$ in. (1.5 mm), the overall dimensional tolerance for one bay is figured as follows:

Overall Tolerance: $= \sqrt{(1/8) + (1/8) + (1/8) + (1/8) + (1/8) + (1/8) + (1/8) + (1/8) + (1/8) + (1/8) + (1/16)}$

$= +/- \ 0.400 \ \text{in.} \ (13/32'')$

Overall Tolerance: $= \sqrt{(3) + (3) + (3) + (3) + (3) + (3) + (3) + (3) + (3) + (3) + (1.5)}$

$= +/- \ 16.5 \ \text{mm}$

**5.** Large components require greater tolerances, especially if they are difficult to alter at the construction site. For example, large precast or cut stone pavers require significantly larger tolerances for joint width and finish grade than a brick or small precast pavers. The same is true of large stone or precast wall panels and brick walls with regard to plumbness. This is because a brick pavement is composed of very

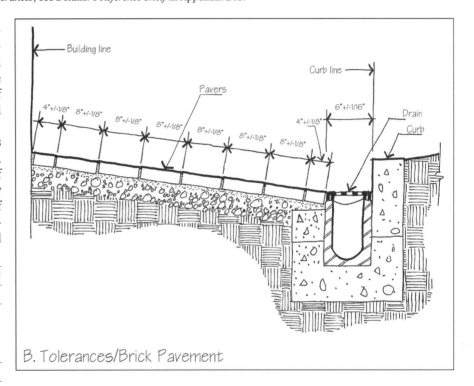

B. Tolerances/Brick Pavement

small pieces; each paver presents an opportunity for correcting the alignment so as to come close to the ideal. Large units limit those opportunities (see B).

**6.** If greater than normal precision is required in a particular project, then it must be clearly specified in the contract documents. Calling for closer tolerances than standard trade practices will likely increase costs. Extraordinarily close tolerances will also result in more elements being discarded or installed work being removed.

**7.** Designers and contractors should collaborate prior to construction to review acceptable tolerances for all stages of construction. When conflicts occur or when tolerances are exceeded, they should again collaborate to find a solution. It is not acceptable to quietly disregard functional features of a detail, such as an expansion joint that is too wide or too narrow, thinking that it is sufficient if it has an acceptable finish appearance. The design needs to work on both functional and aesthetic levels.

■

# Sliding Fit

One of the easiest, most forgiving dimensional relationships between two components is a sliding fit, in which one component overlaps another and can be positioned merely by sliding.

**1.** Overlapping shingles on a wall or fence exemplify a sliding fit. Many wood trim details use a sliding fit to avoid difficult alignment problems. A wood baseboard is installed to cover the ragged gap between the bottom of a picket fence and paved surfaces. A single-piece baseboard works well if the fence and ground surfaces are perfectly flat, but this is seldom the case. The baseboard is simply too stiff to bend into the shallow spots of the fence and pavement. A traditional interior three-piece baseboard addresses this problem by adding two thin, flexible moldings: a cap to hug the contours of the wall and a shoe to mold itself to the floor. The cap and shoe combine, using a sliding fit against the baseboard, to provide the flexibility to adjust to undulating contours. This system is rarely used outside due to the potential for rot where wood members are in contact with the ground, but the lower shoe molding can be replaced with a reveal (see *Reveal*, p. 174) to achieve a similar result. The installer simply slides the base over the pickets until it approximates a line parallel to the pavers, and then secures it to the rear rail (see A).

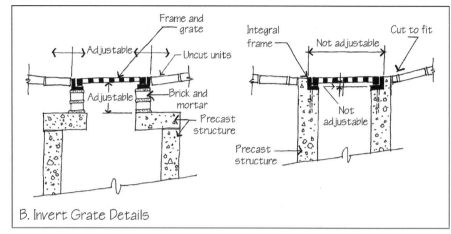

B. Invert Grate Details

**2.** A cast iron frame and grate set over a precast drainage structure is an example of a sliding fit. The frame and grate is installed with the surrounding paving long after the precast base structure is installed. It can slide (and be adjusted vertically) to meet the grades required and to match the paver module (see *Uncut Units*, p. 150). This is not possible with a single-piece unit (see B).

**3.** In general, a sliding fit involves aligning a component to two adjacent, perpendicular planes. The shingle is aligned to the surface plane of the next lower course of shingles and to a perpendicular plane that intersects the course line of the shingle. The baseboard aligns to the vertical plane of the wall and the horizontal plane of the floor. These are all easy fits.

When a third adjacent plane of alignment is added, the problem of fitting becomes more difficult. If the three planes are accurately perpendicular to one another and if the component to be fitted is perfectly square, the fit is easy. However, if there is inaccuracy anywhere in the relationship, the component will have to be trimmed to fit.

If the third plane of alignment is opposite to one of the other planes rather than adjacent, the fitting problem is even more difficult.

When fourth and fifth planes of alignment are added, the fitting problem becomes acute. These situations should be avoided (see C).

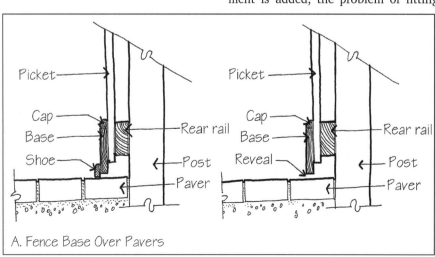

A. Fence Base Over Pavers

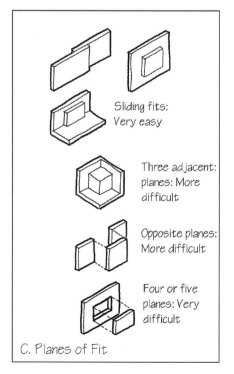

C. Planes of Fit

170    PART 1 ■ DETAIL PATTERNS

**4.** Butt-jointed stone veneer wall panels represent a potentially difficult five-plane fit. It is extremely important that the panels be manufactured to dimension, be square, and be flat within very narrow tolerances. This is generally feasible, because they are made in a factory using precision fixtures and machines.

In attaching the panels to the wall, freedom of alignment in all three axes (X, Y, and Z) must be provided by the connectors (see *Adjustable Fit, p.* 172). This allows the panels to be aligned easily to the same plane, to level, to plumb, and to horizontal and vertical dimension. The width of the joint that surrounds each panel and separates it from its neighbors must be sufficient to allow for any expected deviation in dimension and alignment (see *Joints and Gaskets,* p. 45).

**5.** The common method of mounting large panels of glass into a railing system makes them much easier to fit than cladding panels, because, in reality, they align only to one plane—the plane of the gaskets against which they are placed. The four edges of each light have a sliding fit into the mullions and against the gaskets, allowing for fairly large tolerances in dimension and squareness (see D).

**6.** A valve box cover assembly incorporates a sliding fit to allow the base of the assembly to be placed precisely over the valve and the top section to be set at finish grade. The sliding fit also protects the valve from damage due to impact. Any impact on the top section is taken up in the sliding joint and not transferred to the lower section and damage the pipe or valve (see E).

**7.** A stair made up of stone or precast units that overlap one another can be easily adjusted by sliding the units as they overlap to achieve the required tread dimensions (see F). ∎

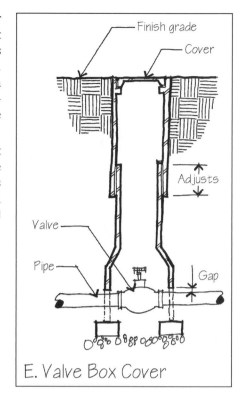

E. Valve Box Cover

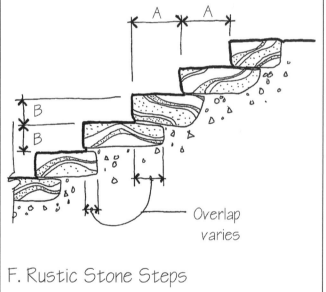

F. Rustic Stone Steps

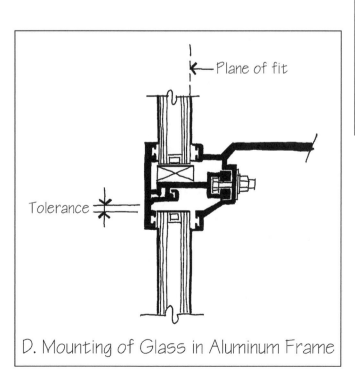

D. Mounting of Glass in Aluminum Frame

Because of the impossibility of maintaining perfect dimensional accuracy in construction, every site component that must be positioned accurately should be detailed so that its alignment can be adjusted during and after assembly.

**1.** This manufactured light fixture is adjustable in three directions. The base plate is shimmed to level the plate and bring it to the required elevation. The yoke rotates around the center screw to allow for angular adjustments (in plan) and the fixture itself rotates within the yoke to allow for aiming the light above a horizontal plane (see A).

**2.** Anchor bolts in concrete are difficult to place with precision and are often out of alignment in two axes. This manufactured metal post base responds to the problem by providing a very large hole, together with an even larger washer in which the bolt hole is off center (eccentric). This allows for adjustment in two axes. If the height of the top of the concrete (the third axis) is inaccurate, steel shims or grout could be used beneath the post base. Usually, however, the wooden post that will be installed in the metal base itself is cut a bit shorter or longer, as required (see B).

**3.** This wedge insert and askew-head bolt allow for vertical adjustment of the location of a steel shelf angle used to support a masonry facing on a concrete backer wall. The inner face of the outer wall of the insert and the head of the bolt comprise an opposing pair of wedges that lock securely together against a downward load in any vertical position.

In case the wedge insert does not align exactly in the horizontal plane with the prepunched hole in the shelf angle, the hole is punched as a horizontal slot. The horizontal orientation of the slot allows the shelf angle to transfer gravity loads directly to the bolt shank without slipping, regardless of the exact position of the bolt in the slot.

A third axis of adjustment is provided by the insertion of steel or plastic shims

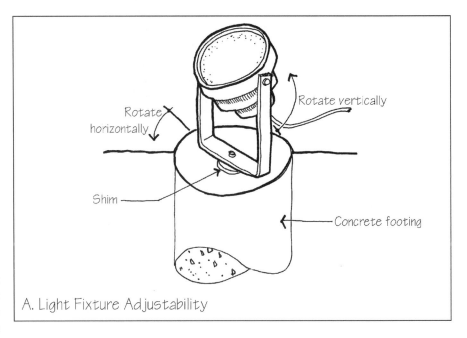

A. Light Fixture Adjustability

of various thicknesses between the shelf angle and the face of the concrete. The shims are horseshoe-shaped so that they will stay in place before the bolt is tightened.

By combining the wedge insert, the slotted hole, and the shims, a connection detail with triaxial adjustment has been created to reconcile the relatively large dimensional tolerances of a concrete backer wall with the closer tolerances of finish brick wall surface. Similar connection details are used to attach shelf angles to steel framing (see C).

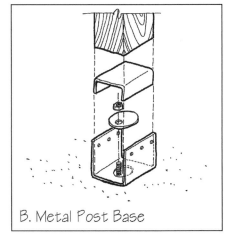

B. Metal Post Base

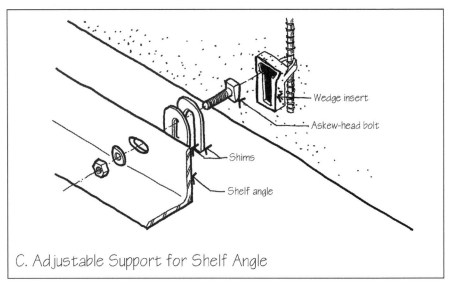

C. Adjustable Support for Shelf Angle

**4.** This is a simple triaxial detail for fastening a stone or concrete panel to the face of a wall. Shims between the slab and the angle clip allow for vertical adjustment. In-and-out adjustment comes from the slotted hole in the base of the clip. Lateral adjustment in the plane of the cladding is provided by the horizontally slotted hole in the vertical leg of the clip. Notice again that the slots are oriented so that they do not compromise the load-carrying security of the connection. It would be a mistake to provide for vertical adjustment by using a vertically slotted hole in the vertical leg of the clip, because this might allow the bolt to slip under gravity loading (see D).

**5.** A covered joint allows for an adjustment in fit at every joint. In a board and batten fence, each joint between the fence boards is covered with a smaller batten board. The joint remains covered over a large range of movement in the fence boards, and the battens can cover a large discrepancy in board width (see E). ■

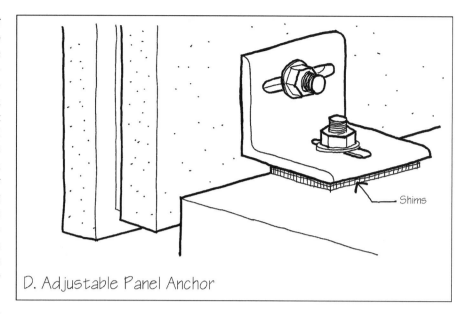

D. Adjustable Panel Anchor

Shims

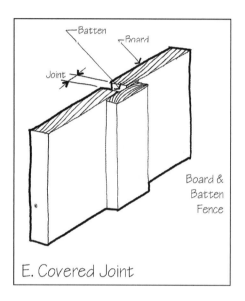

E. Covered Joint

Batten

Board

Joint

Board &
Batten
Fence

 *Reveal*

A reveal is a recess or offset between two pieces of material where they come together. Its function can be to avoid having to make an exact alignment or meet an exact dimension, to cast a shadow line for compositional purposes, or to cast a shadow line that hides minor defects in workmanship.

Carpenters work against heavy odds to create attractive, well-crafted trim: The surfaces being trimmed are often out of plumb, out of level, out of dimension, and wavy. The lumber with which he or she works is often slightly crooked or warped, even out of dimension, and it will change dimension constantly during the life of the structure in response to changes in humidity. These factors make it inadvisable to ask a carpenter to create a flush edge where two planes of trim come together. If a small but significant reveal is included in the detail, slight misalignments, crooks, and moisture movements will seldom be noticed, because they will merely change the dimension of the reveal but not the presence of the reveal. Slender reveals demand more consistent materials and installation than wider reveals. If a flush detail is insisted upon, it will be more expensive to make, and it will be perfectly and reliably flush only at the instant that it is completed, before moisture expansion and contraction begin to take effect.

**1.** A reveal of another type can be used to create a shadow line that conceals imperfections in a joint. In this example, the rabbeted edge of the cap forms a reveal and becomes the apparent joint. A similar detail is often used with a precast or stone wall coping (see A).

**2.** Reveals also work well at joints and exterior corners of stone and concrete facings, both to create shadow lines for compositional purposes and to disguise joinery that may be less than perfect. For another kind of reveal often used in this type of situation, see the quirk miter illustrated on page 177 (see B).

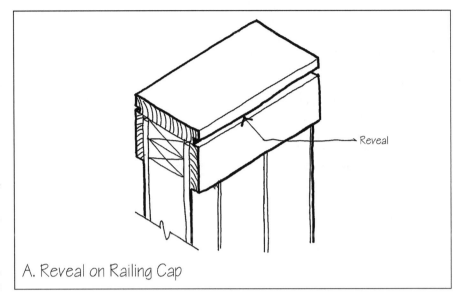

A. Reveal on Railing Cap

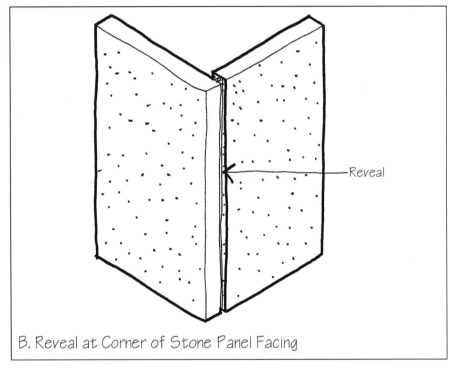

B. Reveal at Corner of Stone Panel Facing

**3.** Rustication strips attached to concrete formwork create shadow lines that conceal irregularities that occur where one pour of concrete joins another or where one panel of formwork butts another (see C).

**4.** A reveal can also be used to hide the junction of a level base of a vertical element such as a stone veneer wall and a sloping ground plane (see D). ■

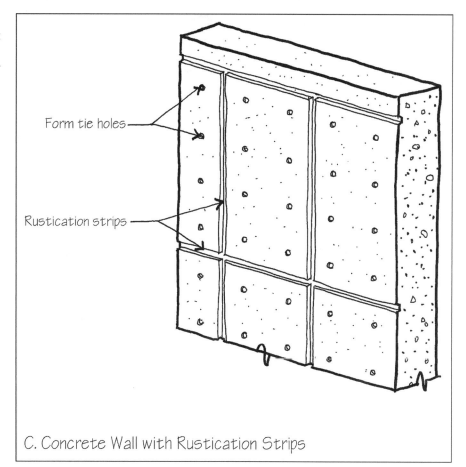

Form tie holes

Rustication strips

C. Concrete Wall with Rustication Strips

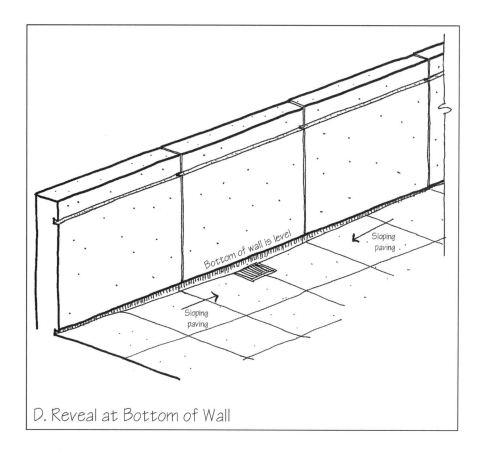

Bottom of wall is level

Sloping paving

Sloping paving

D. Reveal at Bottom of Wall

A butt joint is the simplest way of assembling two components. It is also the most desirable way of doing so under most circumstances.

1. Mitered corners are an attractive concept, but they present several problems. One is that they create a knife edge on each piece of material at the corner, and knife edges are both fragile and potentially dangerous. Another problem is that to realize its aesthetic potential, a miter must be fitted very closely and precisely. This is often difficult to do when the pieces being mitered are long, wide, or warped. A miter between pieces of wood presents a third problem: Because wood shrinks a great deal perpendicular to its grain and very little along its grain, a 45 degree cut across a board will no longer be 45 degrees after the board has shrunk or expanded. Miters in wood tend to open up unattractively as the wood dries out (see A).

2. A simple butt joint avoids most of these problems. It has no knife edges. It is easy to fit. And if it does open slightly when the wood dries, it does so evenly. A butt joint is especially forgiving if it includes a reveal (see *Reveal,* page 174). In this example the reveal is created by simply cutting the top piece of trim a bit longer than it needs to be.

3. Another similar approach can be used with brick paver banding by replacing a miter joint with a square corner brick (see B).

4. It is also possible to butt wood moldings at inside corners of fences or walls to avoid the unattractive opening up that might occur in a miter joint. This special type of butt joint is called a coped joint. It is produced in several steps. The first piece of molding is butted at right angles into the corner and nailed. The second piece of molding is mitered to establish the line of the cope. Finally, a coping saw is used to cut the second piece of molding at an angle of 90 degrees or slightly

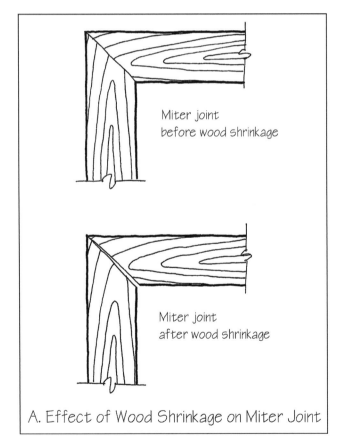

A. Effect of Wood Shrinkage on Miter Joint

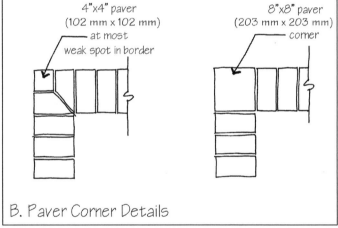

B. Paver Corner Details

less, following the edge of the miter as a guide. The coped end of the second piece butts tightly to the contoured side of the first piece. The coped connection looks exactly the same as a mitered connection but retains its tight fit even if the moldings shrink slightly (see C).

**5.** Sometimes a good compromise for joining long edges of stone or precast panels is the quirk miter. It has no knife edges and is fairly forgiving of fitting problems because of its built-in reveal, but it retains the satisfying visual symmetry of a miter (see D).

**6.** A variation on a butt joint is an offset joint. When two components come together their surfaces can be purposefully offset to allow for variation in joints and in component dimensions (see E). ■

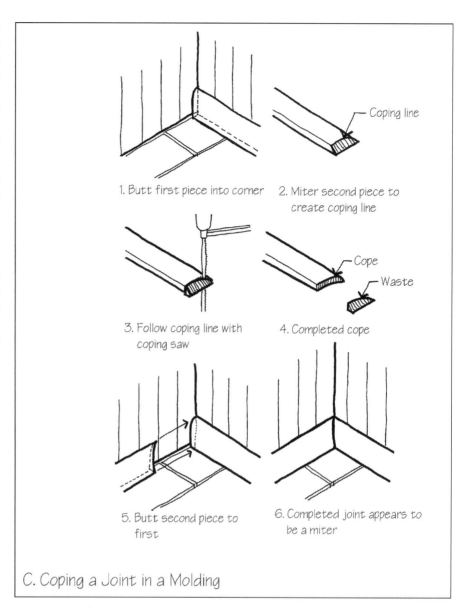

1. Butt first piece into corner

2. Miter second piece to create coping line

Coping line

3. Follow coping line with coping saw

4. Completed cope

Cope

Waste

5. Butt second piece to first

6. Completed joint appears to be a miter

C. Coping a Joint in a Molding

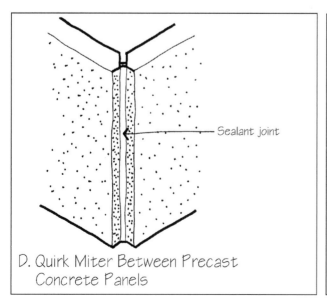

Sealant joint

D. Quirk Miter Between Precast Concrete Panels

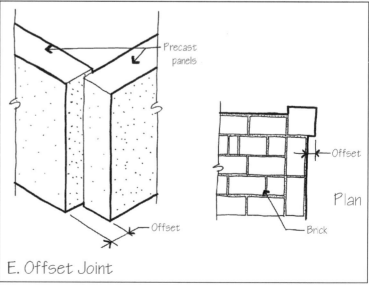

Precast panels

Offset

Plan

Offset

Brick

E. Offset Joint

Where a material or a surface ends, it should do so neatly and decisively.

**1.** Two kinds of edges that are unforgiving are sharp edges and feather edges. Sharp edges are dangerous and are very susceptible to damage before, during, and after construction. If damaged, they are almost impossible to repair. Feather edges are created when we try to smooth one material into another, as in joining a stucco wall to a masonry wall that lies in the same plane by smoothing the edge of the wet stucco onto the face of the masonry. A feather edge looks terrible and is so fragile that it usually cracks apart in a short period of time. It is also impossible to make a smoothly feathered edge in anything but very fine-grained stucco or an asphalt/sand mixture. It does not work, for example, to try to create a feathered wash with mortar on top of a stone wall: The sand in the mortar is too coarse to feather and the thin, insubstantial wash will soon crack and detach itself from the masonry. Instead, a wall should be terminated with a reinforced concrete cap or stone that has a clean, thick edge and a wash on the top (see A).

**2.** Avoid sharp edges on concrete. Sharp edges in formwork often do not fill properly with concrete during pouring and are likely to be damaged when the formwork is stripped—an operation that takes place while the concrete is still weak and very brittle. Use chamfer or fillet inserts in the corners of formwork to eliminate sharp corners on concrete; even 90 degree corners are dangerous, unattractive, and difficult to do well if the designer tries to keep them sharp. Furthermore, they are much more susceptible to damage during construction and occupancy. If sharp corners are required, then the concrete specification and placement methods must be adjusted to be sure that the concrete fills the tight corners. Formwork removal must also be cau-

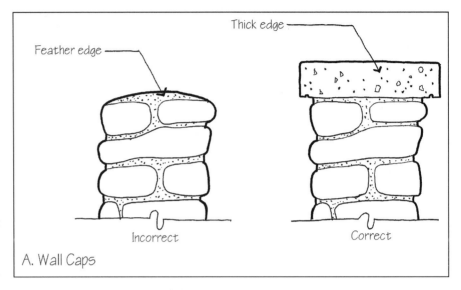

A. Wall Caps

tious to avoid damaging the vulnerable corners. Some damage is virtually certain, and even the best of repairs will be obvious to the eye (see B).

**3.** Sharp angles on stonework and masonry are also unforgiving of minor construction mishaps and are very difficult to repair. Chamfered edges, rounded edges, quirk miters, and reveals are clean, forgiving edge details for sharp masonry corners. To create these types of corners in brickwork, specify specially molded brick shapes. Acute-angle corners that are woven of square bricks have water-catching recesses that lead to premature deterioration. Bricks that are cut to an angle with a hammer or a saw have an unattractive and porous finish on the cut surface (see C).

**4.** Exposed edges of stucco must always be bounded by the appropriate casing beads and corner beads. These

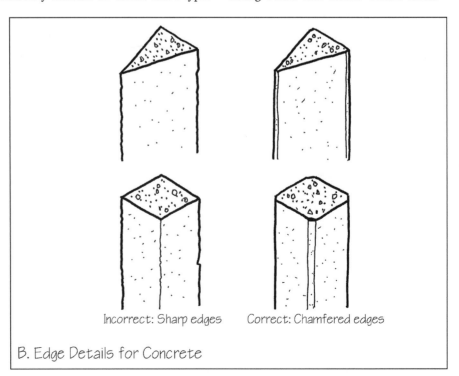

B. Edge Details for Concrete

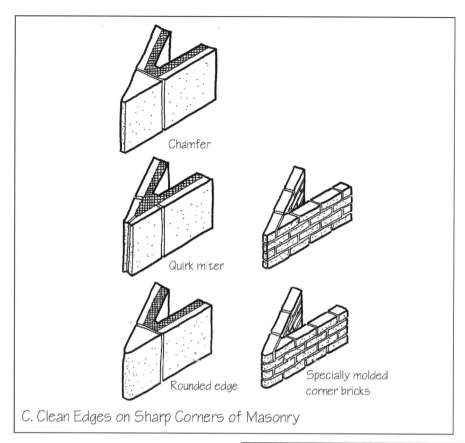

C. Clean Edges on Sharp Corners of Masonry

help the stucco contractor to maintain a constant thickness and to create clean edges that join neatly to surrounding materials. There are also many accessory strips manufactured in metal and plastic that the detailer can use to create crisp, cleanly finished reveals and joints in stucco surfaces (see D).

**5.** A wood ramp intersecting a stone unit pavement can be terminated with a thickened stone section to alleviate the need to install a thin sliver of wood. ■

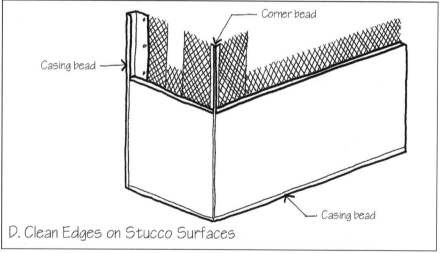

D. Clean Edges on Stucco Surfaces

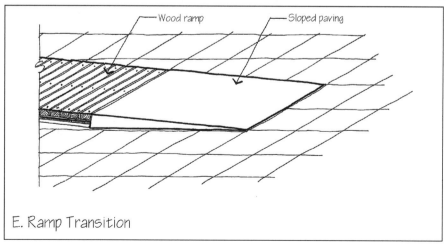

E. Ramp Transition

As a construction project progresses, each stage of work should be more finished than the stages that preceded it, and the installation of fine finishes should be delayed until as late in the construction process as possible.

**1.** The most common example of progressive finish is site grading. From Table 11-1, we see that initially the subsoil on the site is rough-graded to a tolerance of +/- 0.2' or 2 3/8" (+/- 60 mm). This is close enough to install foundations and many subsurface utilities. As the work progresses, finish pavement and planting areas are only installed when the heavy work of constructing buildings and other structures are complete enough to assure that the finish surfaces will not be damaged (see A).

**2.** Imagine two different ways of finishing a wall of poured-in-place architectural concrete. One way is simply to form and pour the concrete very carefully and leave it exposed. The other is to form and pour the concrete somewhat less carefully, and then, late in construction, apply a stucco or tile finish.

The exposed concrete surface would seem to be the more direct, simple, secure, and economical option to choose, because it involves less material, fewer steps, and fewer trades. It is, however, a very unforgiving finish. Any defects in the formwork and ties, any inconsistencies in vibrating the concrete, any cold joints or slight differences in color between batches of concrete, any staining or damage to the wall during subsequent stages of construction will be painfully obvious in the finished surface.

By using stucco or tile, the concrete work can be done in a much less exacting way, and any subsequent construction damage to the concrete surface appearance will be of little consequence. After most construction operations are done, the wall surface can be covered with a scratch coat of stucco, to produce a plumb, flat surface. The finish coat of stucco or tile can then be applied to create a finished surface that is unblemished with crisp edges. The overall cost of the concrete wall plus the tile or stucco finish may be less than the overall cost of simply exposing the concrete wall. This is because the wall with a stucco or tile finish has been finished progressively rather than in a single, irrevocable step. The progression is from rough, crude structural surfaces to scratch coat surfaces to fine surfaces of stucco or tile, with the rough edge covered by a trimboard or strip. Progressive finish involves successively better approximations of the degree of finish ultimately desired, and it delays the finer degrees of finish until as late as possible in the construction process to avoid their being spoiled by rougher operations.

Of course, a stucco or tile surface does not have the satisfying solidity and character of a well-made concrete wall. The client and the designer may prefer the concrete, and they should have it, but they must recognize that it is an unforgiving finish, expensive and risky to produce, and difficult to repair. It

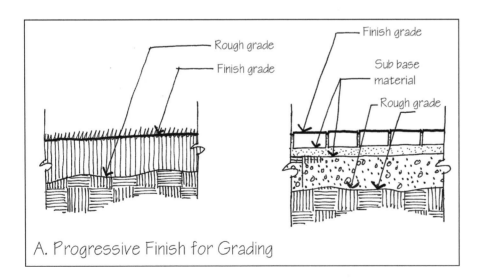

A. Progressive Finish for Grading

must be detailed, specified, supervised, and budgeted accordingly (see B).

**3.** Similarly, an exposed concrete slab is an unforgiving floor finish—one that should be used only if the designer is sure that the contractor will have experienced, reliable, highly skilled concrete finishers to produce it. Even under these conditions, the slab is exposed to a considerable risk of damage or staining throughout the construction process. More forgiving and sometimes less expensive overall is to cover the slab at the very end of the construction sequence with a material such as brick, pavers, or an epoxy-based surface.

**4.** A potential disadvantage of using progressive finish is that initial stages of work may be executed casually and contain flaws, and these flaws may be excused because later steps will cover them up. Standards of workmanship should be established and followed for all segments of construction, based upon objective criteria. For instance, site utilities are often installed when a site is rough graded. If the backfill in the utility trenches is not properly compacted, the subsequent settlement in the trench will be reflected in the finish surfaces. ■

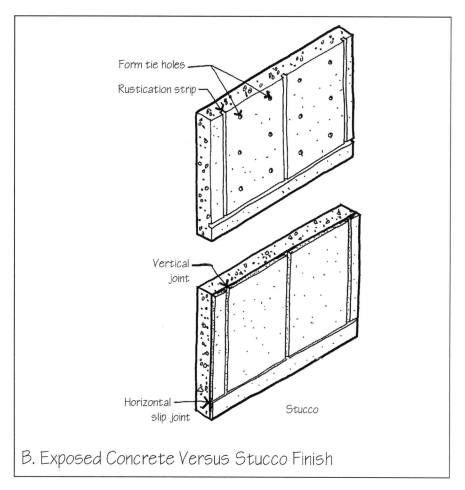

B. Exposed Concrete Versus Stucco Finish

# Forgiving Surface

Some types of finish surfaces make things easier for construction workers, because they conceal or camouflage small inaccuracies and blemishes.

**1.** A smooth, shiny surface accentuates every defect while a rough, flat surface forgives a multitude of blemishes. Benches painted in a glossy paint show every flaw in the surface and every spec of dirt while a penetrating stain does not. A polished stone surface accentuates every flaw in the structure of the stone while a flamed or honed surface makes them less apparent.

**2.** Avoid lighting a smooth concrete or stucco surface with a light fixture that casts light across it at a very acute angle, because such light casts long shadows from otherwise insignificant flaws, making the surface look much worse than it really is. The same surface lit from an angle approaching 90 degrees will appear to be of perfect workmanship. The same is true of bright sunlight washing a wall surface. Alternatively, a very rough-textured surface can be attractive when lit at almost any angle.

**3.** Concrete that has been cast in formwork made of individual boards looks good, even if there are many flaws in the boards or bubbles in the concrete, because such defects become lost in the overall texture. Concrete that has been cast against a smooth steel or plastic surface features any defects prominently, and an attempt to patch them will only make them more blatant. Almost any type of texture will work to hide defects in concrete: sandblasted, bush hammered, corrugated, or ribbed. Integral pigments in the concrete mix can conceal minor color variations when the wall is new and later as it weathers.

**4.** In a wall or pavement constructed of very precisely made bricks in a stack bond pattern, each brick must be laid with extreme care, because any slight dimensional misalignment of a brick will stand out from the rest of the pattern. Traditionally, bricks vary somewhat in size, color, and distortion, and a wall made of such bricks is a richly textured tapestry in which minor misalignments only add to the visual interest. Minor variations in the wall are less apparent when the mortar color is similar to masonry unit colors.

**5.** A closely mown grass surface (1/8″ 3.2 mm) shows every minor roll in the finish grade similar to a golf green while turf mown to a height of 2 to 3 in. (50–75 mm) variations are much less noticeable. A groundcover bed is even more forgiving of an undulating finish grade. ∎

CHAPTER

# 12 Efficient Use of Construction Resources

Efficient use of construction resources is the basis of planning and constructing an economical and sustainable project. By using materials efficiently, waste material is reduced, less energy is expended to produce and transport the materials needed to construct the project, and money is saved on all phases of the project's life. Efficient use of construction resources often follows directly from a project's details. If not thoroughly considered from this point of view, a seemingly simple, straightforward detail can conceal endless problems in materials procurement, tool and machine utilization, construction scheduling, and even labor relations as well as waste. The detail patterns associated with avoiding these problems include the following:

In factory /shop work and onsite work each have their own associated advantages and disadvantages. An important task of the detailer is to allocate the work of making a project judiciously between the two for optimum construction speed, quality, and cost.

**1.** In the factory or shop, the weather is always dry and temperatures are always comfortable. Lighting is good, large machines and tools with impressive capabilities and extreme accuracy can be used, and workers can work in comfortable postures. Wage rates for factory workers are substantially lower than for onsite workers, and worker productivity (because of the factors mentioned earlier in this paragraph) is higher. Pieces can be checked for quality before they become part of the project. But the sizes and weights of the components created by the factory are restricted by the dimensions and capacities of trucks or other transport methods.

On the jobsite, the weather and the light vary greatly in quality. Tooling is not as sophisticated. Access to the work is not always the best. Urban sites may be cramped and difficult to secure. Wage rates at a job site are higher, and productivity ranges from high to low, depending on weather, light, tooling, and access. But very large assemblies can be created and adjustments can be tailored to specific site conditions. With careful field measurement, assemblies can be built to actual required size and shape, which is a particular advantage in matching existing conditions.

**2.** In most smaller-scale projects, the optimum mix of factory and site operations is well established. Foundations, paving, decking, retaining walls, and so forth are done on the site, using simple factory-produced components, such as formwork panels, masonry blocks, bricks, cut stone, precast pavers, and dimension lumber. Site furniture, fence panels, and gates, which require high precision and exacting finishes, are not made onsite but are ordered as prefabricated units from fabricators. Electrical wiring, plumbing, and irrigation systems are installed onsite, but such exacting components as light fixtures, irrigation, and fountain valves and nuzzles are factory made. Finish surfaces for pavements, walls, and some site carpentry are installed onsite, using factory-produced panel products in many cases. In general, the smaller, highly precise, highly finished components are made in the factory, while the larger elements of the building are created onsite from simple, easily fitted pieces of factory-made materials.

**3.** In many larger projects, the choices may not be so obvious. Should a bridge be built onsite or be prefabricated? Should a concrete curb be precast or poured in place? Should a wall be clad with brickwork or stonework that is assembled on the site, or should it be clad with factory-made panels? Should site walls be constructed onsite, or should they be interchangeable with building prefabricated panels? Should mechanical systems for fountains be assembled on-site or pre-fabricated? Pedestrian bridges, park shelters, bus shelters, and seating in public spaces are typically made of factory-produced components for quick and reliable installation at the site, but *can* be built on-site if desired. These are complex choices that involve the entire project design team (see A).

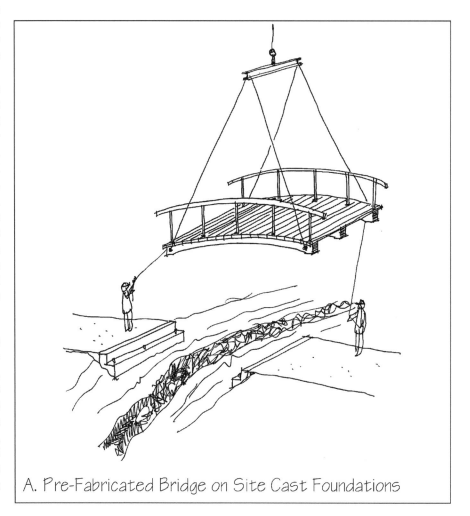

A. Pre-Fabricated Bridge on Site Cast Foundations

**4.** Some projects involve a high degree of integration of factory and site production, calling for increased collaborations between landscape architects, contractors, and product engineers. New materials or products may be developed for use in a particular project, such as a green roof system that integrates drainage and water holding reservoirs. Technically sophisticated factory-made assemblies such as these may be delivered to the site for installation by specialized crews trained by the manufacturer.

**5.** All site projects are adaptive in nature. They must meet existing conditions at their perimeter at a minimum and often must connect a number of existing conditions with new construction. As projects are built, small changes in newly constructed buildings and structures are accommodated in the landscape. Onsite elements are inherently more adaptable to changes

than shop items. Therefore it is crucial that shop-fabricated elements be designed with forgiving details and that their dimensions be field verified prior to fabrication.

**6.** In-factory work generally involves greater capacity for precision, speed, and replication than onsite work. However, exceptions exist; advanced technology is sometimes present at the construction site, and work at factories is sometimes carried out using archaic means. For instance, at the construction site, building elements may be guided into place to within millimeters of their intended location using global positioning satellite (GPS) surveying. While at the factory, specially shaped bricks are still made by placing freshly formed, unfired "green" bricks into a wooden box the shape of the intended brick, then a worker manually pulls a piece of piano wire through the clay to

cut off any portion protruding from the box. Both of these are appropriate levels of technology, meeting the specific criteria for accuracy, speed, volume, and cost unique to each task.

**7.** The balance between site factory fabrications should also weigh the environmental cost both on-site and off-site. Fabrication on-site takes space and creates a waste stream that is not always easy to accommodate. A sensitive site may not have room to accommodate a space for on-site materials storage and fabrication, nor additional soil compaction and runoff water. Offsite fabrication in a factory, on the other hand, can develop recycling programs and efficiencies in using material minimizing waste. However, the cost to transport raw materials to the factory and finished goods to the site can add tremendously to the resources needed to produce the items. ∎

The act of designing and drawing a detail should be based on a mental process that rehearses the sequence in which the detail will be assembled on the project site.

**1.** In the mind of a construction manager or a construction worker, a detail drawing should create a vivid, dynamic picture of actual materials, fasteners, tools, and operations. From the detail drawing, the contractor should easily be able to visualize a sensible, workable process for assembling that part of the project. A good habit for the detailer to develop is to design and draw each detail in the order in which its pieces are assembled, thinking simultaneously of the actual construction operations that are represented by each new element of the drawing and trying to see the detail not as an object but as a process, which is how the builder will see it. This creates the opportunity for the detailer to rehearse mentally the construction sequence, searching for better ways of doing things, looking for "bugs" and for components that will not go together easily on the construction jobsite. For important details and elaborate assemblies, it can make sense for the detailer to sketch out for his or her own enlightenment and scrutiny a series of drawings that show the assembly sequence step by step. If using digital drawing methods, each step could be a different layer of the drawing. In cases where an entirely new and unfamiliar construction sequence is required, these sequential sketches should be cleaned up and used as part of the construction drawings.

To a beginning detailer, a detail drawing may appear almost as an abstraction that has little meaning in terms of actual materials, tools, and processes. Through office experience, reading, and jobsite visits, the beginner should acquire as quickly as possible a critical base of knowledge of what details really mean to a contractor.

This knowledge base is never complete and will grow throughout the detailer's career; the hardest part is to get a strong enough start in this learning process to become a fully effective designer of realistic details. Rehearsing the construction sequence mentally, when drawing each detail, can help materially in this education.

**2.** When rehearsing the construction sequence, look for such signs of inefficiency as excessive numbers of separate trades, repeated visits by the same trade, lack of temporary support for components, lack of alignment references, fitting problems (see *Sliding Fit,* p. 170), and opportunities for spoiling of previously completed work by gouging, scratching, or staining (see *Progressive Finish,* p. 180).

Strive for a detail that requires a minimum number of trades and visits per trade, uses sliding fits only, needs little or no temporary support, requires no special tools, and has a minimal need for shoring, ladders or scaffolding—in short, a detail that will go together like clockwork. In the simplified construction sequence for constructing an intensive green roof, the interim conditions can be analyzed for weaknesses and vulnerabilities of the finished work as well as the need for timely coordination with other trades (see A).

**3.** Rehearsal of a construction sequence can often turn up hidden problems with a detail that appears entirely satisfactory. Consider this detail for a shared edge between a paving system raised on pedestals and a planting bed that is over a built structure. The seam between the planting bed and the raised paving system must be rigid and serve multiple proposes. The edge must hold back the planting medium while allowing drainage to flow through it at deck level. It must also be hard enough to resist burrowing by urban rodents that may use it as a way to access the void space

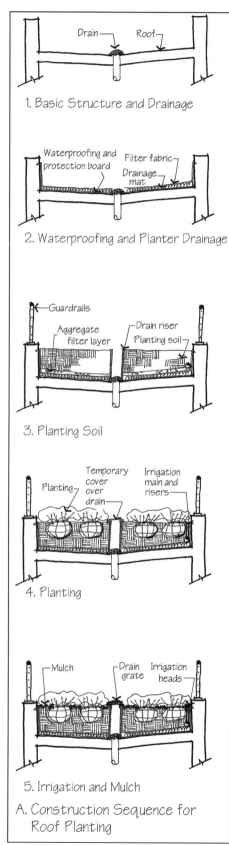

1. Basic Structure and Drainage

2. Waterproofing and Planter Drainage

3. Planting Soil

4. Planting

5. Irrigation and Mulch

A. Construction Sequence for Roof Planting

below the pavers. An early version of this detail used a permeable fabric to separate the soil from the void. The fabric was not sufficiently rigid to prevent the soil from bowing out under the pavers, allowing for settlement in the bed and potential frost heaving of the pavers, as well as being subject to burrowing. A hardware cloth backer was then proposed to add rigidity to the fabric and to prevent burrowing. This further evolved into a backer board set between the pedestals, which would have addressed the rigidity and burrowing objectives, but would have been very expensive to install between each pedestal (it would have required trimming in length and in height for each section). The final version of the detail relocated the pedestals within the outside edge of the pavers rather than at their edges, and attached the edge restraint board outside of the line of pedestals. This allows the edge board to have a sliding fit with any gap at the deck level being covered with the filter fabric. The edge boards can also overlap the individual pedestals, allowing for additional adjustments horizontally (see B).

**4.** The detailer's mental process rehearses the sequence in which the detail will be assembled on the site and how it will be maintained over the life of the project. Components that must be replaced over time should have accessible fasteners to facilitate removal and replacement. Wooden fence or rail members that are attached to a concrete wall or foundation should be anchored to the concrete using accessible steel anchors and not imbedded permanently in concrete (see C). ■

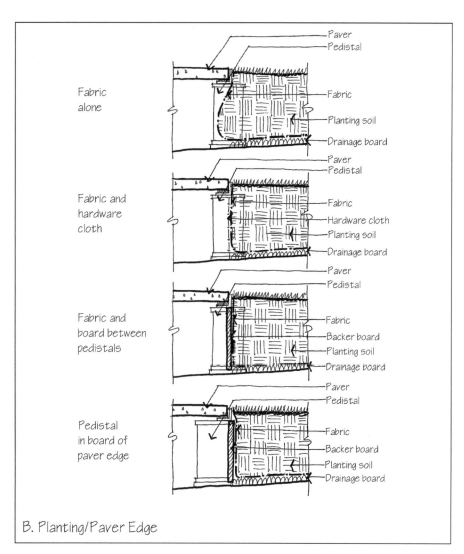

B. Planting/Paver Edge

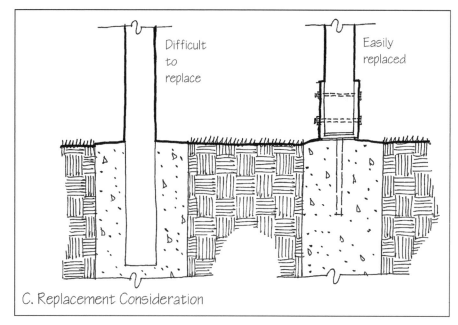

C. Replacement Consideration

Using materials and components that are readily available makes construction easier. Construction project scheduling is more difficult when materials or components are not off-the-shelf.

**1.** Certain site components are found everywhere. A wide variety of paving materials, plant materials, fencing, wall materials, and the like are readily available. But sometimes just one special component can cause the whole process to break down. Suppose your details and specifications call for a new, improved kind of erosion control blanket that has just come on the market. Suppose further that you did not check to see if it was locally available, and it is not. The contractor orders the blanket from a distant supplier, and it takes several weeks to arrive. Meanwhile, a portion of the site cannot be graded because a supporting slope is unstable without the erosion control blanket, and the construction process has to stop. This causes delays and costs money.

The moral of this not-so-hypothetical story is simple: If speed and ease of construction are the highest priorities, do not use anything but standard, off-the-shelf products.

**2.** If, instead, you have a strong reason to do otherwise, then you should make a preliminary phone call or two to establish availability of the nonstandard product. If necessary, work directly with the contractor to be sure that the product is ordered well in advance of need, and be ready to specify an accept-

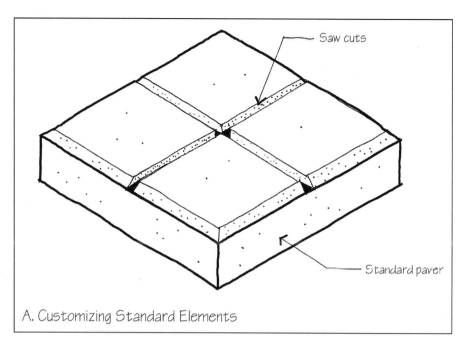

A. Customizing Standard Elements

able alternative product if supply problems persist and construction delays loom. Do not be afraid to use new products, but be aware of potential supply problems. Do your part to solve potential supply problems before they occur. And do not try too many new products on the same project, or these logistical problems may multiply.

**3.** Some landscape architects use off-the-shelf parts in unusual ways, gaining the advantages of stock products without sacrificing novelty and functionality. Simply placing an industrial lighting fixture or steel stair into a residential setting can meet function and

budget objectives with an interesting solution. Even a brick paver can have a noticeable impact on a garden if it is twice or half the size of conventional usage.

**4.** A stock item can sometimes be customized on the construction site to create a fresh effect. It is easy, for example, to cut bricks or pavers to different widths, or to use a saw or grinder to give them new score lines or edge profiles (see A).

**5.** Light fixtures can be modified with alternate bases, poles, fixtures, and lamps to create a number of variations in form (see B).

**6.** Many important elements are not actually stock items, that is, they are not made in advance, waiting for purchase. Steel and precast structural elements, some furniture items, fence panels, and many light fixtures are not usually produced until the order is received. It is wise to contact suppliers and fabricators and find out what the lead time will be, and ask about the availability of particular materials your project will need. For instance, a light fixture with a pole designed for direct burial may require more lead time to be fabricated than one made with a standard bolt circle base that can to be bolted to a concrete foundation, simply because the pole sections are on backorder from the manufacturer. ■

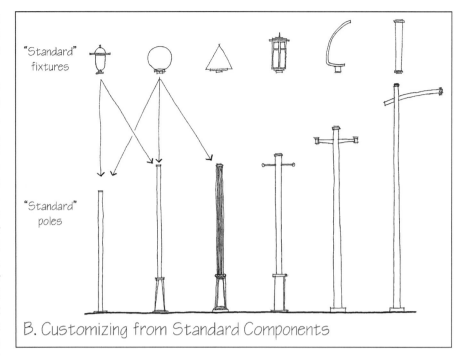

"Standard" fixtures

"Standard" poles

B. Customizing from Standard Components

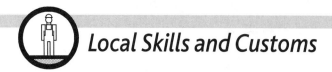

# Local Skills and Customs

A landscape's details should reflect knowledge of the labor force that will construct the project.

1. Know what kind of contractors and work force will be executing your details. Sometimes the project will require field collection of plant material and/or salvaging building materials. Knowledge about the expertise of the local contractors can have a substantial impact on the final project results. Greenroofs and greenwalls require a great deal of coordination and knowledge of building construction to be successful. Not every contractor, even within a specific trade, has the same set of expertise.

Conversely, if your project will likely bring together a pool of creative, skilled craftspeople, consider including in the design features that will display their talents. Our drawings and specifications assume that all builders are equally capable of executing the project, but of course this is seldom true. Many landscape architects and contractors work together on successive projects because they form a productive and complementary team.

2. Sometimes the project sequence or location presents constraints. For instance, if water will not be available on the jobsite until construction is well along, then the early stages of construction must be designed to require as little water as possible, postponing planting until very late in the sequence. Sometimes the project location presents special opportunities. For example, if you know that there are local sources of relatively inexpensive stone, brick, precast concrete, or plate steel, perhaps the design should include them. The local labor force is likely to be familiar with local materials, so the necessary skills will also be available at a reasonable cost. Be prepared to adapt the design to constraints and opportunities associated with the location.

3. It is important to be familiar in advance with the local labor practices. Are the building trades unionized, and, if so, what are the union rules regarding jurisdictions and work practices? Are plumbers required for irrigation work or masons for stone pavement? Does a particular mason's union, for example, specify the maximum weight of masonry unit that a mason can handle alone? Which union has jurisdiction over the operation of small excavators and compactors? If the trades are not unionized, what are their usual ways of going about things? Try to detail in such a way that the labor force will have no trouble dividing the work among the trades and that it can follow its usual practices.

4. Builders in various regions have their own customary ways of doing things. In some areas of North America, most small scale foundation walls are made of poured concrete, and, in other areas, they are made of concrete blocks. The predominant material in any one area is usually cheaper and is practiced by a larger group of competing subcontractors (such as granite curb in New England verses poured in place curb and gutter used in most of the rest of the U.S.). Steel fabricators in some areas prefer to bolt even their shop-fabricated connections, while others like to weld them. Certain regions have excellent stucco, tile, or concrete flatwork contractors, whereas others do not. Do not restrict yourself to these customs, but exploit them whenever you can. And, when your design runs counter to the customs, be prepared to do the additional work necessary to help line up subcontractors and materials.

5. Local wisdom is not always correct. Common practice in a given location may simply be the residue of countless ad hoc episodes over many years and may not actually constitute good practice. The old saying, "What is good is not always popular, and what is popular is not always good," may apply here. The construction industry changes constantly as new knowledge, materials, and regulations alter the way we design and build. Many practices once in common use are now discredited (such as the use of tree paint). The detailer is expected to incorporate relevant current conditions into the design. Part of every built project is the give and take between landscape architect and contractor regarding what each believes to be the best practice. The landscape architect initiates this dialogue and ultimately is responsible to conclude it, after considering a wide array of sources.

6. Not only are there differences in the relevant codes and ordinances from one city to another, but there are also slight differences in how they are enforced. Do not assume that a code interpretation granted in one jurisdiction will be honored in another. When uncertain whether a detail is going to be acceptable, it is wise to look for precedents in the area or contact the relevant officials.

7. If unfamiliar with customary practices in the area, invest some time to visit construction sites or recently completed projects comparable to the one you are designing. Landscape architects may also collaborate professionally with local counterparts to tap into this kind of local wisdom.

8. Local builders may be hired as consultants during the design development phase of the landscape architect's work in an effort to fully integrate local skills and customs into the construction documents. The cost of this consultant is often offset by reduced construction bid prices. Contractors inflate their bids if they are uncertain about the materials or methods to be used. Drawings and specifications that present the project in terms that the contractors understand will generally be rewarded with lower costs and better quality. ∎

# Refining the Detail

Even good details can be improved upon. Do not limit yourself to familiar or stock solutions, especially when addressing new circumstances. The concept "truth through making" (*verum ipsum factum,* Latin) recognizes that even a well-conceived detail is not fully understood until it is made.

**1.** Details are where the landscape architect's and the contractor's shared interest in quality converge. Craftspeople are excellent resources for the detailer. Their knowledge of construction materials and processes is intimate, and they often have insights about the detail that would be beneficial to the architect. Observe them as they work, and make note of what things they do easily and well, and what things give them problems. Speak to the contractors to see if they have any suggestions about how a detail could be improved or more easily built.

**2.** In some offices, the designer and detailer may never visit the construction site, making an unfortunate disconnection between design and construction. It is important to establish a routine process through which comments about the details can be conveyed from the construction site back to the office, providing a needed feedback loop through which the details can be improved. The person from the office who is responsible for construction administration should prepare specific notes regarding materials, details, and specifications that were found especially successful or unsuccessful during the construction phase. These notes should be reviewed by designers, detailers, and specifications writers as a base for later project phases, and for future projects.

**3.** Never discard a carefully thought out detail hastily because a contractor or supplier thinks an alternative is better. Listen to the alternative, but also take the time to thoroughly consider its implications on other aspects of the project. Substitutions sometimes have secondary effects on adjoining elements, functional aspects, or finished appearance that are not obvious initially. On large projects there is often a lag of many months or even years between the drawing of the detail and its actual construction. As memories dim over the intervening time, the reasons behind the choice of a particular detail may be temporarily lost. A hesitation in accepting alternate methods of detailing may allow a bit of time to rediscover the reasons behind the initial detail.

**4.** Each completed project is potentially a learning laboratory for the detailer. It is often gratifying and enlightening to revisit projects years after occupancy to observe the performance of materials and details. Some owners may even be willing to invest in a formal post-occupancy evaluation of construction systems at intervals, as part of their maintenance program. The detailer can assemble a manual of successful details that have been refined through use, ready for further improvement in the next project. ∎

Details should be designed with consideration of the weather sensitivities of the various construction operations and the time of year when those operations are likely to occur.

**1.** Certain construction operations are very weather sensitive. Grading is not possible when weather is too cold or wet to work the ground. Planting should occur when plants are dormant and before seasons of rain and new growth: Digging dormant plants and holding them for later planting can make out-of-season planting less hazardous. Asphalt is not available in very cold parts of the year. Exterior painting should not take place under rainy conditions, hot windy conditions, or cold conditions; this may indicate that prefinished exterior materials are preferable for certain projects. Concrete and masonry work can be problematic in very hot or very cold weather, which might lead the designer to select a precast concrete, steel, or heavy timber system instead if extreme temperatures are anticipated during construction. Stucco work cannot be done in very low temperatures, but precast concrete panels can still be placed.

**2.** The dimensions of large prefabricated components such as steel, precast concrete, and glue-laminated beams are established inside factories where temperatures are moderate. When moved outdoors they will change in size, especially in very hot or very cold weather. Surveyors may have to factor this into their calculations when these members are erected.

**3.** Select materials and components for each project with an eye to the time of year and the temperatures and precipitation expected when it will be built. Anticipate potential problems with weather-sensitive operations and eliminate the problems in advance by selecting appropriate systems and components, if you can. In any case, be ready to propose alternative ways of doing things if weather problems develop. ■

# Pride of Craftsmanship

Rare is the construction worker who does not have a love of good work and a pride of craftsmanship that can be brought out by an inspired detail.

1. Most bricklayers spend months or years at a stretch laying nothing but running bond facings and are delighted (if sometimes tentative at first) to have an opportunity to create a more decorative pattern bond, a corbelled ornament, a curving wall, or an arch. Stone masons can work in a variety of styles, from dry-stacked rubble to precisely set cut stone. Certain plasterers still know how to do decorative texturing. Painters can easily be persuaded to do masking, striping, and stenciling to create colorful patterns. Most heavy timber framers readily apply chamfers, quirks, and lamb's tongues to their beams and columns.

Proceed cautiously into these areas. Some of these traditional expressions of pride of craftsmanship can be exceedingly expensive if they are misused or overused; but it is often possible within even a modest construction budget to add a few small touches to the project that will lift it above the ordinary level of craftsmanship. It is very important that these details be clear and well documented to assure that the contract will reflect a fair price for these elements.

2. Even where you do not use these overt expressions of pride of craftsmanship, workers appreciate intelligent details that make the best possible use of their skills, and they dislike arbitrary, uninformed details that force them to do things that are awkward or difficult to do well. Learn what workers in each trade can do best and most economically, and detail accordingly. This will result in a lower contract price, and, just as importantly, it will get the workers on your side, helping to make the landscape the best that it can be. ∎

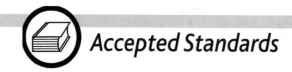 **Accepted Standards**

Details should conform to norms that are known, understood, and accepted throughout the construction industry. These norms are embodied in the published standards of a number of construction-related organizations. By conforming to these norms and referencing them in the written specifications for each project, the detailer eliminates many ambiguities and potential sources of misunderstanding from the construction documents.

**1.** Suppose, for example, that the detailer specifies a paving brick simply as "suitable for use as paving in the Chicago climate." This leaves considerable uncertainty as to what is "suitable." The masonry contractor may have had good experiences with a particular brick on previous jobs, but the bricks of the same type that are purchased for the current job may be manufactured for a different purpose and may deteriorate rapidly in winter weather. The detailer could remedy this situation by specifying the maximum water absorption that the brick may have, but this leaves the contractor with the task of requesting absorption test results from the manufacturer. The entire dilemma could be avoided by merely specifying that the paving bricks must be Class SX pavers, as defined by ASTM C 902. ASTM C 902 is a standard specification for paving bricks that is promulgated by the American Society for Testing and Materials (ASTM), a major standards-setting organization in the construction industry. ASTM C 902 is known and understood throughout the masonry industry, and bricks that conform to it are so designated in manufacturers' literature. It includes standards for strength, water absorption, saturation, abrasion resistance, warpage, chippage, dimensional tolerances, efflorescence,

and other criteria, as measured by standard laboratory tests. By citing ASTM C 902, the detailer not only avoids potential communication problems and misunderstandings but also adds to the construction contract a very powerful, well-considered set of requirements that avoid a number of potential disasters.

**2.** Voluntary consensus standards are set by various organizations, which then carry out conformity assessment and safeguard integrity of the standards in manufacturing and construction.

In the United States, ASTM is a major source of accepted standards in the industry; it publishes standards for many construction materials. Many other organizations have also established standards for other materials and assemblies that have become widely accepted. These include the American National Standards Institute (ANSI), a private, nonprofit organization that develops standards for many industrial products used in buildings. Agencies within the U.S. Department of Commerce also produce standards, as do many nongovernmental organizations (NGOs) that are affiliated with particular industries. For instance, the American Nurseryman's standards for plant material are codified in ANSI Z-60. The standards are invaluable to the detailer when working with plant material. They stipulate minimums and maximums for root ball and container sizes, heights and widths of plant material ranging in size from groundcovers to trees.

In Canada, standards corresponding to those by ASTM are set by the Canadian Standards Association (CSA). The Swiss-based ISO (International Organization for Standardization) is the world's largest developer of technical standards. It has representatives from

many countries and seeks to build consensus between governmental and commercial interests globally.

**3.** Standards underlie much of a landscape architect's work and are essential to the construction of projects. If there were no standards, we would soon notice that materials or products are of poor quality, incompatible with equipment we already have, unreliable, dangerous, or simply do not fit. When products meet our expectations, we tend to take this for granted. When detailing and writing specifications, we become aware of the role played by standards in raising levels of quality, safety, reliability, efficiency, and interchangeability of building elements. Standards are used to establish that building products and assemblies that originate from foreign sources conform to established norms, thereby allowing manufacturers to compete in the global market.

The publications of some of the more prominent standards-setting organizations are included in the reference list at the end of the book (see p. 241). The detailer should become familiar with the accepted standards for all construction materials and assemblies, and he or she should use these standards as much as possible in specifying and detailing.

**4.** At times, the detailer purposely breaks with accepted norms. Plant material that is a particular shape or size or root condition may be desired for a particular application. The detailer should be aware of the standards and be clear in the documents that the desired plants are different than the norm and where the differences lie. By knowing the standards and pointing out the differences to the contractor, the detailer is more likely to get the results intended. ∎

# CHAPTER 13 Sustainability

## INTRODUCTION

The first tenant of sustainability should be to build something of enduring value and quality that will merit preservation and perpetual use, thereby minimizing decommissioning and the reuse/recycle debate. Designed landscapes for human use are not self-sustaining. They should be designed to resonate with their users and be valuable enough to them to guarantee stewardship over many generations. Landscape will evolve and must evolve to stay relevant. Consider the Emperor's summer palace, the Alhambra, Versailles, and New York's Central Park. All have survived and evolved to support human activity unthinkable to their original designers. All have survived because their design assured that generations of users would care enough about them to maintain them for themselves first and secondarily for future generations. That investment of generations of stewards was not assured by material selection, resource usage, or a specific plant palette. They were sustained because they were designed as special places that are loved by their visitors and emotionally owned by them. Many of the patterns described in Chapter 1 deal with aesthetics. These are inherent quelities that affect the look and inherent attractiveness of the project.

In order to be sustainable, landscapes must be built well. The patterns described in Section 2, "Function," and Section 3, "Constructibility," are present in all enduring sustainable landscapes.

The detailer should keep in mind the current research on sustainable materials and techniques but should analyze new techniques and the claims of new materials using the patterns set out in the other chapters of this book. Details that are appropriately resolved on an aesthetic basis and are durable and constructible will tend to be sustainable.

Projects that are versatile and adaptable to a multitude of uses are also sustainable.

Research into sustainability has focused on planning and design, materials, and techniques. Planning and design are beyond the scope of this book, as is a detailed discussion of materials, but a short discussion of these aspects of construction is needed to put the sustainability patterns in context.

The *Sustainable Sites Initiative* is one set of guidelines and benchmarks for the development of sustainable landscapes. The issues addressed in Sustainable Sites are grouped into 9 categories:

1. Site Selection
2. Pre-Design Assessment and Planning
3. Site Design - Water
4. Site Design - Soil and Vegetation
5. Site Design - Materials Selection
6. Site Design - Human Health and Well Being
7. Construction
8. Operations and Maintenance
9. Monitoring and Innovation

The four patterns included in this section (Minimizing Site Impacts, Maximizing Site Benefits, Moderating Peaks, and Efficiency) are useful in addressing almost all of the issues included in the list above.

The patterns addressed in the previous chapters are most useful in the Site Design, Construction, and Operations and Maintenance sections of the guidelines.

**Site – Design Water** deals with enhancing the surrounding hydrologic systems with new projects. It is addressed in the following patterns:

*Drainage Diversions* (p. 23)

*Redundant Drainage Systems* (p. 27)

*Roof Drainage* (p. 31)

*Control Velocity* (p. 56)

*Sumps* (p. 57)

*Progressive Filtering* (p. 58)

*Level Drainage Surfaces* (p. 62)

*Water Level Reduction* (p. 63)

*Overflows* (p. 64)

**Site – Design Soil and Vegetation** deals with appropriate design of soils and planting to manage and enhance the soil and vegetation of a new project. It is addressed in the following patterns:

  Progressive Filtering - Chapter 3

  Geotextile Separation- Chapter 3

  Structural Tree Planting Soils- Chapter 3

  Root Zone Growth - Chapter 5

  Trunk Zone Growth - Chapter 5

  Branch Zone Growth - Chapter 5

  Succession - Chapter 5

  Site Specific Hazards – Chapter 8

  Planting Life Cycle- Chapter 9

**Site – Materials Selection** deals with appropriate material selections from sustainable sources as well as detailing for ease of maintenance and removal. It is addressed in the following patterns:

  Nontoxic Materials – Chapter 8

  Material Life Cycle – Chapter 9

  Expected Life – Chapter 9

  Surfaces that Age Gracefully – Chapter 9

  Repairable Surfaces – Chapter 9

  Cleanable Surfaces – Chapter 9

  Maintenance Access – Chapter 9

  Less Absorbent Materials – Chapter 9

  Building and Landscape Armor – Chapter 9

  Accessible Connections – Chapter 10

  Installation Clearance – Chapter 10

  Non-conflicting Systems – Chapter 10

  Factory and Site – Chapter 12

**Site – Human Health and Well-Being** deals with equity in project design and use as well as health, safety and welfare. It is addressed in the following patterns:

Safe Footing – Chapter 8

Fall Protection – Chapter 8

Safe Edges – Chapter 8

Safe Glazing – Chapter 8

User Appropriate Features – Chapter 8

Nontoxic Materials – Chapter 8

Site Specific Hazards – Chapter 8

Barrier Free Design – Chapter 8

**Construction** deals with minimizing impacts on the site and surrounds during construction. It is addressed in the following patterns:

  Seasonal Cycle – Chapter 9

  Material Life Cycle – Chapter 9

  Expected Life – Chapter 9

  Factory and Site – Chapter 12

  Rehearsing the Construction Sequence – Chapter 12

  Weather Dependant Construction – Chapter 12

**Operations and Maintenance** deals with minimizing the use of materials and energy over the life of the project. It is addressed in the following patterns:

  Expected Life – Chapter 9

  Surfaces that Age Gracefully – Chapter 9

  Repairable Surfaces – Chapter 9

  Cleanable Surfaces – Chapter 9

  Maintenance Access – Chapter 9

  Less Absorbent Materials – Chapter 9

  Robust Assemblies – Chapter 9

  Building and Landscape Armor – Chapter 9

  Forgiving Surface – Chapter 11

Any development will create impacts on the site and surrounding area. The detailer should be aware of the relative susceptibility of the site and its context to degradation and incorporate measures to minimize them.

**1.** On sites with porous soils, stormwater can be infiltrated into the ground or infiltration can be used to reduce the stormwater flow into the watershed (see A).

**2.** Unshielded light fixtures cast light in many directions and can contribute to light pollution. Shielded fixtures and using low light level systems with good uniformity can greatly reduce energy consumption and decrease harmful impact on the night sky. In some cases, urban flora and fauna also benefit if artificial lighting is not excessive (see B).    ▷

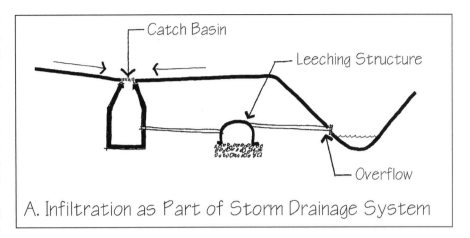

A. Infiltration as Part of Storm Drainage System

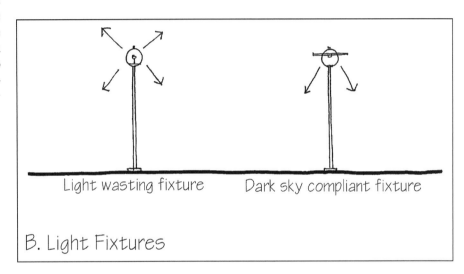

B. Light Fixtures

**3.** Tall buildings and dense plantings can cast shadows over large areas. Shadow lines should be considered in every project both on- and offsite. Microclimates in shaded areas may be different than those of unshaded areas, and especially different than areas that receive both direct sunlight and light reflecting off of glass or metal building exterior surfaces (see C).

**4.** Aggressive plants can invade nearby planting areas and sites. Prudent plant selection, efficient maintenance, and proper detailing can reduce the impact of potentially invasive plantings. Some bamboos and other species that propagate via runners should be enclosed with root barriers to prevent unwanted spread out of their beds (see D).

**5.** Design and material selection can contribute to the reduction of wildfires in fire ecologies. Maintenance operations should remove combustible debris in hazardous areas, and products such as pine needle mulch should be avoided near vulnerable features. ■

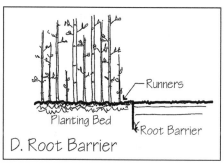

D. Root Barrier

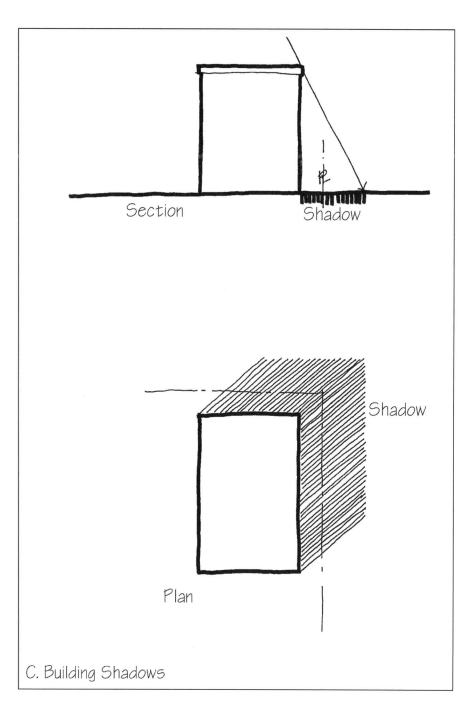

C. Building Shadows

# *Maximize Site Benefits*

Every site has some positive attributes that can be exploited in a site design and detailing.

**1.** Some sites have existing vegetation, topsoil, rock, or building materials that can be saved in place or reused onsite. Details that conserve and use existing tree root zones, rock outcroppings, or reused salvaged man-made materials are possible on many sites. Tree protection details that minimize the impact of construction on existing plant material can be very cost effective (see A).

**2.** In areas where water rights permit, runoff water can be harvested for reuse. The simplest system of this kind is a rain barrel, but more complicated systems involving filtration, pumping, and irrigation connections can be designed.

**3.** Some sites lend themselves to local energy production via solar, wind, low head hydro, geothermal, or other means.

**4.** On sites with porous soils, permeable pavement can be used to reduce icing by reducing winter surface flow. This in turn can reduce the amount of salt required for deicing and reduce the impact on nearby plants and on water quality downstream and plant damage at the source (see B).

**5.** Many additional sources of waste water can be harvested for irrigation and/or water features. Graywater, air conditioning condensate, blowdown water from cooling towers and boilers are all potentially available for use.

**6.** Many sites have a prevailing winter and/or summer wind direction. Windbreaks can be used to reduce winter heating loads if they are optimally positioned far enough away from the building wall to break the prevailing wind without shading it. Windbreaks can also be used to harvest snow to increase soil moisture, and to precipitate dust out of the air, and to disperse odors (see C). ■

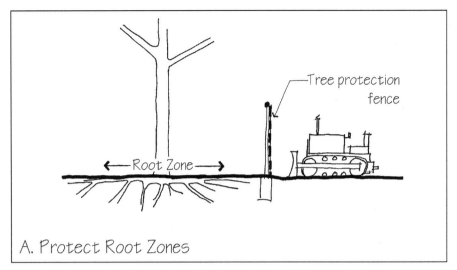

A. Protect Root Zones

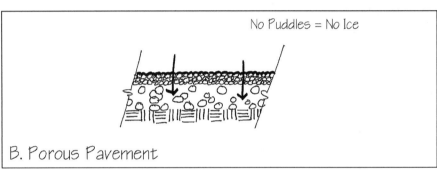

B. Porous Pavement

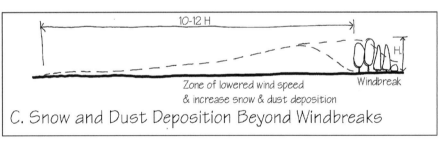

C. Snow and Dust Deposition Beyond Windbreaks

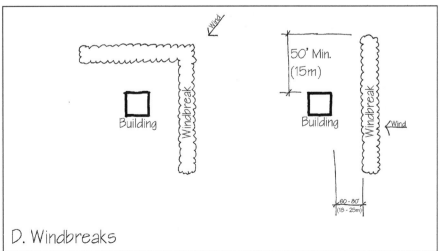

D. Windbreaks

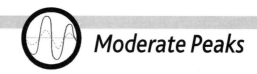

Many environmental events come in cycles. Storm flows start out small and rise to a crest and subside, temperatures go through a daily and yearly cycle. Man-made events can be cyclical; traffic flow and parking demands vary daily and seasonally. The detailer should use strategies that minimize the peaks of these cycles.

**1.** Rain gardens and retention and detention basins are used to minimize peaks in stormwater by holding back water at peak flow times and slowly releasing water after the peak has passed. This allows the downstream storm channels to be smaller and better utilized. Green roof systems can also add some stormwater storage, but the stormwater capacity must be balanced against the structural cost to support the weight of the water on the roof (see A).

**2.** Summer sun can cause dark materials to heat up and radiate heat well after the sun stops shining, contributing to the heat island effect. Trees in paved areas, green roofs, green walls, and green screens reduce solar gain and air-conditioning loads for buildings. Lighter-colored pavements and wall materials also contribute to heat reduction. In addition, respiring plants can cool the air and clean it of particulates and carbon dioxide.

**3.** Site plans that disperse pedestrian and vehicular traffic can use smaller widths and result in less paving and less cost and reduced environmental impact than wider travel ways. Dispersed circulation lanes tend to better accommodate the different speeds of pedestrians, cyclists, and drivers (see B).

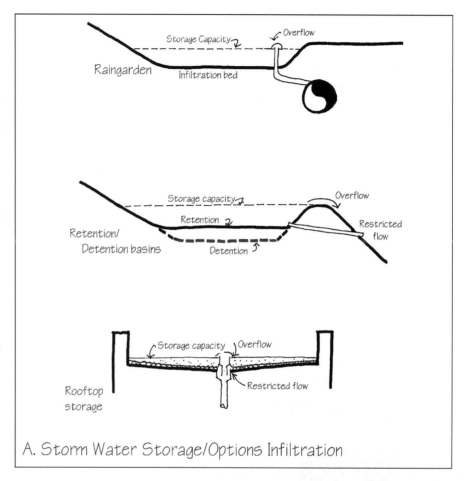

A. Storm Water Storage/Options Infiltration

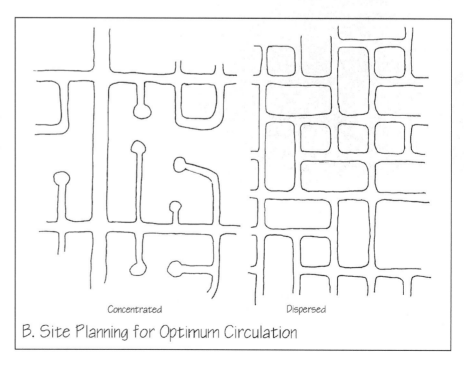

B. Site Planning for Optimum Circulation

**4.** Creating sittable edges in public areas can reduce the amount of formal seating required in the space. Walls and rails that are the correct height to accommodate sitting and leaning serve a double use and reducing the need for dedicated seating (see C).

**5.** Lime mortars, unsealed concrete, or concrete masonry surfaces can be used to absorb carbon dioxide out of the atmosphere. If environmental circumstances allow, it is beneficial to leave surfaces of these materials unpainted and unsealed so that atmospheric gasses can be absorbed, reducing the peak carbon dioxide in the air.  ■

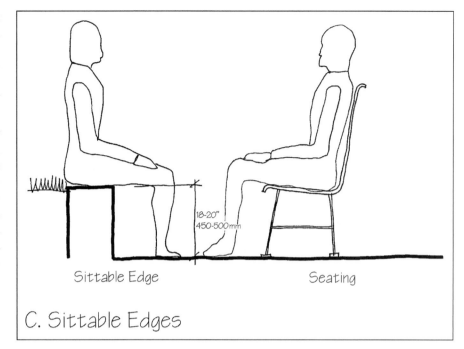

Sittable Edge                    Seating

C. Sittable Edges

Doing more with less is a core sustainable design concept. Any increase in the site's efficiency is intrinsically more sustainable than the same site with less efficient systems. Doing more with less is a core sustainable concept.

**1.** Energy efficient lights, pumps, and the like add to a site's sustainability. For example, LED lights are much more efficient and long-lasting than incandescent bulbs.

**2.** Drip irrigation systems decrease water usage and more effectively deliver water to the plants. Superabsorbants are also used in the planting media to hold water and increase the time between waterings. The use of mulch also reduces evaporation and conserves soil moisture.

**3.** Frequent fertilizer application can be minimized if it is efficiently applied to reduce runoff and waste. In irrigated sites, fertilization can be delivered through the irrigation (or "fertigation") system. ∎

# PART

# II

# DETAIL
# DEVELOPMENT

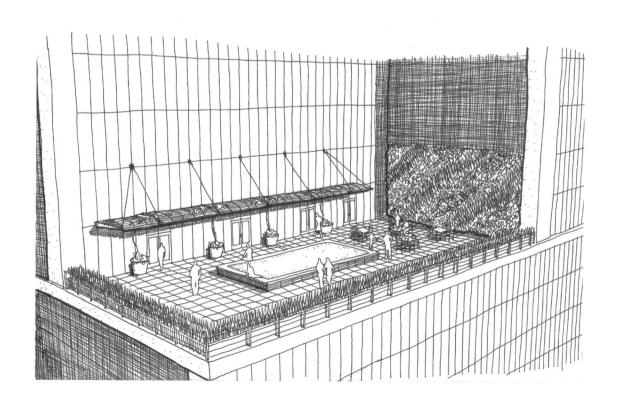

# SECTION

# 1

# APPLYING THE DETAIL PATTERNS

This section of the book consists of three illustrated narratives. These describe the process of designing the key details of specific projects in various styles and uses. The intent is to show how a hypothetical landscape architect goes about designing the details of a project and to reveal something of the concerns, mode of thought, and way of working. Throughout these narratives, special emphasis is given to showing how the detail patterns are a natural part of the detailing process. Pattern names are given in italic so that they are readily identifiable.

These narratives, though they display many twists and turns, have been simplified a good deal to reduce their length and to make them easier for the reader to follow. The drawings, similarly, have been cleaned up and reduced in number from the innumerable freehand scribbles, countless tracing paper overlays, and smudged, densely overdrawn sections that are the usual interim products of the detailer. An attempt has been made to relate the drawing styles on these pages to the qualities of the actual drawings that the detailer produces along the way, starting with freehand sketches and ending with precise, computer-drafted details.

It is readily apparent in these narratives that, in addition to a knowledge of the detail patterns and some conventions of drafting, detailing requires a familiarity with construction materials, tools, processes, and standards that must be acquired from sources other than this book. It is assumed that the reader has at least a beginning understanding of these areas and that this understanding is being augmented constantly by reading the technical literature, consulting more experienced colleagues, and observing actual construction operations.

The three examples presented here break no new stylistic ground. They aspire only to contribute to an initial understanding of mainstream detailing practice. As one acquires more experience, it is even more challenging and a good deal more fun to work on the detailing of an out-of-the-ordinary design.

There is a crucial theme that runs through these three examples: The design of the details of a landscape is a process that establishes with considerable precision both the technical means of its construction and its appearance. In each of the three examples, we begin the design of the details with only a crude idea of the form and direction of the project. By the time the mere handful of key details have been developed to a preliminary stage of completion, the landscape has come alive, not only because it has become patently constructible, but also because it has assumed a character and a personality of considerable depth. It follows that the design of the details of a project should begin while its form and space are still fluid. In this way, the materials selected, the processes by which they are assembled, and the developing character of the details can inform the form-making process for the landscape as a whole.

There are few greater mistakes that a designer can make than to create a finished form for a landscape and only then begin to consider how to build it. Landscapes designed in this way (and there are a great many of them) generally end up with the design concepts or the project durability being severely compromised. Every truly great landscape, ancient or contemporary, incorporates its handling of materials and processes as an integral part of its aesthetic, showing that its designer expended as much love and expertise on its details as on its space and form.

# CHAPTER

# 14 Detailing a Traditional Plaza

## THE PROJECT

The project is a small plaza in a larger development of traditionally styled townhomes in the northeastern United States. The plaza has a pergola set within a bosque of trees, enclosed on two sides with a low fence and fronting a residential street. The ground plane of the plaza will be brick and the planting areas will be edged with the low curb.

## SETTING PERFORMANCE STANDARDS

The client wishes the plaza to convey the image of a traditional urban park with materials and detailing reflecting premodernist norms of the early twentieth century. The pergola will have wood beams and rafters with substantial columns. The light fixtures will meet current energy and dark sky requirements but reflect a more traditional style. The plaza will not contribute to surface runoff on the project. Surface runoff will be captured and infiltrated under the plaza.

## KEY DETAILS TO DEVELOP

The key details that will establish the visual character of the plaza and its methods of construction are listed below.

1. Pavement
2. Grading and Foundations
3. Trellis
4. Site Furniture
5. Foundation
6. Fence

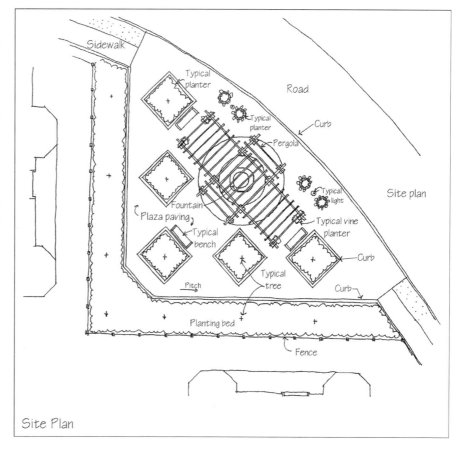

Site Plan

These must be developed as a consistent set of *Contributive Details* (p. 5) that work well with the surrounding building's architecture and with one another. They are the most basic of the plaza's details. Details of special situations, such as the ends and corners of curbs and edges of paving patterns, will be developed using the general details as a point of departure.

## EARLY WORK ON FORM, MATERIALS, AND DETAILS

### PAVEMENT

One of the first choices to be made in detailing the plaza is to choose a paving system. Paving systems can be either modular or monolithic and either rigid or flexible.

Modular systems are constructed of individual units such as brick, concrete, or stone pavers that are installed in a specific pattern and typically trimmed to fit at the edges. Monolithic systems such as crushed aggregate, cast-in-place concrete, and asphalt are installed (poured, spread, and so forth) in place to form a homogeneous plane.

Rigid systems such as cast-in-place concrete and mortared bricks allow for precise surface gradients and clean surfaces, free of loose setting bed material, but require care and detailing of all joints. Flexible systems such as asphalt paving and interlocking concrete pavers with sand-swept joints, on the other hand, accommodate a great deal of movement in the material itself or in its numerous joints (see *Accommodating Movement,* Chapter 4). The flexible systems accommodate much more movement internally in the rigid systems and that movement can result in puddling in flat gradients.

Neither cast-in-place concrete nor asphalt paving are particularly in the traditional style we want to use. Although the roadways are asphalt and many of the sidewalks are cast-in-place concrete, the park is a key amenity area and a richer, more historic material is called for. The traditional aesthetic favors a modular system of bricks and/or stone (see *Timeless Features,* p. 7). The monolithic pavement used in most traditional designs is a fine, crushed aggregate of stone, brick, or seashell. These flexible monolithic systems are very forgiving of

movement but because they are loose materials, the surface is easily worn away and can be tracked onto the other rigid pavements.

Brick, stone, or precast pavers can be set over a flexible crushed stone or asphalt base with a mastic and sand-swept joints, or set on a rigid mortar bed with mortared joints over a concrete slab. The placement of expansion joints visible in the finished surface must correspond with expansion joints in the base slab, the joint pattern must be consistently worked into the overall design (see *Expansion Joints,* p. 81). In addition, all the joints are much more visually prominent in the rigid systems than in a flexible system where they are much narrower. The visual expression of the joints between the pavers can be minimized with the use of the colored mortar, but due to their width they will always be more prevalent than a sand-swept joint. In a flexible system, there must be a rigid edge restraint (see *Edge Restraint,* p. 77) around the perimeter of the paving system and around the edges of all penetrations. Without this edge restraint, individual pavers at the edges will move to not support the rest of the field. Joints will open up with frost and/or heavy use causing the whole system to fail.

Paving systems can be designed to be porous with water penetrating through the joints between units or through a monolithic matrix. Porous paving systems must be designed from the bottom up. The water that percolates through the surface needs to be evenly conveyed to soils that are permeable enough to absorb it without softening the subgrade soil supporting the system, with additional provisions for removing excess water. This necessitates grading a level subgrade picking up the difference between level steps and a sloping surface in the subbase material (see *Level Drainage Surfaces,* p. 62). In order for water to penetrate the surface, the paving units often have lugs on the paving edges to retain a gap between them and the joint filter, which is a very coarse material. In addition, most porous pavement systems require periodic maintenance to remove the air-blown fines that could clog the *system* (see *Maintenance Practices,* p. 102).

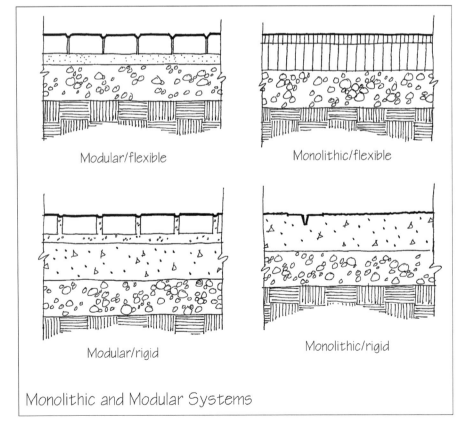

Modular/flexible

Monolithic/flexible

Modular/rigid

Monolithic/rigid

Monolithic and Modular Systems

We will select a brick porous pavement system to facilitate infiltration and reduce runoff. With the selection of a paving material we can start to develop sections through the site. The section will show the surface gradients, the finish grade relationships between the levels of the site and between sloping and level elements, and subgrade and finished relationships. In addition to the section, a plan of the subgrade conditions is developed. Not all the water running over the surface will percolate through the joints. Additional surface water will need to be picked up in area drains and conveyed to the basins. The reservoirs are shown as an open-graded stone. An alternate would be a system of concrete or plastic infiltration chambers, dry wells, or similar. The edges of the recharge reservoirs is worked out and the relationship of the basins and the foundations is reviewed and additional details are developed, if needed, to reflect the different foundation conditions inside and outside the basins.

Once the paver is selected, the module of the pavers and joints should be compared to the space between planters. Some adjustment to the dimensions of the site elements may be needed to allow for a clean installation (see *Uncut Units,* p. 150 and *Dimensional Tolerance,* p. 166). Paving patterns should also be examined and evaluated at this time. A running bond pattern throughout the plaza would result in few cut pavers, but could result in a number of "slivers" of pavers at the curb edge. Examining the orientation of the paving pattern relative to its edges may result in one orientation being superior to another (all other things being equal).

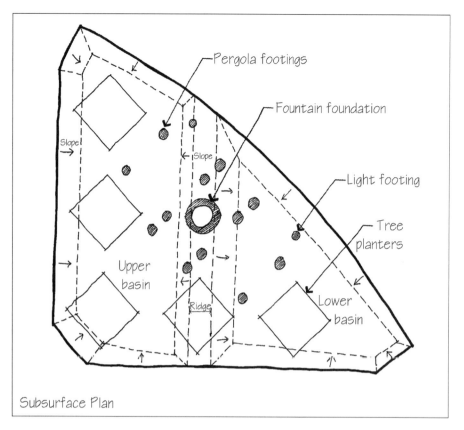

Subsurface Plan

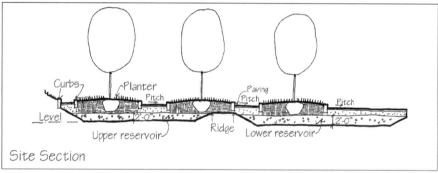

Site Section

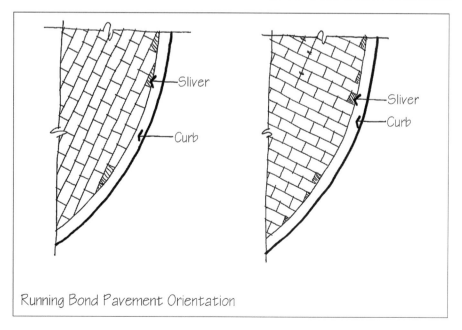

Running Bond Pavement Orientation

## GRADING AND FOUNDATIONS

This section through the site, starting at the curb and proceeding to the units at the back of the plaza, shows that with a minimal 1 percent pitch (to facilitate water filtration) the site will drop 1-4 in. (25-100mm) from back to front. Checking the pavement finished grade in each of the column bases we see that grades vary by 6″ (150mm) in elevation from the highest spot next to the pergola columns to lowest. The structure of a pergola is usually level and will be for this exercise. Therefore, we need to develop a detail that can accommodate the difference in the base elevations. This is a small structure bearing relatively little weight so we have some options for supporting columns. We can install columns that will extend to good bearing soil below the frost line *(see Foundation Below Frost Line,* p. 75*)* or we could float the structure on a thickened concrete slab (see Foundation Options). If we were using a rigid paving system, a thickened slab might be very economical. Given our choice to do a flexible paving system, the introduction of the thickened slab below the pavement may unduly complicate the construction process, cause differential settlement, and be just as costly as a full depth foundation.

The concrete footings could extend to the surface but that would give us little opportunity to adjust the finish grade

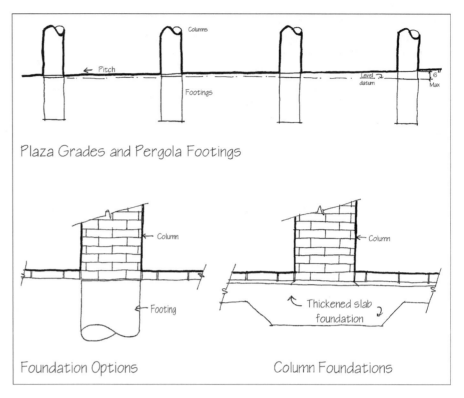

Plaza Grades and Pergola Footings

Foundation Options

Column Foundations

of the plaza surface (see *Adjustable Fit,* p. 172) and would expose potential rough concrete next to more finish work (see *Progressive Finish,* p. 180). A better detail might be to recess the top surface of the foundation below the finish grade.

## PERGOLA

This leads to material choices for the pergola columns. The tapered shape of

a neo-classical column could be constructed in a number of different materials. The columns could be fabricated in stone as a single unit or in pieces; constructed of concrete either precast or cast in place, as a single unit or pieces. The columns could also be constructed of wood or fiberglass; there are many manufacturers of these types of columns. As a further alternate, columns could be constructed of bricks or

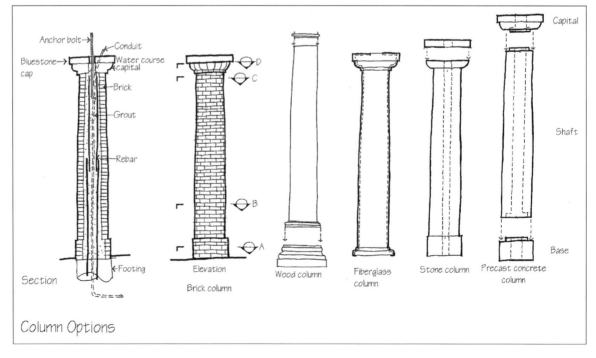

Column Options

smaller pieces of stone to make up the desired shape.

The wood and the fiberglass columns are typically fabricated as hollow shells with an interior cavity. This means any moisture that accumulates in the cavity must be collected and weeped (see *Drain and Weep,* p. 38) to the outside. In addition, wood columns should be installed with a gap between the bottom of the wood and the foundation to prevent premature rot in the wood base.

The tops of the columns also need to be considered. The hollow sections require a cap to keep moisture out of the cavity and to secure the beams to the column. The cap should also allow for air movement through the cavity to the outside. A solid cap over a column composed of stone or brick will also

benefit from a cap to shed water from the top joints.

The stone, concrete, or masonry alternates can be constructed without a cavity and avoid the complications of venting and weeping. A wood or fiberglass column is considerably lighter and would also influence the foundation details. Weighing the significance of all the patterns mentioned above, we have selected a brick column with a stone cap. Curved, shaped bricks for the shaft of the column come in various radii from 8 in. (203 mm) to 8 ft-0 in. (2,438 mm) and can be custom formed to any radius. Small radii—less than 12 in. (305 mm)—usually have slanted radial ends with the sides being square to the back in larger radii. Radii a little smaller or larger than standard sizes

can be approximated by varying joint widths (see *Dimensional Tolerance,* p. 166) and accepting some variation in overlap (see drawing below). A 9½ in. (241 mm) not tapered base section can be made up of 7 to 8 in. (203 mm) uncut exterior radius bricks with joints that are a bit larger than the standard ⅜ in (9 mm). A similar method can be used with different brick sizes. The 8½ in. (216 mm) radius straight section is similarly made up of 7 to 8 in. (203 mm) exterior radius bricks with joints slightly larger than ⅜ in (203 mm). The tapered section is made up of between 6 and 7 to 8 in. (203 mm) exterior radius bricks with joints set at ⅜ in. (9 mm) on the exposed face and ⅛ in. (203 mm), minimum at the rear edge of the brick on the interior of the column. It will be

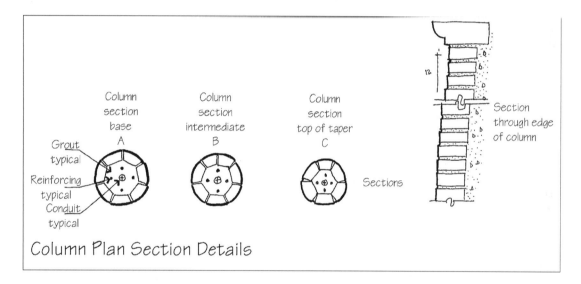

Column Plan Section Details

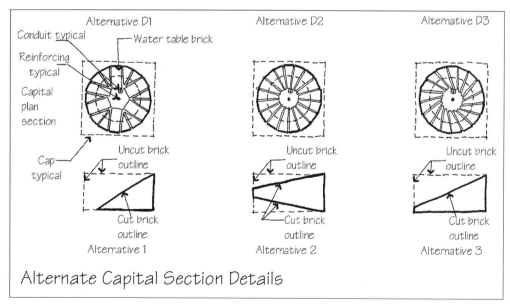

Alternate Capital Section Details

necessary to cut one or two bricks for every course (see Column Plan Section Details).

The detail we are considering for the capital utilizes a formed water table brick that is widely available in a variety of shapes, usually with a standard brick module 2¼ in. by 3⅝ in. by 7⅝ in. (51 × 92 × 194 mm). To achieve the 11 in. (279 mm) radius that we have designed, we will need to cut most of the water table bricks that make up the capital. The drawing below shows three options for making up the cap from standard units. We first consider an option that requires the least number of cuts (see *Uncut Units,* p. 150), using uncut bricks and cut bricks in a pattern of one uncut brick followed with two cut bricks. This Alternative 1, has fewer cut bricks and an interesting pattern, but the pattern is not symmetric, and the cut bricks do not have much support from the column section below, extending only 2⅝ in. (67 mm) over the body of the column. Alternative 2 requires a single cut to each brick. This option allows all the bricks to extend 4¼ in. into the body of the column. The cut on one side of the brick will be evident in the curved section of the water table and will add a spiraling effect to the cap. Alternative 3 requires two cuts to every brick. This option is similar to the second and extends all bricks over 4¼ in. into the body of the column and each brick is symmetrical in the cap. The second and third options could be mocked up (see *Simulated Assemblies,* p. 158) and evaluated to see if the spiraling effect of the second option overweighed the cost of the third (see *Alternative Capital Section Details*).

The core of the column will be filled with grout or mortar and reinforced with rebars that connect the column to the foundation. The core can also include conduits for lighting and sound (see *Vertical Chase* p. 108).

The column is capped with a 24 in. by 24 in. by 3 in. (610 × 610 × 76 mm) slab of bluestone. In the northeast United States, bluestone is readily available and cheaper than granite or other native stones. Its dark-gray color is often beautifully paired with blended red/gray bricks. Bluestone is a sedimentary

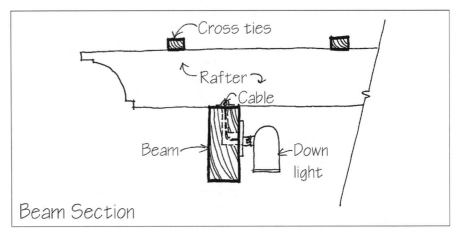

Beam Section

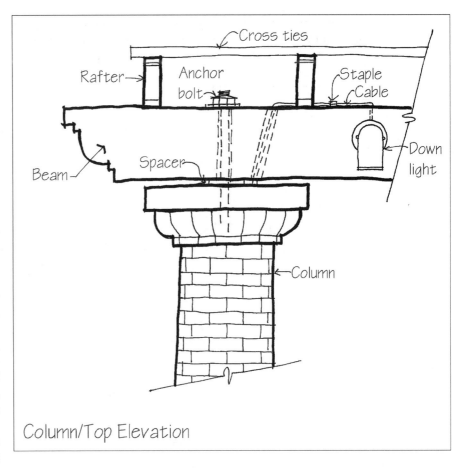

Column/Top Elevation

stone that is quite durable if set with its natural bedding horizontally. It is usually split to a desired thickness, then accurately saw cut to a plan dimension. It is easily sawn and core drilled at a stone fabricator's shop. The monolithic slab will cover the joints in the column and prevent moisture from infiltrating into the core. The detailer may consider flashing below the bluestone to prevent moisture from entering into the

column base, but the flashing will prevent a solid mortar bond between the bluestone cap and the brick. If moisture bond is a concern (with hollow construction etc.) then a drip edge cut into the cap should be considered (see *Overhang and Drip,* p. 40).

The beams, rafters, and purlins that make up the pergola are being detailed in wood. Synthetic materials were considered but not selected because they do not match the rustic look of the trellis and they often are not as stiff in long spans as natural woods. The detail of the attachment of the beam to the column includes a neoprene spacer to keep the beam from direct contact with the bluestone cap preventing moisture from rotting the beam (see *Capillary Break,* p. 43). The beam is connected to the cap via a threaded rod or J bolt imbedded in the core of the column and extended through the cap. The rod keeps the beam from shifting on the column and the washer and nut keep it from lifting up off the cap due to wind, warpage, or vine growth (see *Robust Assemblies,* p. 144). The purlins on the top of the rafters add another visually interesting layer to the pergola (see *Intensification and Ornamentation,* p. 10). They also keep the rafters from warping. The small sectional area is enough to restrain a twisting rafter but would not be adequate to withstand an aggressive vine like wisteria. The beams can also be bored to receive wires for lighting or sound systems. Wires can be run along the tops of the beams out of sight, and connected through them to fixtures mounted on the sides of the beams (see *Horizontal Distributions,* p. 110). The rafters and purlins can be attached via galvanized or (preferably) stainless steel fasteners to prevent corrosion and staining (see *Surfaces That Age Gracefully,* p. 132).

The paving is detailed with voids (cut outs) at the base of each column, which are edged in steel to firmly define the brick edge and allow space for the vines to grow up to the pergola (see *Root Zone Growth,* p. 96, and Vine Planting Detail).

## SITE FURNITURE

The plaza is designed to have pedestrian scale lights, wooden benches, and terracotta planters. The lights are designed to be bolted to the concrete footing. The bolt attachment detail allows the contractor to adjust the light to be plumb even if the footing is not, and to adjust the base of the light to meet grade (see *Adjustable Fit,* p. 172). J bolts are typically cast into the footing with the threaded ends extending above finish grade. If the

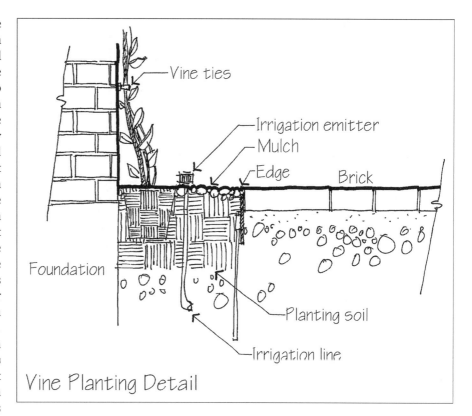

Vine Planting Detail

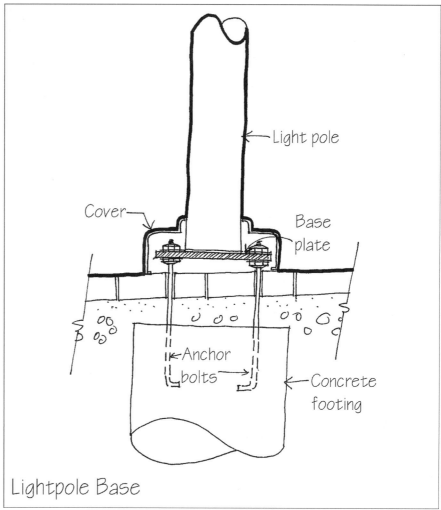

Lightpole Base

top of the foundation is intended to be exposed, flush with grade or above, the base of the light can be bolted directly to the foundation and shimmed to be plumb. If the foundation is not meant to be exposed, the foundation is poured below the finished grade and the bolts are installed to extend through the finished paving material. After the foundation and the paving are installed around the anchor bolts, the lights can be installed on the anchor bolts using nuts on both sides of the base plate. In either case most lights are designed with a decorative housing that covers the structural connections; they may also cover the electrical connections (see Lightpole Base).

The benches are to be positioned on a slightly sloping surface. The maximum change in grade over the four legs is ¾″ inches (19mm). The legs can be cut or shimmed to level the bench. The benches are anchored in two locations to prevent them from shifting and to prevent theft (see Bench Base).

The planters are shimmed to level and the bottoms have a hole to accommodate a drip irrigation line as well as drainage. A filter fabric is installed between the inside of the planter in the planting soil mix. The planters are designed with sloping interior walls so that if the planting media freezes it will lift up and not crack the outside walls. The planters are intended to be planted every year with annual flowers so the vacillation of freeze and thaw will not be detrimental to plant growth. If the planters were intended to be planted with evergreen woody plants that are more sensitive to multiple freeze-thaw cycles, the inside edges of the planter may need to be insulated. Traditional terracotta was considered for the planter, but it is not suitable for use as a planter that will be left filled with planting media through the winter. In the Northeast, traditional terracotta pots need to be emptied and dried prior to winter. Moisture absorbed by the terracotta would likely freeze and crack the pots. Precast concrete and fiberglass or other composite materials can be designed to withstand freezing and can approximate the look of a terracotta

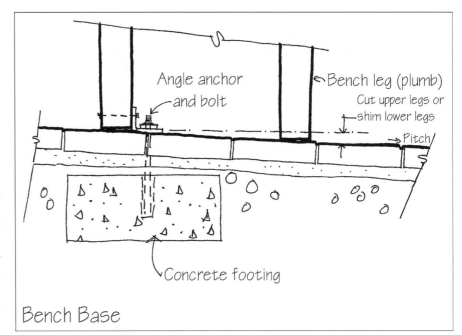

Bench Base

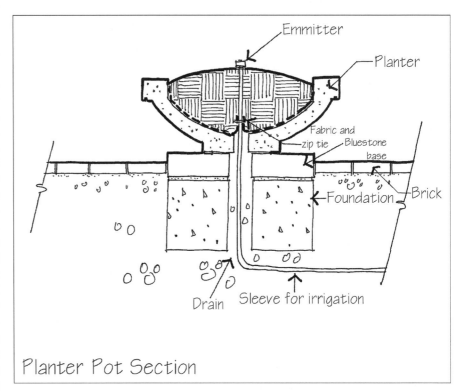

Planter Pot Section

pot. These are deemed more suitable for this project (see Planter Pot Section).

## FOUNTAIN

The fountain under the trellis is envisioned as a simple basin with a single jet that would animate the space and provide a pleasant background noise in the plaza. To match the vocabulary

of materials in the plaza, the exterior of the basin will be built of brick with the bluestone cap. The interior of the basin will be stucco with tile band at the water line. The structure of the fountain basin will be reinforced concrete to minimize cracks (see Fountain Section).

The source of water for the jet comes from a submersible pump.

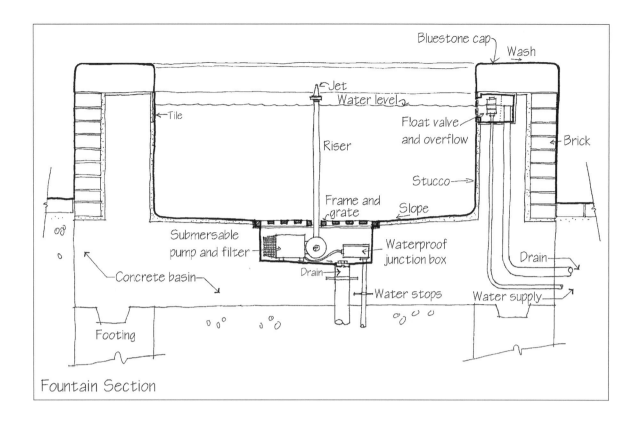

Fountain Section

The pump will include a filter, and it will draw power from a submersible junction box in a sump at the center of the fountain. A removable grate will cover the sump and allow an opening for the riser and jet to go above the surface of the water (see *Accessible Connections,* p. 161). Submersible lights will also be connected to the junction box and hung from the grate. The bottom of the sump has a drain line with a threaded connection. While the fountain is active the drain line can be sealed with a plug, but during the winter, the plug can be replaced with a domed drain. The water level indicator will be recessed into the wall to provide makeup water and to be an emergency shutoff for the lights and pump if water levels drop precipitously. The same recessed box can also accommodate overflow water during heavy rains (see *Redundant Drainage Systems,* p. 27). The fountain controls are fairly sensitive to changes in water level therefore, the foundations for the basin should extend below the frost line to prevent settlement (see *Foundation below Frost Line,* p. 75). Cracks in the basin and penetrations through the basin could cause leakage. Therefore any penetrations through the wall of the basin should include a water stop and the basin structure should be cast in a monolithic single pour.

## FENCE

The plaza is bound on two sides by residences. The residences are separated from the plaza by an 18 in. (460 mm) change in grade, a curb, fence, and planting. The change in grade together with the fence and planting create a visual edge to the plaza and a sense of privacy and defensible space for the units. The fence will be level on one side, but will slope a total of 1' – 6″ (460 mm) on another. The fence panels should be detailed to be "rackable," or individual fence panels should be stepped along the run (see *Adjustable Fit,* p. 172). The steps bring visual attention to areas that don't merit such attention (see *Active and Recessive Details,* p. 12), so we will use a sloping rackable picket fence with base boards that will follow the finish grade.

At the top of the slope, the fence will mark the boundary between the public space of the plaza and the private space of the front yard. With the base of the fence 18 in (460 mm) above the plaza, the overall height of the fence itself can be fairly low. With the addition of planting, the fence can also be fairly transparent and still provide privacy. A traditional picket fence has been chosen for this project. The fence will be fairly low, 30 in. (920mm), with somewhat wide spacing of the pickets (openings equal to the width of the picket). The low height and wide spacing are less imposing and unfriendly than fence constructions with more opacity. The wide spacing and simple construction of the rails will make racking fence panels down a slope more feasible. The top of the pickets are cut to shed water as are the top of the posts (see *Wash,* p. 33). The gate posts are built up to provide additional strength for the gate and a chase for wiring a light (see Vertical Chase). In addition, the larger gate posts can mark the entrance

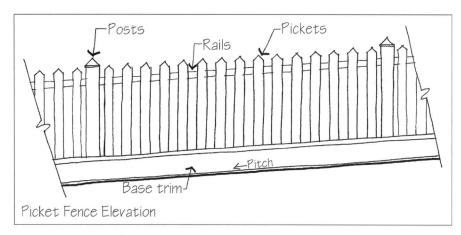

Picket Fence Elevation

way to the residence (see Picket Fence Elevation).

## NEXT STEPS

There has been an important aesthetic component to our work: The character of the landscape has emerged in a very exciting way as we have developed these key details. Unsympathetic detailing can destroy the aesthetic of an otherwise well-designed landscape, while thoughtful detailing can make it even better.

As we prepare to draft the final drawings of all the details for this project, we gather and organize the notes that we made to help us remember key aspects of these details from all phases of the project. We make a list that reminds us to include in the specifications such special items as the specialty bricks for the columns, the porous pavement reservoir construction, the planters and fountain mechanical items, as well as the more usual components, such as lighting, pavers, curbs, stone fabrications, planting, and coordination items for site engineers and irrigation designers who coordinate power and water services.

We also make some notes regarding things to keep in mind as we visit the site again and again during the construc-

tion process. It would be good to call to the contractor's attention in advance of construction the project's special features or challenges. For instance, the pergola columns are complex enough so that we should discuss them in detail with the general contractor and the mason before they are constructed. The first column to be built will be carefully checked as the exemplar for the others (see *Simulated Assemblies,* p. 158). Other than this, these details are largely based on common practice and probably need no special mention on the jobsite. Though always gratifying and even exciting, site visits for this project should largely be rather routine exchanges between designers, consultants and contractors. The constructive dialogue begun months ago will continue until the project is complete.

## KEY REFERENCES

The following are important reference materials that were used in developing this set of details. Full bibliographic information on these publications is given in the reference list at the back of this book.

1. Relevant building codes.
2. Manufacturers' catalogs.
3. National Forest Products Association, Span Tables for Joists and Rafters.

# CHAPTER 15  Detailing a Rooftop Garden

## THE PROJECT

The project is a small urban rooftop garden with intensive green roof and green wall as well as a steel trellis located in a large city in the southern, semitropical (zone 9) United States. The garden has a ground plane of large pavers and is contained on two sides by a perimeter parapet planter. The opposing two sides include a green wall and a glass walled lobby opening to the garden. The glass wall is shaded by the steel trellis. At the center of the garden is a rectangular planter of turfgrass.

## SETTING PERFORMANCE STANDARDS

The garden is on the 15th floor of a contemporary style building and is part of the adjoining lobby/restaurant space. Building tenants will have access to it for casual use and the restaurant will use it for expansion dining and event seating. The details should be contemporary and foster exterior use as weather permits. Some weight restrictions exist, but additional structural capacity is provided at the perimeter and the structure can support shallow planting soils or a pavement system throughout. The windows on the north side of the garden offer significant views, especially at night.

## KEY DETAILS TO DEVELOP

The key details that will establish the visual character of the garden and its methods of construction are highlighted in the plan and are listed below.

1. Pavement system
2. Perimeter planter with safety railing
3. Trellis
4. Turfgrass planter with integral lighting
5. Green wall system

These must be developed as a consistent set of *Contributive Details* (see p. 5) that work well with the surrounding architecture and with one another. They are the most basic of the garden's details. Details of special situations such as the ends and corners of

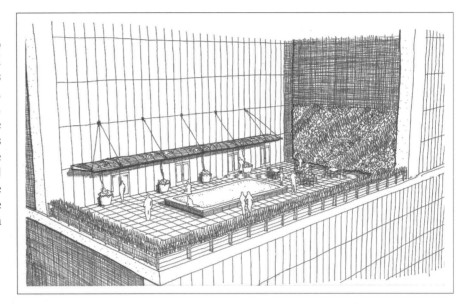

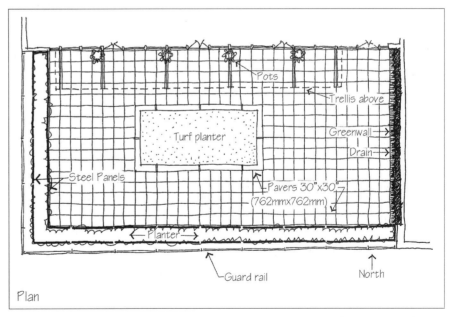

Plan

curbs, and edges of paving patterns will be developed using the general details as a point of departure.

## EARLY WORK ON FORM, MATERIALS, AND DETAILS

### PAVEMENT SYSTEM

As examined in the previous chapter, the type of paving system is one of the first choices to be made in detailing the garden. Being over a roof complicates the decision but it also offers some opportunities. As with the Traditional Plaza in Chapter 14, the paving choices are between either modular or monolithic and between rigid or flexible systems.

Flexible modular systems are constructed of large, individual units such as concrete or stone pavers and can be installed without a slope on the finish surface if supported above the sloping finished roof surface with premanufactured plastic pedestals. Rigid systems such as cast-in-place concrete or stone are installed over a concrete base to form a sloping surface. Rigid monolithic systems are installed above a redundant drainage system at the layer of the waterproofing below (see *Redundant Drainage Systems,* p. 28).

Both of these systems require some depth at the thresholds of the doors that open onto the garden. The pedestal system has some important advantages over the monolithic system. The modular units can be removed for maintenance of any pipes or wires that will feed the irrigation or lighting in the garden as well as surface below (see *Maintenance Access,* p. 136). If structure allows, the void below the pavers could be used for temporary stormwater storage. The free drainage through the open joints also allows for the level of the garden to be close to the finish floor elevation of the adjacent lobby.

For this exercise we have selected a pedestal support system with 30 in. (762 mm) square precast pavers, 2 in. (50 mm) thick with ⅜ in. (9.5mm) open joints. The concrete will be a light color in order to minimize heat gain and remain relatively cool underfoot. The paving system will allow for easy

access to the drains below for cleaning and inspection. The trellis is designed to accommodate vine growth, but pots will need to be provided for the roots. The pavers directly below the planters may require additional support and will need to be modified to accommodate irrigation and drainage for the planting.

When the selection of a paving material is complete we can start to develop sections through the garden. This section will show the surface gradients, the finish grade relationships between the levels of the building and the garden paving and planting areas, and between sloping and level planes, and roof deck grade.

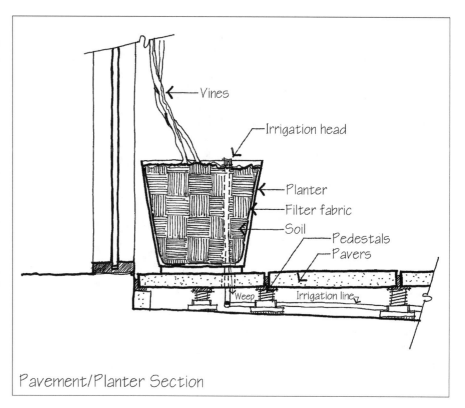

Pavement/Planter Section

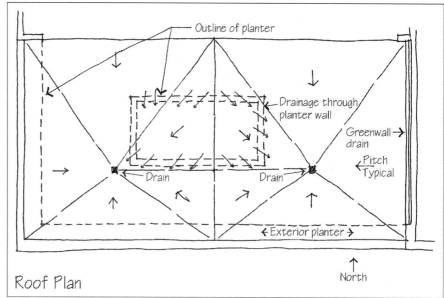

Roof Plan

This plan and section through the garden shows the roof conditions below the pavement system as they will be just below the finish floor elevation of the lobby. The roof slopes away from the building wall to two roof drains positioned in the space just beyond the edge of the planter. The planter at the east parapet can be developed to accommodate necessary soil volume below the level of the pavement to keep the top edge of the planter below eye level of seated restaurant patrons. The top of the turfgrass planter is set at a seat height of 20 in. (500 mm) above pavement level, also below seated eye level.

The section also shows a guardrail at the parapet (see *Fall Protection* p. 116). The guardrail is intended to accommodate window washing and maintenance only (the planter will act as a barrier to the general public). It should be detailed to be as transparent as possible. For this exercise, we have selected a post and cable system at 30 in. (750 mm) above the parapet. The trellis is shown in the section below and provides shade on the south-facing glass and connects directly to the building structural system (coordinated with the architect and structural engineer) (see North /South Section).

## PERIMETER PLANTER WITH SAFETY RAIL

The perimeter planter height is set by the section above as a maximum of 42 in. (1067 mm) above the pavement. The interior finishes of the lobby and restaurant feature painted and unfinished stainless steel as well as a concrete floor. We will use painted steel plate to form our planter walls. We could also use stainless steel but the cost would be higher, which would force us to compromise in other details. The steel can be used with a very thin section and give a very clean and sleek look to the planter edge. The steel planter sections will be shop fabricated to keep the tolerances tight and provide a controlled environment for painting the surface (see *Factory and Site*, p. 184). The edge should be detailed with ample opportunities for field adjustments during installation and movement over time (see *Adjustable Fit*, p. 172).

The design intent is to make it appear as though the sheets of steel have grown up from below as thin, nearly two-dimensional edges forming large planted boxes that contain the garden. The surface and exposed edges need to be detailed as cleanly as possible to reinforce the illusion of a two-dimensional plane. All the connections and stiffeners to prevent distortion of the face of the panels, should be welded to the rear of the panels where they will be buried and out of sight.

Ideally, the joints in the steel panels will line up with the paving module. We will make a note to coordinate the uncut modular paving joints with shop-fabricated joints in the steel planters. We also want the steel panels to be able to expand and contract while remaining in a true alignment. A slip joint in the rear of the panel will allow for the movement (see *Sliding Joint*, p. 89), keep the panels aligned, and keep the soil from escaping through the joint.

We can use the equation from Chapter 4 for sizing expansion joints (see p. 49). Working through a preliminary calculation to determine widths and spacing of these open joints in the steel construction, we first check to see what size of an expansion joint we need for a joint coinciding with every second paving joint which is 60″ (1524 mm) O.C. An open joint without sealant accommodates 100 percent of the movement in the adjacent edge panels so sealant joints for an open, sliding joint results in the following:

$$W = \frac{100}{X}(\varepsilon L \triangle T + M_o) + t$$

X = 100 (open joint is capable of 100 percent movement)

E = (.0000065 = expansion coefficient of steel),

L = 60 in. (1524 mm) (The length of two paving modules)

$\triangle$ T = 180 degrees F (42 degrees C) as the expected maximum range in temperature of the painted steel,

M = 0.04 in. (1 mm) from structural engineer,

t = + 1/8 in. (3.2 mm) construction tolerance of the assembly.

Placing these project values into the formula:

W = 100/100 [(.0000065) (60) (180) + 0.04"] + 0.125

This results in a joint 0.235 in. (6 mm) wide or about ¼ in. Our paving joints

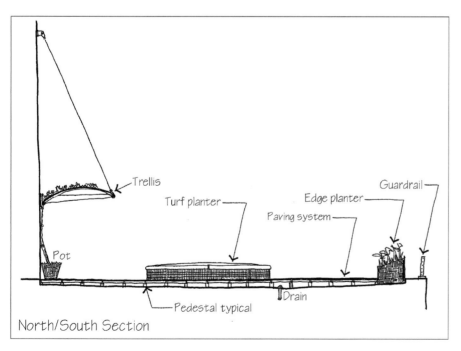

Trellis
Turf planter
Edge planter
Paving system
Guardrail
Pot
Drain
Pedestal typical

North/South Section

are ⅜ in. (9.5 mm) wide so we will try a wider spacing of 120 in. (3,048 mm) (four modules). This results in a width of .2694 in (7 mm). If we simplify the equation, setting our joint width at ⅜ in. (9.6 mm), we can solve for the joint spacing. This results in a maximum spacing of 210 in. (5,334 mm) or seven paving modules. We will lay out the joints on the plan and not exceed a distance of seven paving modules. We will also need to explore the corner and end condition for the planter edge to be sure that movement will not be restricted in these locations, and for accurate fit (see Planter Edge Joint).

Corners are notorious for misalignment. Expansion can come from both directions and if a joint occurs at a corner it needs to accommodate two perpendicular forces. Many times it is better to design a corner that is solid with nearby joints on either side in a straight run. The end condition will have to contain the soil and allow some space between the planter and the building face. It will also have to slope to accommodate the different heights in the front and back panel. We have designed an end panel that can be bolted to the side panels from the inside allowing for adjustments in all three directions (see *Sliding Fit*, p. 170).

The planter will be irrigated and we will specify a free draining soil mix and compatible geotextile to keep the soil from migrating through the joints (see *Geotextile Separation,* p. 59) or into the space below the planter and pavers. We want the geotextile to terminate below the soil surface so we have called for a bead of adhesive to keep the fabric in place during planting and to keep soil from migrating behind it. We have included a plastic drainage grid at the bottom of the planter to facilitate drainage (see *Progressive Filtering,* p. 58). We have also included a layer of insulation on the outside (predominantly south-facing) surface to protect the plant roots from overheating on hot sunny days.

Similar details are sometimes used in northern planters to keep planters subject to winter sun from repeatedly heating up and thawing once they are frozen. The frequent oscillations between freezing and thawing can

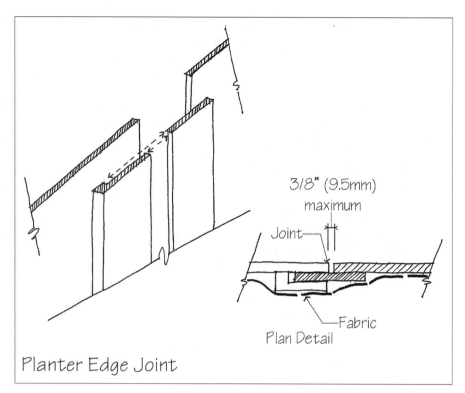

Planter Edge Joint

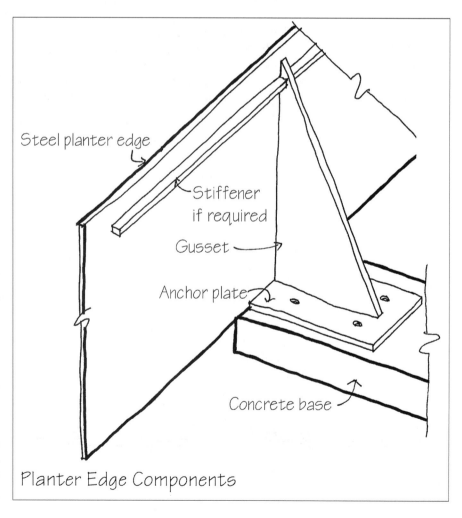

Planter Edge Components

also harm plant roots; soil expansion in planters can also cause structural damage to the planter walls.

The building has been designed with a wide and low parapet. This will keep the planters out of view from below and will allow for access to the edge of the building for glass cleaning and other maintenance activities. In conjunction with the architect and structural engineer, a series of anchors for window washing rigs have been sized and a cable rail will be added to the parapet as an added safety measure. The safety rail will be a series of stainless steel cables supported by simple painted steel posts. The architects are including the safety rail on their drawings, but the intent of the planters is (in part) to screen the railings from view. To assure that this design intent is met, it is vital that both fabrication drawings be reviewed at the same time. This is a critical coordination issue between the architect, landscape architect, fabricator, and the contractor (see Planter Section).

## TRELLIS

To shade the south-facing windows from direct sunlight a trellis is included in the design. The trellis will be supported from the building wall with rods or cables and clean functional hardware in keeping with the building detailing. The horizontal trellis members will be made of a painted steel frame and canopy. We will explore two options for the trellis. One option has a canopy of woven stainless steel fabric panels stretched within the frame with steel rods and tendons. The alternate will be a series of closely spaced pipe rafters and oversized connectors of threaded rods and fabricated connectors. As with the safety rail, the design of the trellis must be coordinated with the work of the architect and structural engineer from design through fabrication and installation (see Canopy Detail).

The trellis can be designed to combine stock components and custom fabrication. The frame can be designed from standard steel bar and flat stock, the rods or cables can be designed with stock fasteners, and the fabric panels can also be selected from standard sections. Rods and cables are available in a large number of diameters and are usually cut to length

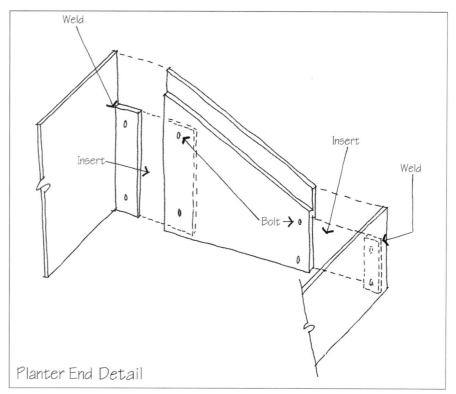

Planter End Detail

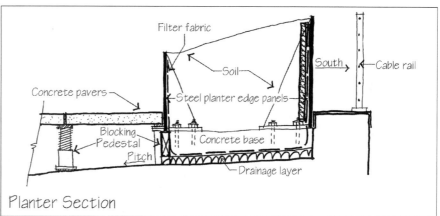

Planter Section

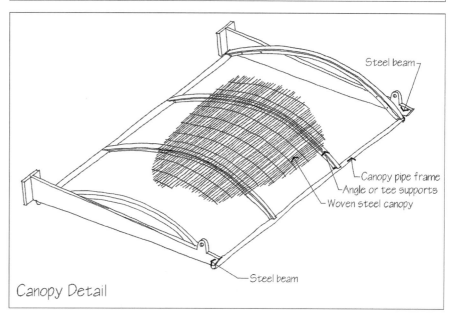

Canopy Detail

for each application. Similarly, steel fabricators usually cut stock members to the sizes needed for each project.

However, the woven steel meshes or fabrics come in stock widths that are difficult to alter, so the design of the trellis should reflect this modular width (see *Uncut Units*, p. 150). The main structural beams that support the trellis will be attached directly to the building and should correspond to its structural grid. The building's columns are located just behind the building skin and the rod/cable connections and beam connections will attach to the columns (see *Providing Structural Support*, p. 103).

The building column grid will determine the spacing of the main beams and the width of the woven fabric will determine the module of the panels that will be supported by those beams. The basic structure of the first trellis is a series of painted steel frames fabricated from curved steel angle and pipe sections with stainless steel fabric stretched over those frames. The frames are supported by painted steel beams that are directly attached to the building and further supported by a rod or cable connected to anchor points above (see *Similar Metals*, p. 139).

An early sketch of the system should be developed with the structural engineers and, if possible, with the fabricator. The pros and cons of rods versus cable can be discussed and resolved. The cables provide great support in tension, thus they may be more slender than rods but may not provide the stiffness required to keep the structure from lifting in the wind. The members can be sized and component manufacturers selected.

The frames for the fabric are designed to stretch the fabric within the rigid frame over curved side rails to create an arching ceiling above the passages to the roof garden. The individual panels will have adjustments that will allow the fabric to tighten up over time within the frames (see *Adjustable Fit*, p. 172). The frames will also be adjustable in their connection to the beams and the rods or cables can also be adjusted. The look of a bolted structure with sleek rod or cable connections is consistent with what we are trying to achieve and will give us a lot of flexibility in fabrication and installation (see Canopy Section and Elevation).

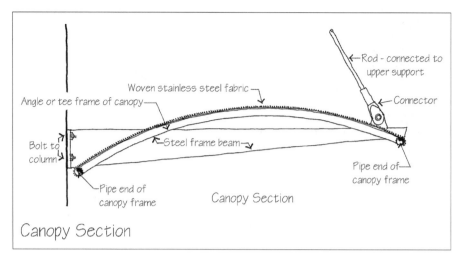

Canopy Section

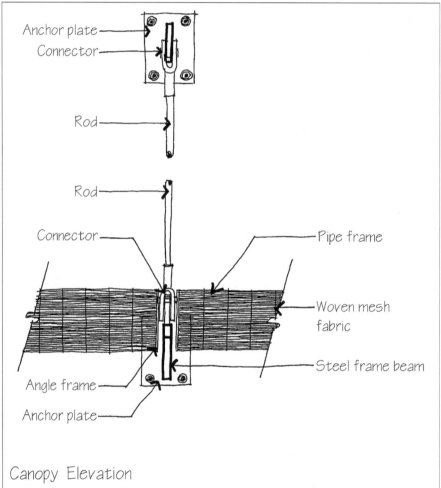

Canopy Elevation

An alternate trellis design was developed that would be constructed entirely of stock components that are easily found in any metal shop. The woven fabric and the tendons were replaced with threaded connectors, some simple fabrications, and a straightforward rafter system. The resulting design does not have the more refined look of the first trellis option, but could be fabricated by a larger pool of fabricators and could accommodate a wider range of field adjustments with its many threaded connectors (see Alternate Section and Elevation).

The curved fabric solution is more appropriate for this project, and can be achieved by our skilled team of fabricators and contractors. This alternate trellis design was therefore not carried forward.

The final trellis components and finished assembly should also be reviewed in a mockup to verify its qualities, and coordinated at every phase of the project.

## TURFGRASS PLANTER WITH INTEGRAL LIGHTING

The planter in the middle of the garden is intended to provide a seat height edge and introduce a cool grass surface for sitting or reclining. The planter should look substantial in the daytime but appear to float above the surface of the terrace at night. The top of the edge is set at 20 in. (500 mm) above the pavement the edge of the turf should be flush with the seat/edge and slightly crowned in order to appear level. The grass will be watered with pop-up irrigation heads, evaporative cooling should further add to the cooling effect of the turf. To reduce the weight of the soil on the structure below, we will replace the soil at depths greater than the 18 in. (375 mm) (needed to support the turf) with polystyrene blocks and an open grid for drainage. It is very important to both crown the polystyrene and provide weep holes through that layer to the drainage layers below. The planter soil and fabric should be treated similarly to the edge planters, but the turf will require much more water than the perimeter planters. It could be aerated periodically to alleviate compaction so a heavier soil mix could be considered for this planter.

The top of the planter wall will serve as seating, so it should have a rounded edge that will not damage clothing (see *Safe Edges*, p. 119). We have selected to use a precast concrete coping to match the pavers.

The coping is durable and light in color; it will be cooler than other materials. To reduce weight and achieve the floating effect we seek, we will support the coping with a narrow concrete wall to contain the planting and with poured concrete wing walls to support the ends of each coping section.

To cover the cavity below the coping, we will add panels of stainless steel woven fabric similar to the trellis. The fabric panels will allow us to backlight the panels and provide a glow below the copings that will be shielded from direct view and not compete with the view of

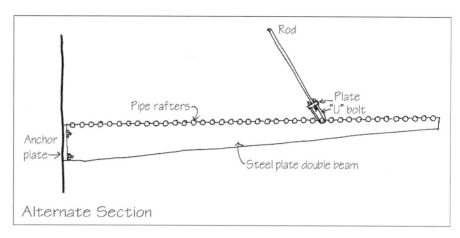

Alternate Section

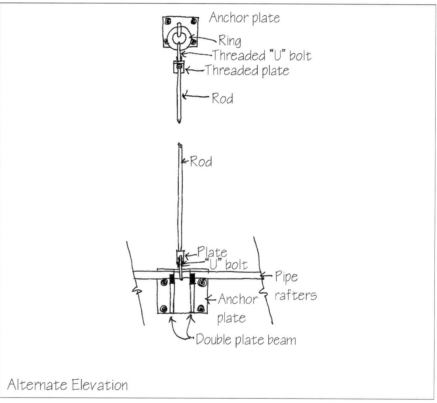

Alternate Elevation

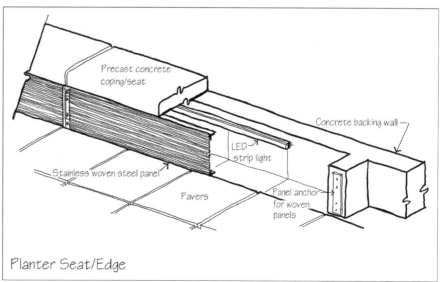

Planter Seat/Edge

the city. The lights can be unshielded, low wattage and very energy efficient. The panels are modular and removable for maintenance of the lighting system. The stainless steel is very durable and will not show heel marks from seated residents or patrons (see *Robust Assemblies*, p. 144 and *Cleanable Surfaces*, p. 135). The modules of the panels should reflect the paving module similar to the planter joints.

A similar calculation to the one above for the open joint of the planter can be carried out for the caulked coping joints. The sealant joint will have a movement capacity of 50 percent, the precast concrete will have an expansion coefficient of .0000055 in./in./degree F (.0000098 m/m degree K), the structure structural deflection is expected to be insignificant, and the construction tolerance for the coping is ⅛ in (.125 in.) (3 mm).

Working backward, a ⅜ in. (9.5 mm) joint would work for up to a 63 in. (1,600 mm) spacing, or two paving modules.

If we try a ½ in. (12.7 mm) joint, we get a spacing of up to 126 in. (10 ft, 6 in.) (3,200 mm), or four modules.

If we seek to relate the joint pattern of the copings with the joint pattern of the front panels and the planter, we can use the four-module joint at 120 in.(or 10 feet) (3,048 mm), or 10 ft-0 in., as the lowest common dimension. At 150 lbs/cf (2,322 kg/m³) of concrete, the coping will weigh 750 lbs (340 kg) each. If a crane is not available, a lightweight aggregate should be considered to make them manageable by hand (see *Parts that are Easy to Handle*, p. 154).

The corners of the coping and lower panels in the planters should be slightly rounded and avoid joints in the corner similar to the planter edges. The coping is easily fabricated with a rounded corner and the selected stainless steel fabric can be rolled in one direction to accommodate a curve. The development of this corner detail will determine the orientation of the fabric and the attachment detail of the panels to the inner frame. These corners will be prominent in the finished project, so this detail deserves our careful attention (see *Hierarchy of Refinement*, p. 8).

## GREEN WALL SYSTEM

The green wall indicated on the plan is sheltered from direct morning sun with a westerly orientation. The green wall will be made up of pregrown panels that will be hung from a steel frame that is attached to the wall. There are a number of manufactured systems that are available for this purpose. The detail will be built around a specific proprietary system and incorporated into the documents.

As with other elements in the garden, the green wall and the frame will have to be closely coordinated with the structural engineer and architect as well as plumbing engineers for water supply and drains. The moisture that runs through the panels will have to be kept out of the building. It may be prudent to incorporate additional waterproofing and a deep edge to prevent moisture from entering the building's exterior wall. Each section of the system is designed to be irrigated from above (often with added fertilizer) and drained into a gutter below. The panels contain a growing medium, structural support, and many systems include a rigid back and flexible geotextile-covered front. Panels can often be pregrown in a nursery, filling in over the geotextile cover and acclimated to a similar light condition.

When planning for green walls, the horizontal depth of the mature planting from the building wall should be considered, as should the maintenance required to keep the wall looking lush. A gutter drain at the base of the wall should be wide enough to catch water dripping off the plants, thereby preventing pavement staining and potential for slipping (see *Safe Footing*, p. 114). A wide drain also acts as a warning for visually impaired users that there may be plants extending beyond the face of the wall.

Fertilizer is likely to be present on some of the runoff water coming from the wall. Fertilizers are salts that can react chemically with concrete and many metals. Barriers on the sides of the wall and materials below the wall should be corrosion resistant.

The detailer should examine the location where the gutter drain is inserted

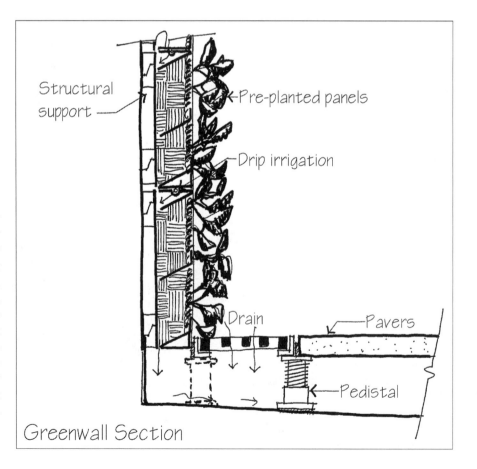

Greenwall Section

in the raised pavement system. Most frame and grate systems are designed to be attached to a rigid base. The pedestal system is flexible. The grate will attach to the green wall or at its base and will abut the pavers or it will be mounted on the pedestals that support the pavers. The water that passes through the grate could be treated the same as any water falling on the pavers and comingle with it on the way to the roof drain. The runoff from the green wall may be chemically very different from that of the terrace. Water from the green wall could include fertilizer and could be harvested and recycled. The terrace water could also be recycled but if the terrace is used for food service, cleaning chemicals used to remove food stains from concrete could contaminate the water for some types of reuse.

## NEXT STEPS

As in the previous example, there has also been an important aesthetic component to our work in this example: the aesthetic ideas suggested solutions and eliminated many others. The precision of the crisp industrial aesthetic lead to the selection of shop-fabricated items that can more reliably achieve the tolerances required to make them work. In the previous example, most of the critical elements were built on-site and could be adjusted at the site. In this example, many of the steel fabrications will be built in the fabricator's shop and shipped to site for installation. The detailer needs to pay particular attention to the fabrication drawings to assure that the details worked out with the fabricator are workable in the field to achieve the design intended. The patterns described in Chapter 10, *Ease of Assembly,* and Chapter 11, *Forgiving Details,* will be particularly applicable.

This project is built upon and is surrounded by a building. Establishing common aesthetic and functional aspirations for the project with those of the building architect and engineers are crucial. The details must be integrated to work on both an aesthetic and function basis. Everyone involved must share an understanding of where the project is going.

The same is true of coordination with the builder. It is sometimes the case that the landscape is looked at as an afterthought by builders. They concentrate on the main building components through the life of the project and only focus on the "landscape" after the project is nearly completed. That would be catastrophic for this project. Every building system, from structure to plumbing and electrical, could be affected by this work. The builder must be engaged early in the project in order to succeed. Access to the Garden and material handling will require use of building elevators or a crane. The staging of material and labor could be critical to the success of the project (see *Rehearsing the Construction Sequence,* p. 186).

Mockups are critical for this project as well. Few of these items are "standard." They are not complicated but they need to be explored in mockup to be assured that they will be executed correctly. Sloppy work will destroy the aesthetic appeal of the elements.

The details developed here are for an intensive green roof. It will require water to be successful. Knowing that, the rest of the project could be examined for water harvesting opportunities. Graywater, condensate harvesting, and runoff recovery all could be explored to assure that the garden will have the water it needs to remain successful.

## KEY REFERENCES

The following are important reference materials that were used in developing this set of details. Full bibliographic information on these publications is given in the reference list at the back of this book.

1. Relevant building codes.
2. Manufacturers' catalogs (particularly the Greenwall components).
3. ANSI Z-60, The American's Nurseryman's Standard.

CHAPTER

# 16 Detailing a Residence

## THE PROJECT

The project is a residence on a hilltop in the Rocky Mountains. The house has been sited to take advantage of views to the north, east, and west. There is a road to the south that will be screened from view and traffic noise. The living room opens out onto a terrace that extends northward to a firepit. The kitchen wing will flow out onto a small grass lawn. The house will be heated and cooled via a geothermal heat exchange unit in the basement, so we will not need to locate and screen air-conditioner units. A small utility yard will be located off the bedroom wing for grill and firewood storage as well as a working surface for potting and outdoor projects. We will also work with the engineers to locate all the meters, backflow preventers, and so forth in the service yard, out of sight.

## SETTING PERFORMANCE STANDARDS

We wish to minimize water usage (except for the small panel of lawn, which is used as a luxurious framed element in lieu of a field around the entire site) in the project. The details should support planting in an arid landscape with generous volumes of planting soil and planned snow storage areas to build soil moisture (see *Root Zone Growth,* p. 96, and *Maximize Site Benefits,* p. 199). The hardscape detailing, should complement the detailing of the house utilizing similar treatments of wood and concrete where a continuity is desirable (see *Contributive Details,* p. 5). The house is built of concrete, with expansive windows and corrugated aluminum siding, and a painted, horizontal ship-lap siding. Some of these materials can be utilized

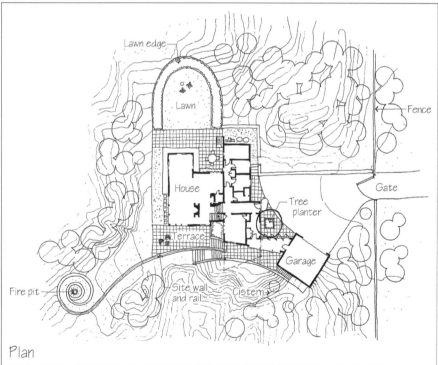

Plan

in the site to detail fences, walls and other elements.

## KEY DETAILS TO DEVELOP

The key details that will establish the visual character of the project and its methods of construction are listed below. These must be developed as a consistent

set of *Contributive Details* (p. 5) that work well with the building's architecture and with one another. These are the most basic of the site's details.

*Fence*

*Water Collection System*

*Site Walls*

*Pavement*

*Railings*

*Tree Planting*

*Lawn Edge*

*Fire Pit*

The plans and details need to be coordinated with the site work for the house; utilities and geothermal system to minimize the cost of rock excavation and to preserve the existing vegetation (see *Minimize Site Impacts,* p. 197 and *Maximize Site Benefits,* p. 199).

## FENCE

The fence separates the property from the road and should have sufficient mass to absorb sound and be detailed without gaps that would allow road noise to penetrate through it. A wall was considered for this purpose, but the client did not like the look of a wall and preferred the look of a wooden fence. The fence is designed to have a continuous rustic façade on the street-facing side and painted ship-lap siding matching the house on the house-facing façade. The fence is an active edge to the property when viewed from the house and rustic recessive when viewed from the road (see *Active and Recessive Details,* p. 12).

The site is extremely rocky, so the posts will be set with post anchors on concrete footings poured into the bedrock. To assure a tight fit, the frame that supports the rustic board façade will be sheathed in plywood and the cavities between the studs will be filled with insulation to further reduce vibration of the fence surfaces and reduce sound transmission. To prevent sound from "leaking" under the fence, a trim board will be added at the base of both sides of the fence to plug the gap. The sound attenuating properties need to be weighed against the snow deposition patterns generated by the prevailing winds. The gap at the base of the fence is required to block sound, but interferes with the passage of wind and snow deposition patterns. The rustic boards will be a split redwood "grape stake" and the baseboards will be a composite material to resist rot in contact with the ground. To reduce the exposure of the grape stake end grain,

the tops will be cut at an angle to shed water (see *Dry Wood,* p. 137).

Facing the house, the fence is clad in western cedar siding matching the house but it is turned vertically, to better conform to the irregularities of the site. The end grain of the siding is covered with a composite cap that will resist rot and is easily bent to conform to the flowing profile of the fence (see *Dry Wood,* p. 137). The cap laps over the siding behind the grape stake façade and includes a trim piece to cover irregularities in the top of the siding (see *Sliding Fit,* p. 170).

The gate will match the corrugated aluminum used on the house façade. The lighter weight and contrasting

color and texture will work well for the gate (see *Continuous and Discontinuous Details,* p. 14).

Where the driveway will penetrate the fence, we have a different set of criteria to meet. The gate will have to ride above the ground and be able to operate in the snow as well as in other seasons. A gap below the fence will allow road noise to enter the property, but the front of the house is somewhat separated from the main outdoor spaces that most need shielding from road noise, so this is less of a concern here.

We can choose from among several options for the gate operation. The gate can swing on a hinge (or hinges, if it is

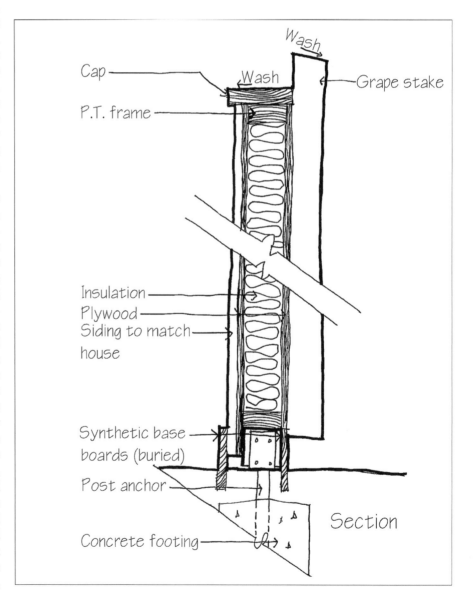

detailed in two sections) or it can slide behind the rest of the fence. It could also retract into the ground or lift above the drive on tracks. Both of these last two options are quite costly and were eliminated from consideration for that reason. Of the two remaining options, the sliding gate would work best under heavy snowfall provided the area needed to retract the fence was covered and protected from snow accumulation. The swing gate requires the clearing of snow from the arc of the gate's swing before it is opened. With the gate swinging into the property, a snow plow would not be able to come to the property and clear the gate from the outside prior to opening it. A plow operator would have to hand-dig the snow away. To minimize the snow accumulation, the gate is detailed to allow wind to penetrate the structure through a series of slats and act as a snow fence (see Elevations).

On the aesthetic side of the ledger, the swing gate is simple and fits into the plane of the fence. The slide gate is set behind the fence and requires additional structure for the track and to act as a counterweight, almost doubling the length of the gate itself. Both gate types can be automated. The swing gate was chosen to make the gate simpler and use fewer resources.

## WATER COLLECTION

As much water as possible will be collected for reuse. Chapter 13, *Sustainability*, contains the driving concepts behind this, especially the pattern *Maximize Site Benefits* (p. 199).

A cistern will be located in one of the lowest spots on the site near the building. A collection system of plastic piping will connect to the cistern. A pump will convey the water in the cistern to a subsurface drip irrigation system under the lawn and to a temporary drip system to help get the new plantings established. The cistern system could also be expanded to accept graywater from the house.

Roof water will be collected at the downspouts or rainchains and drains

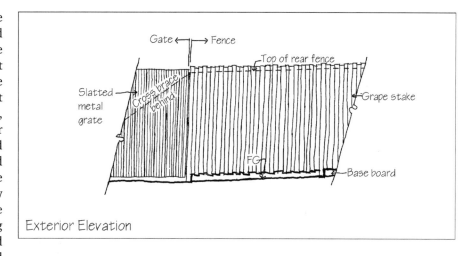

Exterior Elevation

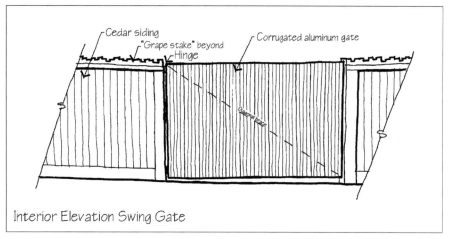

Interior Elevation Swing Gate

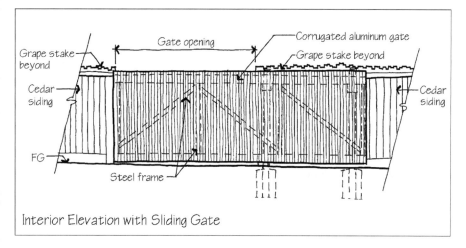

Interior Elevation with Sliding Gate

(see *Roof Drainage,* p. 31); the paved surfaces will drain to area drains and be connected to the roof drainage system that empties into the cistern. The drainage structures will all include sumps and or filters to catch the particles that will be washed into the drainage system (see *Sumps,* p. 57) in the beginning of each storm keeping the sediment from entering the cistern.

We will locate the cistern at a relative low point near the house in an area we can screen from view that we can connect to each of the drain lines via gravity. The cistern should have a vent to allow air to displace the water as it is used, an access hatch for cleaning (*Maintenance Access,* p. 136), an overflow (see *Redundant Drainage Systems,* p. 27) with the outfall reinforced with stone to prevent erosion (see *Building and Landscape Armor,* p. 145) and a submersible pump to supply the irrigation system (see Rain Harvesting Diagram).

## SITE WALLS

The site will require a number of retaining walls to support the terrace and lawn and to hold back the existing slope at the driveway. Concrete is aesthetically compatible with the rocky site and is used extensively in the house details, so concrete walls are a logical choice for the site walls. We wish to create a special character for the site retaining walls that come out of the rock to create a plinth that the house sits upon. We will use coarse-textured form liners to create a rough textured finish on these site walls. These walls will be related to the family of concrete walls of the house, but will have details giving them a separate character from the house walls.

The form liners will make a rough vertical pattern in the wall face, allowing us to incorporate wall joints in the recesses of the pattern. In our effort to harvest as much site water as possible, we will not use weep holes in the wall face, but will incorporate a continuous perforated drain to intercept any groundwater buildup behind the wall and transmit it to our central cistern. We will cast a concrete wall cap with a separate texture to facilitate the creation of a smooth-flowing line at the edge of the terrace below the rail and above the rough wall face. The cap will ride above the rough wall and a reveal will create a shadow line below the cap and give us a very forgiving transition from the rough to the smooth (see *Reveal,* p. 174). The pavement behind the wall will rest on a haunch formed by the wall below; it will be detailed to allow for the expansion joint to move

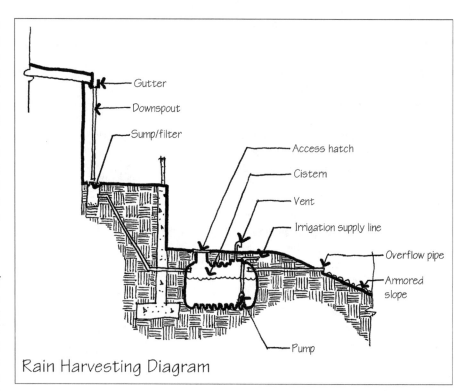

Rain Harvesting Diagram

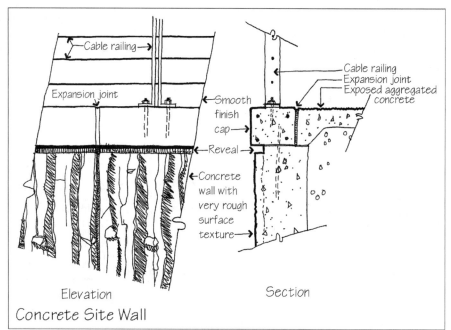

Elevation — Section

Concrete Site Wall

without vertical settlement (see *Expansion Joint,* p. 81).

### PAVEMENT AND RAILINGS

To allow for collection of all water running off of impermeable surfaces, the pavement systems should be monolithic to minimize the number of joints and through which water loss could occur. The pavement in the driveway will be asphalt with an aggregate rolled into the surface for added color and to

lighten the surface to reduce the heat island effect. The patios and terraces will be detailed in exposed aggregate concrete with a delicate grid of expansion and control joints.

There are several options for creating control joints in exposed aggregate. A tooled joint is effective when installed prior to the washing of the surface and the exposing of the aggregate. With seeded (placed) aggregates, however, the tool often drives the decorative aggregate too deep into the slab to be exposed, leaving an excessive amount of cement "paste" at the joint and changing the look of the surface along the joint. Saw cutting joints is also an option but cutting can dislodge the aggregate if the concrete has not set sufficiently to retain them. Similarly, thin plastic strips called "zip-strips" can be placed in the slab prior to seeding the aggregate, but care must be taken not to dislodge their alignment. Alternative saw-cut options with different mixes of aggregate should be tested and compared to thin "zip strip" joints to refine the design in mockup prior to final installation (see Joint Options in Exposed Aggregate).

Expansion joints and tooled joints should also be included in the mockup so that a full range of joint types and sizes can be evaluated. The wider expansion joints or larger tooled joints can be used as a primary pattern with the narrower saw-cut or strip joints forming a secondary overlay pattern (see Intensification and Ornamentation, p. 10).

The pavement in the east terrace will extend over the retaining wall to minimize the visual presence of the edge and allow the view to the east to be as seamless as possible. The railing on the edge of the wall will also be detailed to be as transparent as possible, in steel and cable. The rails are intended to flow with the line of the concrete wall and pavement, so we will curve our rails in plan and in elevation to follow the concrete surfaces. This choice to fabricate the rail frame in curving sections as opposed to straight segments will greatly increase the cost of the rail system, but without contribution of the curved rail, the sweeping curves of the wall and terrace will not have the integrity implied in the design (see Contributive Details, p. 5). As the cables are tightened, they exert a great deal of pressure at the end of their runs, so the end of the cable run must be rigid enough not to be bowed out of alignment when the cables are tightened. We will look at four options to reinforce the ends while maintaining the look of the overall fence (see Typical Rail Elevation).

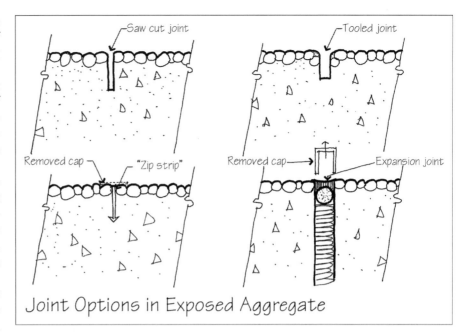

Joint Options in Exposed Aggregate

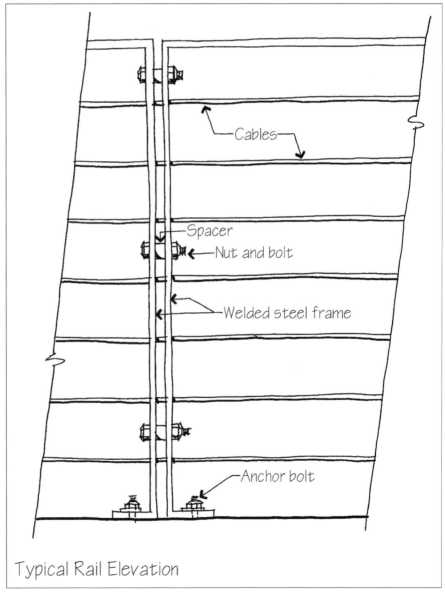

Typical Rail Elevation

The first option is to mimic the double posts between every section of railing and add a stiffener to the assembly on the back side of the railing. This heavier section should resist bowing when the cables are tightened and is compatible with the detail of the rest of the railing. It ends the railing abruptly with a minimum of accentuation. The downside of this option is that it creates a front and a back to the railing, a complicating factor we may not wish to introduce into the design (see Elevation Option 1).

The second option is similar to the first in that it uses a stiffener on the back side of the top rail while sloping the railing down to the top of the wall. This heavier section should also resist bowing when the cables are tightened and is compatible with the detail of the rest of the railing. It ends the railing as a flowing element that dies into the surface with a minimum of accentuation (see *Active and Recessive Details*, p. 12, and Elevation Option 2).

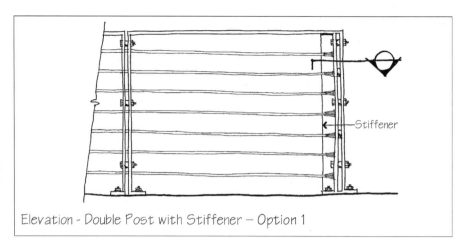

Elevation - Double Post with Stiffener – Option 1

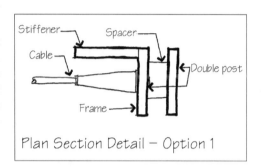

Plan Section Detail – Option 1

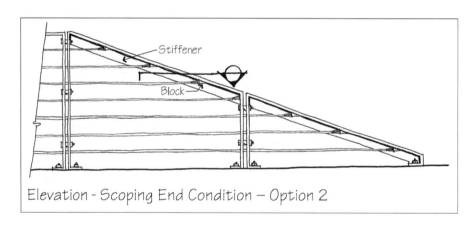

Elevation - Scoping End Condition – Option 2

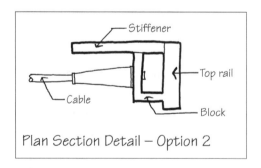

Plan Section Detail – Option 2

The third option uses a thicker end post to stiffen the assembly at its end. The built-up "I" section is similar to the rest of the detailing of the railing with the advantage that it does not favor one side over the other (there is no back side) as do the first two options. This heavier section should also resist bowing when the cables are tightened and is compatible with the detail of the rest of the railing. It ends the railing with an element that is somewhat different than the rest of the railing, accenting the termination of the railing (see Elevation Option 3).

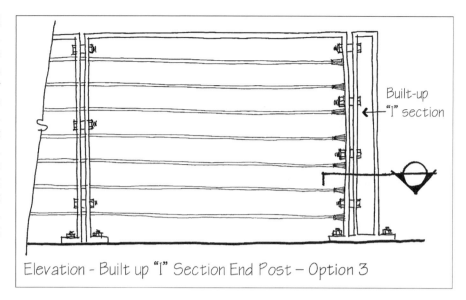

Elevation - Built up "I" Section End Post — Option 3

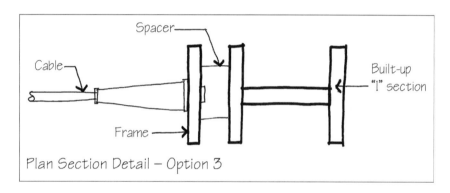

Plan Section Detail — Option 3

The fourth option also uses a thicker end post to stiffen the assembly at its end; it extends that thicker post to become a light fixture. The built-up tube section is somewhat similar to the rest of the railing detailing, and it does not favor one side over the other (there is no back side). This heavier section should also resist bowing when the cables are tightened and is compatible with the detail of the rest of the railing. It ends the railing with an element that is somewhat different than the rest of the railing, heavily accentuating the termination of the railing (see *Hierarchy of Refinement,* p. 8, and *Off the Shelf Parts,* p. 188). We will use options 3 and 4 in appropriate locations in this project (see Elevation Option 4).

## TREE PLANTING

Geologically, this site presents some special challenges. The site has very shallow bedrock so the tree planting details need to address the bedrock subgrades to assure sufficient drainage and root zone for long-term health of the new plantings (see *Root Zone Growth,* p. 96). Plant species that are compatible with the anticipated soil and water conditions must also be carefully selected.

Of particular interest is the planter between the house and the garage. We have selected two monolithic impermeable pavements in this area, so we will need to add aeration provisions as well as irrigation. The drain at the bottom of the excavation can be connected to a vent which will allow air to penetrate the planting soil mix. The planting detail for this location includes limits in plan and section for rock excavation and replacement of the rock with a planting soil mix that will structurally support the pavements and allow space for root growth. The roots will be limited in their horizontal growth, so we will make the depth of planting soil deeper than a usual planting pit. Care must be taken to provide adequate support below the tree roots to prevent settlement.

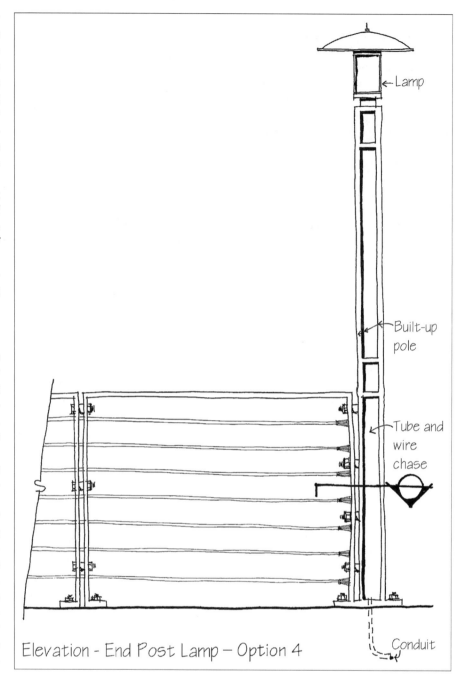

Elevation - End Post Lamp – Option 4

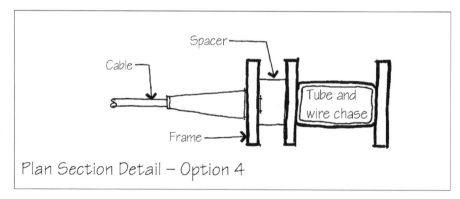

Plan Section Detail – Option 4

The section also will include an under-drainage system (see *Water Level Reduction,* p. 63, and *Structural Tree Planting Soils,* p. 65) to keep the water table below the root zone, vents to the surface to facilitate air flow to the planting soil, and a drip irrigation system that will water the tree and groundcovers in the planter. The edge of the planter will include a short integral curb that will reinforce the edge without thickening it below the surface. This will facilitate root growth into the planting soil below the pavement (see *Root Zone Growth,* p. 96). The detail will also indicate an eased edge at the bottom of the curb to further facilitate root growth into the structural planting soil below (see Section).

## LAWN EDGE

The design concept of the lawn edge is that it will be a green surface perched at the edge of the cliff. The lawn is a stark contrast to the native mountain vegetation of the rest of the plant palette. To achieve the illusion that the green extends to the edge while providing a safe barrier along the precipice (see *Fall Protection,* p. 116), we will incorporate a concrete retaining wall at the edge with a tapered top edge that will minimize its presence. Just beyond the wall the grade will slope up toward the wall.

To reinforce the illusion of the green surface extending to the edge, we will plant the zone between the concrete wall and the turf with a fine, textured deciduous shrub that can be pruned to maintain the horizontal plane of the turf to the edge. We will further reinforce the illusion by reducing the view of the wall by painting the inside of the wall to match the color of the shrubs' branches. The color match will camouflage the wall in the winter when the shrubs are not in leaf. The shrubs can be pruned to take up the height difference between the 12 in. and about 36 in. (305–914 mm). To make up the difference of the last 12 in. (305 mm), we will install a custom steel edge to retain the turf and allow the shrubs to meet the finish grade of the turf surface (see next page, Lawn Edge Section).

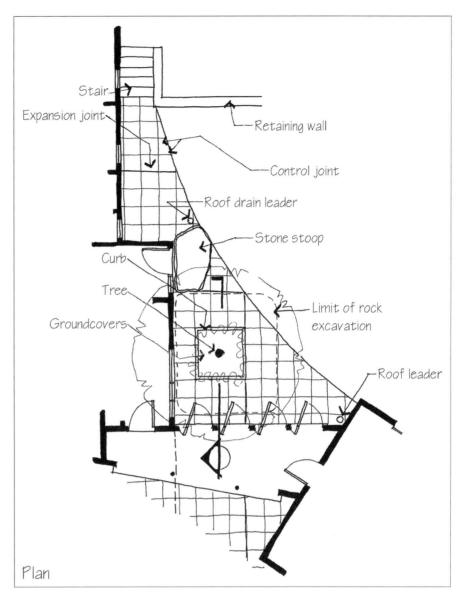

Plan

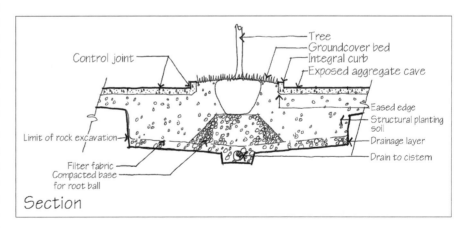

Section

## FIRE PIT

The fire pit is at the center of a small gathering spot located out on a beautiful rock outcrop. It is a bit removed from the back of the house by a narrow plateau edged by an extension of the wall that supports the terrace. In an arid environment where wildfire is often a threat (see *Site-Specific Hazards,* p. 125), the fire pit is only for seasonal use as appropriate, but at all times it creates a central focal point and a place to go to get away from the house.

Since the site is often windswept, the wall will spiral down into the pit to form terraced steps for seating and to create a sheltered spot for the pit. Because the pit is depressed, we will add a drain at the bottom of it. To assist in starting the fires and to counteract high winds, we will install a weatherproof fan connected to the drain line to blow on the fire from below. It will be controlled with a rheostat and will be attached to the outfall pipe that drains the pit. The fan can be located in a spot that is away from the pit, relatively easy to access for maintenance and out of sight (see Section Through Fire Pit).

## NEXT STEPS

Aesthetics have also played a large role in the selection of which details to use for this project and the character of the landscape has emerged as we have developed these key details.

Before we draft the final drawings of all the details for this residence, we review all of the notes that we made while developing those details. We develop specific plans for tree protection and rock excavation that are coordinated with the excavation for the building foundations, the utilities that will service the house, the geothermal and rainwater collection systems, and the new planting. These plans must be coordinated with the architect and engineers as well as the builder and subcontractors.

We will include in the specifications such special items as the exposed

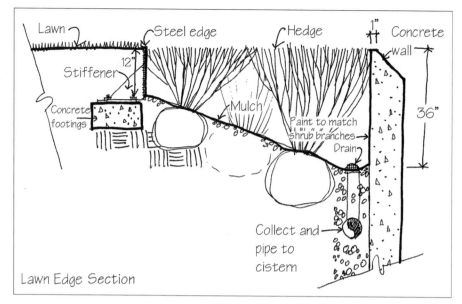

Lawn Edge Section

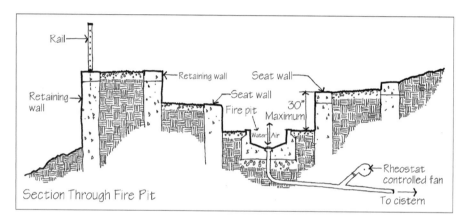

Section Through Fire Pit

aggregate joints, the rail fabrication, the steel edge at the lawn, and so forth. We will also outline the more usual components such as grading, lighting, pavers, steel fabrications, planting, and items for site engineers and irrigation designers to coordinate power and water service both during construction and after.

We also make some notes regarding things to keep in mind as we visit the site again and again during the construction process. The fence and rail details are complex enough so that we should discuss it in detail with the contractor before they are constructed. The exposed aggregate and wall formwork should be viewed in mockup

(see *Simulated Assemblies,* p. 158). The water harvesting and specific wall details and grading also merit special mention but, other than these, these details are pretty straight-forward and probably don't need special mention on the jobsite.

## KEY REFERENCES

Relevant building codes and manufacturing catalogs were important reference materials that were used in developing this set of details. Full bibliographic information on these publications is given in *The Detailer's Reference Shelf,* Appendix A.

# SECTION

# 2

# GETTING STARTED

Designing details is not a neat, linear, fully logical operation. Like any design process, it is engagingly messy and complex. It involves false starts, wrong turns, mental blocks, dead ends, backtracking, and moments of despair as well as purposeful progress, intelligent decisions, creative synthesis, and gratifying moments of inspiration, insight, and triumph.

Begin the process of detailing a project by clarifying your aspirations for the project in terms of aesthetics, function, and constructibility. If you have been involved in the project's schematic design, then it should be easy to outline these goals.

Next, set specific performance standards for the project and identify the key details from which other details of the building are likely to be derived. Develop these details in sketch form, preferably on inexpensive tracing paper, with a pen or soft pencil. Supplement these sketches with photographs of similar details. Analyze the photographs and sketches to look for visual clues toward developing the new details. Also look for structural precedents. Is a vertical structure more like a fence or a wall? Should the pavement float above the adjacent planting beds or be sunken below them? Which design moves are most important and dominant? Is there directionality to the forms that should be reinforced in the details? Should the elements be monolithic or modular? Most digital media are too hard-edged and rigid to be appropriate for this stage of detail development. Begin by drawing the "given" site conditions: basic patterns and elements that will unify portions of the site, key sections through the site that will focus the scale of the elements that will be addressed and the transitions between elements. The first ideas for the key details will emerge logically from these given conditions as you follow the detail pattern, *Rehearsing the Construction Sequence* (page 186).

At this early stage of detail development, it is best to think freely and not be too constrained about the regulatory, economic, or logistical challenges associated with the project; those will be addressed soon enough. It is more important to work rapidly to establish a tentative set of key details.

At this point, rigorously assess each detail in terms of the particular criteria you stated at the outset. How does each meet the broad goals you stated regarding aesthetics, function, and constructibility? How does each compare to the more specific performance standards that you set for the detail? Beyond those criteria, now look at the compositional or spatial implications of your first efforts. Refine your aesthetic goals to make them more precise than they were previously.

Make notes graphically or in writing, summarizing important items in each detail that may have bearing on other parts of the project or that may need to be investigated further. These notes may also record items that need to be incorporated into the final working drawings or into the project's written specifications.

Repeat this process for all of the key details. Carry the findings from each detail investigation forward to positively impact the next detail in the series. Be sure that all of the project's details grow from a common source, with each detail influencing the others.

After bringing all of the key details up to a fairly advanced level of development, test them in greater depth. Explore their less typical conditions. How does the detail turn the corner? How does it terminate? How does another intersecting material meet it? Are its edges articulated? Perhaps your studies to this point have been done at a relatively small scale, such as ¾ in. equals 1 ft (1:16), a scale at which it is impossible to draw the smaller features of a detail. If so, then step up to $1\frac{1}{2}$ or 3 in. scale (1:8 or 1:4, or the more customary metric scales of 1:10 or 1:5) to study the detail more closely. All detail studies must include three-dimensional sketches or a study model, preferably of a corner or termination.

Though the detailing process is seldom neat and linear, it should not be chaotic or wander pointlessly. It should always be pursued with one's eyes fixed firmly on the objectives that were established at the outset, and with reference to the detail patterns elucidated in this book.

As with your learning of the landscape architectural design process in general, with experience you will become more efficient in the process of designing details. The design of a landscape's details, like the design of its form and spaces, is never completely finished. Expect to continue to refine the details as the project evolves, including at the construction site.

## The Detailer's Reference Shelf

## Formulating Exercises for Self-Study or Classroom Use

APPENDIX  The Detailer's Reference Shelf

EVERY DETAILER will have his or her favorite selection of essential references. These are ours. The list is selective rather than exhaustive.

It would be unwise and expensive to try to assemble this entire shelf of references at one time. It is better to acquire references one or several at a time as they are needed, and the collection will gradually fill itself out. If you are determined to acquire a minimum shelf of detailing references immediately, start with the most essential publications, indicated by an asterisk (*). Ordering information is given for all references, except books by recognized publishers. There is a charge for most of these publications; the main exceptions are manufacturers' catalogs, most of which are free.

The Internet is usually the most powerful, immediate, and direct path to detailing information. Most resources that were formerly available only through personal correspondence and catalogs are now available for download in Adobe PDF (portable document format) as well as other formats.

## 1. CODES

Contact the building department of the city or town in which a building will be built to determine the relevant codes. The building codes in most U.S. states are now derived from the International Building Code:

1.  International Building Code. Online at www.iccsafe.org. (This code and others produced by ICC have replaced the National Building Code, the Standard Code, and the Uniform Building Code as the model building code for almost all states in the United States).

2.  National Building Code of Canada. Institute for Research on Construction, National Research Council, 1200 Montreal Road, Ottawa, Ontario, Canada, KIA OR6. Online at http://irc.nrc-cnrc.gc.ca/index_e.html.

## 2. STANDARDS

1.  *Accessible and Useable Buildings and Facilities. ANSI A117.1. American National Standards Institute, Inc., 25 West 43 Street, New York, NY 10036. Available online at http://www.ansi.org. (This book contains specifications for making buildings and sites accessible to and useable

by people with disabilities. Many other standards are also available from ANSI.)

2.  *ANSI Z60.1. American Standard for Nursery Stock. New York: American Association of Nurserymen, 1997.

3.  *ANSI A300 Parts 1, 2, 3, and 4: American National Standard for Tree Care Operations—Tree, Shrub, and Other Woody Plant Maintenance—Standard Practices for Pruning; Fertilization; Support Systems: Cabling, Bracing and Guying; and Lightning Protection.

4.  ASTM Standards in Building Codes. American Society for Testing and Materials International, 100 Barr Harbor Drive, West Conshohocken, PA 19428-2959. Available online at www.astm.org. (This four-volume compilation, updated frequently, covers all the ASTM standards under which building materials and assemblies are specified and detailed.)

5.  *The Sustainable Sites Initiative: Guidelines and Benchmarks, 2009. American Society of Landscape Architects, Lady Bird Johnson Wildflower Center at the University of Texas at Austin, and the United States Botanic Garden, 2009. www.sustainablesites.org/.

## 3. GENERAL REFERENCES ON DETAILING

1.  ASLA and AIA MASTERSPEC. Published by ARCOM. Available online at www.arcomnet.com. (Updated continually, this is an encyclopedic reference on selecting and specifying materials and components for landscapes. Individual sections on specific materials can be downloaded separately.)

2.  *Allen, Edward, and Joseph Iano. Fundamentals of Building Construction: Materials and Methods, 4th ed. New York: John Wiley & Sons, 2004. (This is a solid, general reference on how buildings are put together and gives a basic set of details for each type of construction.)

3.  Iano, Joseph. "Iano's Backfill." Available online at www.ianosbackfill.com/. (This website is maintained by the authors of Fundamentals of Building Construction to provide information, extensive weblinks, updates, supplementary information, resources for the classroom, and

ideas for further study or research. It is intended to increase the value of the text to students, teachers, and practicing professionals and to foster a stronger community among all those dedicated to building well.)

4. Construction Specifications Institute. The Project Resource Manual—*CSI Manual of Practice*, 5th ed. New York: McGraw-Hill, 2004. (Updated frequently, this is the standard by which nearly all construction specifications are written.)

5. *Construction Specifications Institute. National CAD Standard. Alexandria, VA. (This is a booklet that establishes standard symbols and electronic data conventions for use on construction drawings and details.)

6. *Hopper, Leonard J. *Landscape Architectural Graphic Standards*. New York: Wiley, 2007. (This large handbook, which is updated frequently, is the standard reference for architectural detailing. Also available as CD-ROM.)

7. *Sweet's Catalog File. (The print version is a weighty collection of bound volumes of manufacturers' catalogs, covering every area of architectural construction. It is issued yearly by the McGraw-Hill Book Company to architectural and engineering firms that design a sufficient volume of buildings to meet McGraw-Hill's qualification criteria. The only way for individuals and small firms to obtain this file is to solicit year-old copies from larger firms. Electronic versions of individual sections are available for download at http://sweets. construction.com. CAD details from manufacturers are also available.)

8. *Harris, Charles and Dines, Nicholas. *Time-Saver Standards for Landscape Architecture Design and Construction Data*. New York: McGraw-Hill, 1998. (This is similar in breadth to *Landscape Architectural Graphic Standards* and in some areas better, and it is also updated frequently. Includes companion CD-ROM.)

9. *Zimmermann, Astrid, Ed. *Constructing Landscape: Materials, Techniques, Structural Components*. Basel: Birkhauser, 2009. (This is a European-oriented reference. It is very comprehensive and deals with many more contemporary applications than *Graphic Standards* and *Timesavers*).

10. Allen, Edward, and Patrick Rand. *Architectural Detailing: Function, Constructability, Aesthetics*, 2nd ed. Hoboken: John Wiley & Sons, Inc., 2007.

11. Hegger, Manfred, Hans Drexler, and Martin Zeumer. *Materials (Basics)*. Boston: Birkhäuser Basel, 2006. (A good basic series.)

12. Ballast, David. *Handbook of Construction Tolerances*. New York: Wiley, 2007.

13. Kirkwood, Niall. *Art of Landscape Detail: Fundamentals, Practices, and Case Studies*. New York: Wiley, 1999.

14. Kirkwood, Niall. *Weathering and Durability in Landscape Architecture: Fundamentals, Practices, and Case Studies*. New York: Wiley, 2004.

15. Pinder, Angi and Alan Beazley. *Beazley's Design and Detail of the Space between Buildings*. London: E. & F.N. Spon, 1990. (Good UK detail reference.)

16. Sauter, David. *Landscape Construction*. Belmont: Thomson Delmar Learning, 2010. (A good hands-on basic book.)

17. Thallon, Rob. *Graphic Guide to Site Construction: Over 325 Details for Builders and Designers*. Newtown: Taunton, 2003. (A good hands-on basic book.)

18. *Allen, Edward, David M. Foxe, and Michael H. Ramage. *The Boston Structures Group, Form and Forces, Designing Efficient, Expressive Structures*. New York: John Wiley & Sons, 2010. (This is a solid, general reference on structural design with great examples.)

## 4. INTERIOR PLANTING DETAILING

1. *Guide to Interior Landscape Specifications*, 5th ed. Knoxville: Interior Plantscape Division of Associated Landscape Contrators of America, 2003.

2. Hammer, Nelson. *Interior Landscape Design*. New York, NY: McGraw-Hill, 1992.

## 5. DETAILING WOOD

1. *Allen, Edward, and Rob Thallon. *Fundamentals of Residential Construction*. 2d ed. New York: John Wiley & Sons, 2006.

2. *American Institute of Timber Construction. *Standard Specifications for Structural Glued Laminated Timbers of Softwood Species, Design and Manufacturing Requirements*. Order online at www.aitc-glulam.org/. (This is a good general reference on the topic, including section properties, span tables, and typical details. It is updated frequently. Available for download online at no cost.)

3. American Institute of Timber Construction. Typical Construction Details. See above for AITC url. (This pamphlet contains dozens of examples of how to detail heavy timber frames. Available for download online at no cost.)

4. American Wood Council. National Design Specification for Wood Construction. Order or download online at www.awc.org. (This is the basic reference from which wood structures are engineered, and it is updated frequently. It is especially useful to the detailer for working out structural connections between wood members.)

5. Architectural Woodworking Institute. *AWI Quality Standards Illustrated*, 8th ed. (Technical and design illustrations regarding architectural woodwork from raw lumber and veneers all the way through factory-finished and installed product.) Order or download online at www. awinet.org.

6. Canadian Wood Council Website. www.cwc.ca. (Information on all types of wood construction, including heavy

timber, glue-laminated, and light wood frame. The site has typical details for download in CAD format.)

7. *National Forest Products Association. Span Tables for Joists and Rafters. Order or download online at www.awc.org/technical/spantables/index.html. (Using this booklet of tables, you can easily design structures for residential floors, ceilings, and roofs.)

8. Natterer, Julius et al. *Timber Construction Manual*. Basel, Switzerland: Birkhauser, 2003. (One in a series by the publishers of *DETAIL* magazine, this manual has in-depth coverage of the material properties of wood, its history in construction, and numerous contemporary examples of heavy timber detailing.)

9. *Simpson Strong-Tie Company, Inc. Connectors for Wood Construction. Order online at www.strongtie.com/. (This annual catalog is the best single reference on metal framing connectors for wood light framing and heavy timber framing.)

10. *Western Wood Products Association. Dimensional Stability of Western Lumber Products. Available online at www.wwpa.org. (The charts in this booklet are extremely useful in estimating moisture movement in wood.)

11. George, Nash. *Wooden Fences*. Newtown, CT: Taunton, 1999.

12. *Winterbottom, Daniel M. *Wood in the Landscape: A Practical Guide to Specification and Design*. New York: Wiley, 2000.

13. Steiger, Ludwig. *Basics Timber Construction (Basics)*. Boston: Birkhäuser Basel, 2007.

## 6. DETAILING MASONRY

1. *Beall, Christine. *Masonry Design and Detailing for Architects and Contractors*, 5th ed. New York: McGraw-Hill, 2003. (This is the best general detailing reference for masonry of all types.)

2. *Brick Industry Association. BIA Technical Notes on Brick Construction. Available online at www.bia.org/. (Updated frequently.)

3. Indiana Limestone Institute of America, Inc. *Indiana Limestone Institute of America, Inc. Handbook*. Address for ordering: Indiana Limestone Institute of America, Inc., Suite 400, Stone City Bank Building, Bedford, IN 47421, or at http://www.iliai.com. (Updated frequently, this manual gives complete information for detailing limestone.)

4. Marble Institute of America. *Dimensional Stone*. Order online at www.marble-institute.com/. (This large looseleaf binder, updated frequently, emphasizes the detailing of marble, but it is applicable also to granite and other architectural stones.)

5. *National Concrete Masonry Association. *TEK Manual for Concrete Masonry Design and Construction*. Herndon, VA 20171. Available online at www.ncma.org/. (A complete

manual of facts on designing and building with concrete masonry and related concrete units. Updated continuously; 140 titles to date.)

6. National Concrete Masonry Association. *Annotated Design and Construction Details for Concrete Masonry, 2003*. Available online at www.ncma.org/. (Contains masonry details commonly used in construction. Each section covers a specific concrete masonry application and includes details with side-by-side commentary. A companion CD includes all of the details in a format that allows them to be imported and edited using CAD programs.)

7. Pfeifer, Gunter et al. *Masonry Construction Manual*. Basel, Switzerland: Birkhauser, 2001. (One in a series by the publishers of *DETAIL* magazine, this manual has in-depth coverage of the material properties of masonry, masonry's historical uses, and numerous contemporary examples of masonry detailing.)

8. J.A. Farney, William C. Panarese, and W.C. Panarese, *Concrete Masonry Handbook for Architects, Engineers, and Builders*. 6th ed. Skokie, IL: Portland Cement Association, 2008. Order online at www.cement.org. (This is an excellent, well-illustrated reference on detailing concrete masonry.)

9. *Architectural Precast Concrete*. Chicago, Ill: Precast/Pre-stressed Concrete Institute, 1989.

10. Kummer, Nils. *Basics Masonry Construction (Basics)*. Boston: Birkhäuser Basel, 2007.

11. *Sovinski, Rob W. *Brick in the Landscape: A Practical Guide to Specification and Design*. New York: John Wiley & Sons, Inc., 1999.

12. Farney, James A., J. M. Melander, and W. C. Panarese, *Concrete Masonry Handbook for Architects, Engineers, Builders*, Skokie, Illinois: Portland Cement Association, 2008.

## 7. DETAILING STEEL AND STRUCTURAL METALS

1. The Aluminum Association. Aluminum Standards and Data. (Updated every two years, this is a basic reference on aluminum alloys and product forms.) Address for ordering: The Aluminum Association, 1525 Wilson Boulevard, Suite 600, Arlington, VA 22209. Order online at www.aluminum.org.

2. *American Institute of Steel Construction. *Manual of Steel Construction*, 13th ed. Chicago: AISC, 2000. Order online at www.aisc.org. (This contains basic information on available steel shapes, their properties, and steel connections.) American Institute of Steel Construction. *Detailing for Steel Construction*, 3rd ed. Chicago, AISC 2005 Order online at www.aisc.org. (This is a textbook for beginning detailers of structural steel.)

3. Schulitz, Helmut C. et al. *Steel Construction Manual*. Basel, Switzerland: Birkhauser, 2000. (One in a series by the publishers of *DETAIL* magazine, this manual has

in-depth coverage of the material properties of steel, its historical uses, and numerous contemporary examples of steel detailing.)

## 8. DETAILING SITECAST CONCRETE

1. *American Concrete Institute Committee 303 R-04. Guide to Cast-In-Place Architectural Concrete. 2004. Order online or download at www.concrete.org. (This is an excellent guide to detailing and specifying exposed concrete surfaces.)

2. *American Concrete Institute 117-10, Standard Specifications for Tolerances for Concrete Construction and Materials, 2010. Order online or download at www.concrete.org. (Dimensional tolerances for concrete work are spelled out in detail.)

3. *Architectural Concrete Form Liners. Available for download online at www.greenstreak.com. (This small catalog illustrates standard form-liner textures. Rustication strips, chamfer strips, and waterstops are illustrated in other catalogs online from the same source.) For a wider selection of form liners only, try www.scottsytaem.com or www.symons.com. There are also numerous manufacturers of surface "stamps." Try www.stampcrete.com, www.matchcrete.com, or www.brickform.com.

4. *Hurd, M. K. Formwork for Concrete. 7th ed. Detroit, MI: American Concrete Institute, 2005. (This is an excellent and comprehensive general reference on the detailing of concrete.)

5. Kind-Barkauskas, Friedbert, et al. Concrete Construction Manual. Basel, Switzerland: Birkhauser, 2005. (One in a series by the publishers of DETAIL magazine, this manual has in-depth coverage of the material properties of concrete, its history in construction, and numerous contemporary examples of concrete detailing.)

6. *Concrete Floors on Ground. New York: Portland Cement Association, 2001. (This is a good reference for flatwork, forming, curing, and the design of joints.)

## 9. DETAILING GLASS AND PRECAST CONCRETE

1. Glass Association of North America. GANA Glazing Manual. Topeka, KS: GANA, 2008. Order online at www.glasswebsite.com/. (This booklet, formerly published by FGMA and frequently updated, shows standard methods of supporting and sealing glass in windows and cladding systems.)

2. *PPG Industries, Inc. PPG Architectural Glass. Order online at www.ppg.com. (Updated annually, this is PPG's glass catalog, which includes valuable information on specifying and detailing glazing.)

3. Precast/Prestressed Concrete Institute (PCI). Architectural Precast Concrete, 3rd ed. Chicago: PCI, 2007. Order online at www.pci.org. (This is a complete,

lavishly illustrated guide to detailing precast concrete cladding.)

4. Precast/Prestressed Concrete Institute (PCI). Recommended Practice for Glass Fiber Reinforced Concrete Panels. Chicago: PCI, 2001. (This is a complete guide to designing GFRC cladding.)

5. Schittich, Christian. Glass Construction Manual. Basel, Switzerland: Birkhauser, 1999. (One in a series by the publishers of DETAIL magazine, this manual has in-depth coverage of the material properties of glass, its history in construction, contemporary glazing technology, and numerous contemporary examples of glass detailing.)

## 10. DETAILING SOILS AND PLANTING

1. *Craul, Timothy A., and Phillip J. Craul. Soil Design Protocols for Landscape Architects and Contractors. New York: Wiley, 2006.

2. Harris, Richard Wilson. Arboriculture Integrated Management of Landscape Trees, Shrubs, and Vines. Upper Saddle River, NJ: Prentice Hall, 2003.

3. *Keefer, Robert F. Handbook of Soils for Landscape Architects. New York: Oxford UP, USA, 2000.

4. *Urban, James. Up by the Roots: Healthy Soils and Trees in the Built Environment. Champaign, IL: International Society of Arborculture, 2008.

5. Puhalla, Jim. Sports Fields: A Manual for Design, Construction, and Maintenance: An Illustrated Guide to the Design, Construction, and Maintenance of Sports Fields- 2nd ed. Chelsea, MI: Ann Arbor, 2010. (A good all-around turf manual.)

## 11. DETAILING GREEN ROOFS

1. Cantor, Steven L. Green Roofs in Sustainable Landscape Design. New York: W. W. Norton & Company, 2008.

2. Dunnett, Nigel, and Noël Kingsbury. Planting Green Roofs and Living Walls. New York: Timber, 2008.

3. Hoffman, Leslie and McDonough, William. Foundation, Earth Pledge. Green Roofs Ecological Design and Construction. Grand Rapids: Schiffer, 2004.

4. Weiler, Susan, and Katrin Scholz-Barth. Green Roof Systems: A Guide to the Planning, Design and Construction of Building Over Structure. New York: Wiley, 2009.

## 12. DETAILING GRADING AND DRAINAGE

1. Ferguson, Bruce K. and Debb, Thomas N. On-site Stormwater Management Applications for Landscape and Engineering. Mesa, AZ: PDA, 1990.

2. *Ferguson, Bruce K. Porous Pavements. Boca Raton, FL: Taylor & Francis, 2005.

3. Gray, Donald H. and Sotir, Robbin B. *Biotechnical and Soil Bioengineering Slope Stabilization: A Practical Guide for Erosion Control*. New York: John Wiley & Sons, 1996.

4. Field, Richard, Chin, Kee and O'Shea, Marie. *Integrated Stormwater Management*. Boca Raton: Lewis, 1993.

5. Petschek, Peter. *Grading for Landscape Architects and Architects*. Basel: Birkhauser, 2008.

6. Schor, Horst J., and Donald H. Gray. *Landforming: An Environmental Approach to Hillside Development, Mine Reclamation and Watershed Restoration*. New York: Wiley, 2007.

7. Strom, Steven. *Site Engineering for Landscape Architects*. Hoboken, NJ: John Wiley & Sons, 2009.

8. McIntyre, Keith, and Bent Jakobsen. *Practical Drainage for Golf, Sportsturf and Horticulture*. New York: Wiley, 2000. (A good hands-on book for turf and planting bed drainage and grading. It focuses on USGA systems.)

9. Koerner, Robert M. *Designing with Geosynthetics*. Upper Saddle River, NJ, Pearson Prentice Hall, 2005.

## 13. DETAILNG WATER FEATURES

1. Lohrer, Axel. *Designing with Water (Basics)*. Basel: Birkhauser Verlag AG, 2008.

2. C. Douglas Aurand. *Fountains and Pools, Construction Guidelines and Specifications*, New York, Van Nostrand Reinhold, 1991.

3. Dreiseitl, Herbert, and Deiter Grau, *New Waterscapes, Planning, Building and Designing with Water*, Basel: Birkhauser, 2005.

4. Bahamon, Alejandro (Ed.). *Landscape Architecture: Water Features*, Gloucester, MA, Rockport Publishers, 2007.

## 14. DETAILING LIGHTING

1. *Moyer, Janet Lennox. *The Landscape Lighting Book*. New York: Wiley, 2005.

2. Narboni, Roger. *Lighting the Landscape, Art, Design, Technologies*, Basel: Birkhauser, 2000.

## 15. MATERIALS

1. *Sovinski, Rob W. *Materials and Their Applications in Landscape Design*. Hoboken, NJ: Wiley, 2009.

2. Caleb, Hornbostel. *Construction Materials: Types, Uses and Applications*. New York, NY: Wiley-Interscience, 1991,

3. Shan, Somayaji. *Civil Engineering Materials*. Upper Saddle River, NJ: Prentice-Hall, 2001.

## 16. SUSTAINABLE DESIGN

1. Thompson, J. William, and Kim Sorvig. *Sustainable Landscape Construction: A Guide to Green Building Outdoors*. New York: Island, 2008.

2. Calkins, Meg. *Materials for Sustainable Sites*, New York: Wiley, 2008.

3. Ferguson, Bruce K. (Editor), *Porous Pavements*, Boca Raton, FL: Taylor Francis Group, CRC Press, 2005.

4. Dunnett, Nigel and Clayden, Andy, *Rain Gardens, Managing Water Sustainably in the Garden and Designed Landscape*, Portland, OR: Timber Press, 2007.

# Formulating Exercises for Self-Study or Classroom Use

IT IS IMPOSSIBLE to become good at detailing without repeated practice. Such practice is most effective when the resulting details are used to construct actual landscapes, because then it is possible to experience the results of one's decisions and to see what has turned out well and what could be done better in the next project. However, this actual experience may not be fully available to students and interns, and one may wish to become more expert before attempting details that will actually be built. In these cases, it is easy to formulate several types of exercises that will help develop detailing skills.

## 1. ANALYZE AND MODIFY EXISTING DETAILS

A good way to begin the study of landscape architectural detailing is to analyze existing details from available sources, such as actual working drawings, books of details, details in landscape architectural journals, details in manufacturers' catalogs, and details in this book.

### Identify Detail Patterns

Photocopy or plot a detail, reducing it if necessary to allow plenty of white space around it on the sheet. Add notes and arrows in the white space to identify all the detail patterns that are embodied in the drawing. Consider whether there are patterns that should have been explored that are missing.

### Modify Existing Details

Use the pattern analysis of a detail to help identify deficiencies in its design. Then lay tracing paper over the detail and modify it to correct the deficiencies. Make a list of the patterns employed in your redesign.

## 2. DESIGN VARIATIONS ON EXISTING DETAILS

A logical next step in this progression of exercises is to start with a photocopy or a print of an existing detail and then arbitrarily change one important parameter and redesign the detail accordingly. An easy example would be to start with a detail of concrete paver walk intersecting a dry-laid stone wall. Next, change the materials to a poured-in-place concrete sidewalk intersecting a stuccoed concrete block wall. A slightly more difficult exercise relating to the same site would be to change a precast unit retaining wall to a concrete wall with stone facing.

A variant of this exercise is to design an additional detail that is not present in the given set of details, such as a decorative railing or a pergola that will harmonize with the rest of the design.

## 3. DESIGN NEW DETAILS FROM SCRATCH

Difficult, but the most realistic, are those exercises that involve developing details for a new landscape design. Three examples of this process are illustrated in the Detail Development (Part II) portion of this book.

Starting from a basic concept of the space and form of a project, a good plan of action would be the following:

1. Write a list of descriptions of the intent of the design with the most important things first. This list will give an aesthetic checklist to judge the effectiveness of the details in aesthetic terms.

2. Create a list of appropriate materials.

3. Select the key details to be developed.

4. Check the applicable building code for provisions relevant to the detailing process, and keep the code book or a list of code requirements close by for ready reference.

5. Develop the details in stages, aided by studio-style critiques at frequent intervals from a teacher or a senior colleague.

This exercise is most effective if the original design can be modified as the details are developed. This teaches the positive effect that detailing can have on the form and space of a landscape and the integrated nature of the design process—a lesson that will be lost if the original design is considered to be complete and inviolable.

## 4. USE THE PATTERNS TO DO DIAGNOSTIC WORK

Once the patterns have been learned and understood, they can become a powerful basis for figuring out the causes of various detail failures. Problems in real projects make the most effective vehicles for these exercises. As practice exercises and problems for classroom discussion, you can invent or find such situations as the following:

1. The leading edges of walls and curbs are broken and soiled by skateboard use.

2. A stucco wall is cracking badly.

3. An outdoor deck of pine 2 by 6s traps puddles of water during rainstorms.

4. Brick paving is spalling badly.

5. A steel handrail is loose at its connection to a cheekwall.

6. A retaining wall is cracked and bowed.

7. Concrete pavement is cracked outside of its control joints.

8. Street trees are stressed and stunted.

9. Pavements have settled over utility lines and are holding water.

10. A roofdeck planting bed is not draining sufficiently and soils are becoming anaerobic.

## 5. TRY SOME FREESTYLE DETAILING EXERCISES

It can be refreshing and instructive to step outside the world of landscape architecture now and then to attempt to detail other kinds of useful objects. Imagine designing and detailing an end table, a child's wagon, an improved nail hammer, a refrigerator container system, a shelving system, or an automobile trash container. Materials can be mixed and matched as desired: Within a class, for example, everyone might attack the same design problem, but students could be assigned different materials to work with. Comparisons of design solutions and details then become all the more meaningful.

This approach can be useful in exposing students to the experience of designing with materials and systems that are too complex for them to face in standard classroom situations, such as aluminum and glass construction. Success with simple projects will build confidence and encourage students to engage more complex projects.

# INDEX